MOHAMMED RAFI

Golden Voice of the Silver Screen

MOHAMMED RAFI

Golden Voice of the Silver Screen

Sujata Dev

(Authorised by Shahid Rafi)

OM
Om Books International

Reprinted in 2015 by

OM
Om Books International

Corporate & Editorial Office
A-12, Sector 64, Noida 201 301
Uttar Pradesh, India
Phone: +91 120 477 4100
Email: editorial@ombooks.com
Website: www.ombooksinternational.com

Sales Office
107, Ansari Road, Darya Ganj,
New Delhi 110 002, India
Phone: +91 11 2326 3363, 2326 5303, 4000 9000
Fax: +91 11 2327 8091
Email: sales@ombooks.com
Website: www.ombooks.com

ISBN: 978-93-80070-97-1

Printed at Thomson Press India Ltd

10 9 8 7 6 5 4 3 2

For all the Rafi fans
who have kept him alive in their hearts…

Contents

Acknowledgements

I sincerely thank:

Shahid Rafi, who trusted me to do justice to his legendary father, Mohammed Rafi's biography. This book would not have been possible without his support;

Nasreen and Yasmin, Rafi's daughters, for presenting the legend as a doting father and a family man;

Firdaus, Rafi's youngest daughter-in-law, for her warm hospitality, even at odd hours;

Mohammed Siddique, Rafi's younger brother, who, despite his age, spent hours detailing Rafi's childhood with his siblings and parents during the growing-up years in Kotla Sultan Singh, then Lahore;

Bakshish Singh Samra and Kundan Singh Samra, Rafi's childhood friends in Kotla Sultan Singh, for enthusiastically walking down memory lane;

Ajay Mago, Publisher, Om Books International, for encouraging me to write this biography;

Dipa Chaudhuri, Chief Editor, Om Books International, for her support;

Raashid Zaffar, without whom I would never have met Shahid Rafi;

Anupriya Nayyar, who passionately assisted me in my research on Rafi's life;

Hosang Kattrak and Shirish Kulkarni, ardent Rafi fans who were always there to answer all my queries on the singer's rich repertoire;

Rajani Acharya, who helped me to capture the interviews on audio and visual formats, in the accompanying DVD;

Suresh Jethva, the photographer, who travelled with us right through;

Udaya Tara Nair, who helped me reach out to Dilip Kumar, who has given the Foreword for this book; as Rafi's dear friend and contemporary, it marks a befitting start to the biography;

Manoj Soral, for being the first to read the initial draft and for his constructive suggestions;

Raju Naushad, legendary music director Naushad Ali's son, who helped me trace many of Rafi's contemporaries;

SMM Ausaja, cinema historian and my dear friend, for some priceless photographs of Rafi from his personal archives;

Sanjeev Kohli, legendary music director Madan Mohan's son, for sharing some rare photographs of Rafi with his father and other associates for this book;

Sammina, the talented documentary filmmaker from Pakistan for helping from across the border, capture the interview of the only living sibling of Rafi;

Gurdeep Singh and Rajinder Sohal, who accompanied Shahid Rafi and me to Kotla Sultan Singh and facilitated our interviews with Rafi's childhood friends and enabled us to visit Rafi's school;

Virendra Shankar, Apu Rana and Shyam Dutt for co-ordinating some of the interviews for this book;

Shoili Sarkar-Seth, my editor, for taking excellent care of the biography;

My family for believing in me and helping me overcome all hurdles;

My grandmother, who instilled in me the love for music, and my father-in-law, who encouraged me in all my endeavours. I know their blessings and love are a part of this book. I miss both greatly, knowing they would have loved to read this book;

Everyone cannot be named here but who, in their own way, would have supported me in this amazing peregrination.

Last but not the least, I am extremely thankful to the Indian film industry, particularly to everyone who has been kind enough to talk to us on the legend that was Mohammed Rafi. Their words constitute a priceless and important record of the history of Indian cinema and playback singing.

Agam Nigam
Amar Haldipur
Amit Kumar
Anand*ji*
Andalib Sultanpuri
Annu Malik
Anoop Jalota
Anuradha Paudwal
Bhupinder Singh
Biswajit Chaterjee
Burjor Lord
Dev Anand
Dev Kohli
Dinesh Shailendra
Dr Alim K Chandiramani
Dr Devi Chandiramani
Haridas Prabhu
Hariharan
Himesh Reshammiya
Jagjit Singh
Javed Ali
Javed Badayuni
Joy Mukherjee
Jyoti Matwankar
Kailash Kher
Kersi Lord
Khayyam
Kishan Sharma
Krishna Mukherjee
Kunal Ganjawala
Lekh Tandon
Manna Dey
Manoj Kumar
Mohammed Aziz
Mubarak Begum
Nandi Duggal
Nitin Mukesh
Omi Sonik
Pandit Jasraj
Pankaj Udhas
Pyarelal Sharma
Rais Khan
Rajesh Duggal
Raju Naushad
Ram Mukherjee
Randhir Kapoor
Ravindra Jain
Ravi Sharma
Rehman Naushad
Rishi Kapoor
Roop Kumar Rathod
Ruhan Kapoor
Sagarika Mukherjee
Sanjeev Kohli
Satish Gupta
Sawan Kumar Tak
Shaan Mukherjee
Shabbir Kumar
Shailender Singh
Shammi Kapoor
Shamshad Begum
Sharad Waykool
Shikha Vohra
Sonu Nigam
Sudesh Bhosle
Sudha Chitragupta
Sudhakar Sharma
Suman Kalyanpur
Sumit Mitra
Udit Narayan
Usha Khanna
Usha Timothy
Uttam Singh
Vikram Makandar
Vipin Reshammiya
Yogesh Gaur

Dilip Kumar 34-B, Pali Hill Bandra Bombay 400 050

Foreword

First of all, my compliments to the publisher for the thoughtful gesture of bringing to public knowledge the story of the life of a legend about whom the millions who loved the songs he sang from his soul for their enjoyment and inner enrichment know so little about.

Mohammad Rafi was my voice in practically all my memorable films. He was also the voice of all the leading men of Hindi cinema who enjoyed great popularity with the masses in their time. He had the God given ability to mould and adapt his rendering of a number according to the given situation in the film, the character's mood of the time, the overall nature and disposition of the character in the film and the setting or milieu of the film. From my own experience of working with him I can say that it was always a marvel for me when I listened to his effortless rendering of the compositions of the recordings. He was as clear to me as Naushad Sahab was and with Rafi Bhai it was a mystical bonding as if he was a part of me when he sang for me, knowing without being told, how I would perform the song during the filming of the sequence.

He was a humble, unpretentious man who remained unaffected by all the adulation and reverence he received the millions who listened to his songs and soaked themselves in the myriad moods and sentiments he conveyed so gorgeously with his versatile voice. We understood each other not only as actor and his playback voice but also as friends who shared common concerns. I remember an experience when Rafi Bhai and I were at the Indo China border, soon after the conflict of 1962, to entertain the Jawans of the Border Security Force. And suddenly a day prior to the show he lost his voice due to the severe cold causing a throat infection. Rafi Bhai was in tears and inconsolable because he knew he would let down the eager Jawans who were sending us little notes on pieces of paper with requests for the songs they wished to hear live at the show. He kept on praying and I kept on giving him my own concoction of a ginger and honey drink which he drank obediently. And lo and behold it worked! Rafi Bhai couldn't believe it when he woke up in the morning of the day of the show and he cleared his throat and heard his own inimitable velvet voice. He was a karmayogi in the real sense of the word. He won numerous awards and recognition but he believed that his real reward was the admiration of the people, the common man for whose entertainment Allah had gifted him with the incomparable voice he possessed.

I can see that the author has put in painstaking labour to bring out the story of his life and to highlight the exceptional contribution he made to Indian film music and its popularity across the world the documentary on his life which accompanies the book in a DVD should be of equal value to his followers. My compliments once again.

(DILIP KUMAR)

Preface

Rafi Sahab has been one of the most versatile male playback singers in the history of Indian cinema. Even today, 34 years after his death, when one hears his soothing voice rendering a *bhajan* (devotional song of Hindus), or a stirring patriotic number, or his joyful rendition of nature's splendour, the feeling is special. Rafi Sahab was, and still is, an integral part of the average Indian's life, the changing times notwithstanding.

For many, his voice was that of God.

My grandmother was an ardent music lover and the radio was her addiction. As a little girl, I often rested my head on her lap, listening to Radio Ceylon as her wrinkled fingers ran through my hair. On one such occasion, while the song 'O Duniya Ke Rakhwaale' was playing, she explained that it was the voice of God. I looked up at the stars in the sky and said, 'God, what a beautiful voice you have!'

Later, while I was putting this book together, I understood what my grandmother had meant.

Through a common family friend, Raashid Zaffar, I met Shahid Rafi (the only living son of Mohammed Rafi). Over a cup of coffee, he expressed his desire to publish a biography on his father. We looked around for a publisher and decided to go with Om Books International.

I began work on this biography and a short film with the blessings of the family of this legend—a simple, unassuming, musical giant who ruled the country's popular music scene for almost four decades.

The journey began with the interview of Pyarelal*ji*, the prolific music director. He told me, 'You are the blessed one. You have a great task ahead of you.' That gave me the confidence to go ahead with the challenge.

I wanted to unravel the man behind the voice. Drawing inspiration from Paulo Coelho's *The Alchemist*—'When you want something, the entire universe conspires in helping you to achieve it'—I embarked on the task at hand.

Tracking his footprints brought out many facets of Rafi Sahab's life, both as a singer and a human being. My quest to learn more about this man of few words, led me to speak to people from different walks of life who were acquainted with him in some way or the other—actor, music director, contemporary singer, recordist, family members and surprisingly, even a *paanwala* (person who sells prepared Betel leaves) in one of the bustling lanes of Kolkata.

The stories and viewpoints, in this biography, have been retained at their candid best. Who could have described the relationship between Shammi*ji* and Rafi Sahab better than Shammi*ji* himself!

The toughest yet enjoyable exercise has been the research on Rafi Sahab's career. It would have been impossible to cumulate every detail of his career without the support of his contempories. As I sifted through all the information, I realised that the mere mention of Rafi Sahab was an aggregation of love, admiration and respect that the singer garnered from millions of people across the world for the *fankaar* (artiste) and *farishta* (angel) that he was.

Shahid Rafi gave a clear picture of Rafi Sahab as a family man; this included his relationships within the family, the dreams Rafi Sahab and his wife, Bilquis, shared for their children, and how he was the pivot of his close-knit family.

I have tried to ensure that Rafi Sahab's humble persona becomes apparent through the 80-odd interviews featured in this book. When he passed away, millions throughout the world felt a profound and irreplaceable void.

Three of the many matinee idols Rafi Sahab sang playback for—Shammi Kapoor, Dev Anand and Joy Mukherjee—shared their personal equations with the singer in what would sadly be one of each one's last interviews. Music director Ravi Sharma too bared his heart about the legend. Little did he know that it was the last time he would be speaking about Rafi Sahab, who sang some of the gems he created in the '60s. Jagjit Singh, the *ghazal* (a lyrical poem in verse set to music) maestro, spoke about Rafi Sahab as a singer, just three days before he was hospitalised. Shamshad Begum, the yesteryear melody queen recounted many unspoken milestones at the initial phase of Rafi Sahab's career. As destiny would have it, Manna Dey, the prolific singer who during our interaction referred to Rafi Sahab as the greatest Indian singer, passed away before this book went into press. The talented painter Sharad Waykool, who was supported by Rafi Sahab in the early days of his career, also passed away. Rafi Sahab's dearest childhood friend Sardar Kundan Singh, who with his impeccable memory and childhood anecdotes, helped us retrace Rafi Sahab's roots, died on January 13, 2014. Both Mr Waykool and Mr Singh desired to be present for the launch of this book, and I am certain they shall join us in spirit.

And I hope the readers experience the same joy I did as I began my journey of discovering the wonder that was Mohammed Rafi who we have immortalised in our hearts.

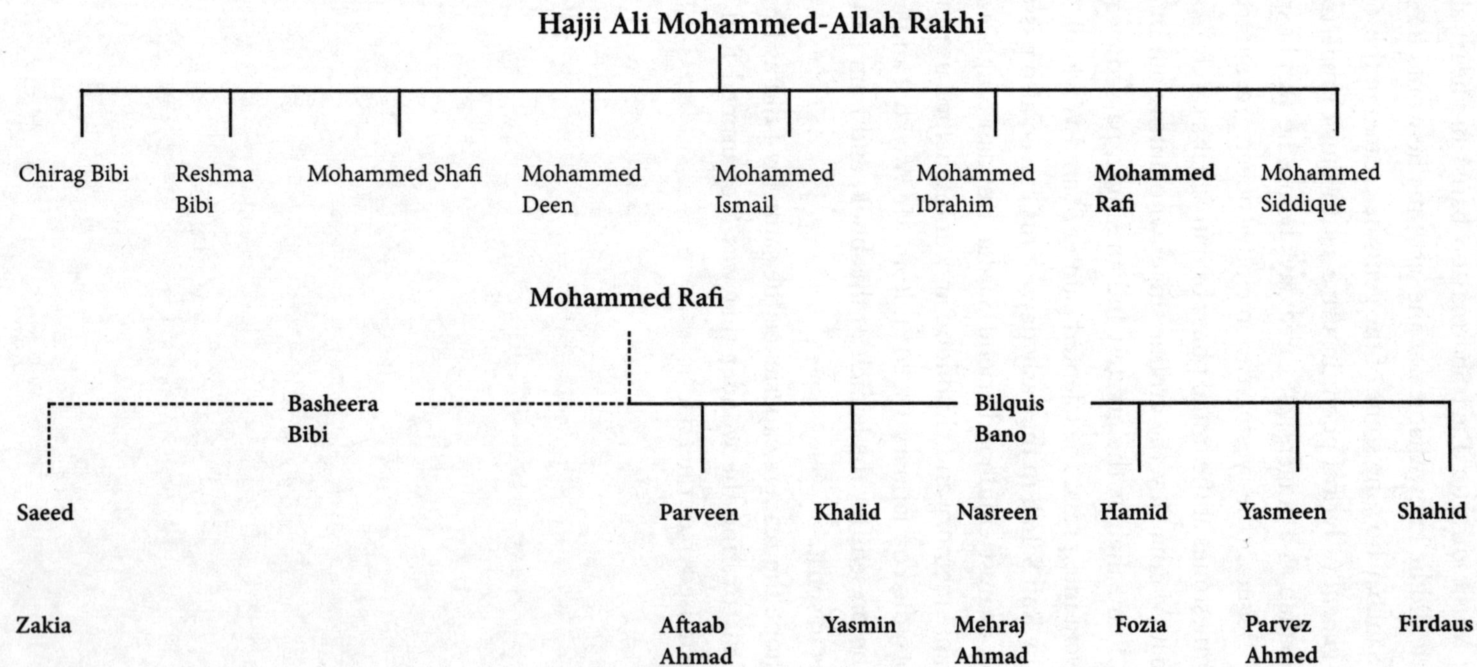
Hajji Ali Mohammed-Allah Rakhi
Chirag Bibi
Reshma Bibi
Mohammed Shafi
Mohammed Deen
Mohammed Ismail
Mohammed Ibrahim
Mohammed Rafi
Mohammed Siddique
Mohammed Rafi
Basheera Bibi
Bilquis Bano
Saeed
Parveen
Khalid
Nasreen
Hamid
Yasmeen
Shahid
Zakia
Aftaab Ahmad
Yasmin
Mehraj Ahmad
Fozia
Parvez Ahmed
Firdaus

1

The Early Years

On the cold night of December 24, 1924, in a home in Kotla Sultan Singh, Allah Rakhi lay shivering and moaning in labour, waiting to give birth to her seventh child. Keemo, the silver-haired midwife had been sent for. Her hands were the most reliable as earlier she had helped Allah Rakhi give birth to her four sons. The midwife now assisted Allah Rakhi give birth to a healthy child. The child cried out loud and strong to announce his arrival in the world.

'*Inshallah! Is bar bhi ladka hua hai,* Rakhi! (By the grace of the Almighty, you have again been blessed with a son, Rakhi),' announced the midwife and with a smile held the child up to the father, Hajji Ali Mohammed, who was anxiously waiting outside the room. Elated Hajji rewarded the midwife with two *ser*s (unit of measure) of wheat, *gur* (jaggery), new clothes and a few *sikka*s (coins).

The child was named Mohammed Rafi, literally, 'The Exalted One'. For the midwife, it was just another successful birth.

In the small village of Kotla Sultan Singh, with limited sources of income, Rafi's was a home shorn of even the bare necessities. The family of nine—including Rafi's brothers Mohammed Deen, Mohammed Shafi, Mohammed Ismail, Mohammed Ibrahim and their sisters Chirag Bibi and Reshma Bibi—was forced to lead a frugal existence. Throughout his childhood, Pheeko, as Rafi was fondly called then, wore the clothes his elder brothers had outgrown.

Situated in the *taluka* (administrative district) of Majitha, 15 kilometres from Amritsar, Kotla Sultan Singh comprised 60 Muslim, 30 Sikh and three Hindu families. The village remained an island of peace even through the traumatic period of Partition. One of the several Sunni Muslim families in the village was that of the Bhattis, who later came to be known as the Rafis.

Crisis loomed large over Hajji Ali's family when it expanded further within the next three years, with Allah Rakhi giving birth to another child, a son. Hajji Ali realised it would be near impossible for him to sustain a family of 10 (including his youngest born, Mohammed Siddique) in the village, with hardly much source of income.

An excellent cook, he would be summoned whenever there was a function in the village—the family's only source of income. Even today, elderly villagers of Kotla Sultan Singh speak fondly of the culinary skills of Hajji Ali who was reputed for a particular preparation, the *satranga chaawal*, which had seven layers of rice in different colours.

In those days, life in rural India was tough for people who did not own agricultural land. Hajji Ali was forced to look at other towns for better opportunities of earning a livelihood for his family.

In 1926, Hajji Ali decided to leave for Lahore, the capital of undivided Punjab, about 50 miles away from their village. Being the closest township where he had a few distant relatives, it was a natural choice. Mohammed Deen, his eldest son, accompanied him.

Hajji Ali's relatives helped him set up a very simple street corner *dhaba* (eatery) in Lahore. Mohammed Deen set up a barber shop at Noor Mohalla, which was well-known for *garam hamaam* (special facial treatment after a shave).

Young Pheeko used to wait eagerly for Eid when his father would buy new clothes from Lahore for all the children and send them home. It was also the time when he would have all his friends come home and his mother would serve *seviyan* (vermicelli-based dessert) to all. Eighty-six-year-old Kundan Singh Samra, one of Pheeko's closest friends, fondly remembered how children from both the communities would wait all year round for Eid and devour the *seviyan*.

Another eagerly awaited occasion was the Baisakhi *mela* (fair). Pheeko would visit the fair with his friends every year. He was very fond of sugarcane juice and Kundan would always pay for his friend's glass of juice. But one day, he discovered that he was short of money; he had just enough to buy one glass. So the two friends drank from the same glass.

In those days, such an act was nothing short of blasphemy. Sure enough, a villager who happened to notice this went and complained to Kundan's father that his son was sharing a glass of juice with a Muslim boy. But to the villager's utter shock, Kundan's father replied, 'He is Kundan's elder brother and my son.'

While Pheeko treated Kundan like his younger brother, there was another boy in this play group, who he loved and respected, just like an elder brother. Sardar Bakshish Singh Samra was two years older than Rafi. The two families shared a common wall, and the two friends, many common interests. One of them was flying kites; they delighted in watching their respective kites reach dizzying heights, competing with the numerous others that dotted the sky. Whenever Pheeko could lay his hands on a kite, all he had to do was come to his terrace and whistle. The next moment, Bakshish's robust frame would be jumping over the wall. The kite-flying began amidst much laughter and jokes. Pheeko would often look up and declare, '*Mennu aasmaan di udai leni hai.* (I want to fly in the sky.)'

A thoughtful child, Pheeko ran numerous errands at home. With their father away at Lahore, the boys in the family had added responsibilities. One of these was to graze cattle in the fields, along with other boys. The vast lush fields of Punjab gave him a sense of joy and freedom. He would hum folk songs and his friends, mesmerised by his voice, would quietly leave everything and sit listening to him. Something in their friend's voice captivated their young hearts.

At times, this spell would be rudely broken by the arrival of jackals, who attacked their cattle. Most of the children would look for things to throw at the jackals. Pheeko would simply stand and let out a loud call, identical to that of the jackals. And the jackals would scurry away, bewildered by the unusual sound. The emergency measure to scare the jackals away would then turn into another form of entertainment, with Pheeko imitating the sounds of different animals till the setting sun forced them to retrace their way back home.

Pheeko never missed a chance to have fun with his close friends. In those days, that meant long sessions of simple rustic games like *pithoo, kokla-chapaki, gilli-danda* and *chupan-chupaai* (popular Indian games) with his friends. One of the most common games was *khedo kundli* (similar to hockey). Allah Rakhi and Bakshish's mother would make the balls for them—these handmade balls would have embroideries and beautiful designs called *pidian*.

The village had one school. Although Bakshish and Pheeko were in different classes, they were together during the school prayers in Punjabi—sung under a banyan tree in the courtyard. It was Pheeko's favourite part of the day at school as he could sing to his heart's content. Here too, his classmates were in awe of his singing prowess. Kundan also went to the same school. Even in those days, he would say, '*Pheeko ik din bott wadda gayak kalakar banega.* (One day, Pheeko will become a great singer.)'

Though Pheeko was older than Kundan, they were in the same class. The reason was that the young singer had failed to clear his fourth standard exams and had to repeat the class. Pheeko would never find academic lessons interesting; his genius lay elsewhere.

When Kundan and he were in the fourth standard, they were once punished. The experience left a mark, quite literally, on both. They had skipped classes to visit Kundan's sister, married and staying in a nearby village. The next day their teacher, Nazir Ahmed, asked Pheeko why he had been absent. He replied that he was missing his sister and had gone to see her. The teacher knew that his sisters lived in the same village. He asked Kundan if his friend was lying. Kundan blurted out that they had gone to visit his sister. The angry teacher thrashed them for being dishonest. But the 12-year-old Pheeko was puzzled by the punishment. Even as the tears flowed, he protested, 'But Kundan's sister is my sister.'

The old school has now been taken over by the government. The classroom where Pheeko had once learnt his lessons in Urdu is now used to teach English to the present generation of students. But the old banyan tree, witness to his earliest days of singing, still stands in the centre of the school compound.

Even as young Pheeko's love for music grew by the day, little did he realise that his life was about to change. It was now a decade since his father had moved to Lahore. What had started out as a small *dhaba* was now thronged by people from the neighbourhood and also nearby localities. His income was now stable; he was earning many times more than what he did in Kotla Sultan Singh. It was time to call his family over to Lahore.

It was now Pheeko's turn to bid adieu to his familiar surroundings, the beloved, dusty lanes and his friends. The most heartbroken of them all was his dear friend, Kundan.

'How will I spend my life without you?' He asked Pheeko in anguish.

Choking with emotion and unable to utter a word, his teary-eyed friend etched out his and his friends name in Urdu on the rough trunk of a tree that still stands in the village.

Many moons ago, his friend Pheeko had said, 'Whenever you feel my absence, our names inscribed on this tree will fill my void.' The octogenarian now stares fondly at the tree trunk and slowly caresses it with his wrinkled hands. The names are no longer there. The flood of memories triggers a stream of tears that course down Kundan's face. Once again, his mind darts to the distant past, to his beloved friend, Pheeko.

Little did young Kundan realise that this dear friend would one day become the legendary playback singer Mohammed Rafi, worshipped by countless fans across the world.

In 1936, Pheeko, all of 12, along with his mother and other brothers and sisters, left Kotla Sultan Singh for Lahore to join his father and eldest brother. The family moved into a small two-room house at Bilalgunj in Lahore. Around this time, three of the seven families related to the Rafi family also left Kotla Sultan Singh for Lahore.

2

At Home in Lahore

Pheeko never went back to school. He joined his elder brother's salon as a barber. But he was obsessed with music. Hajji Ali wanted to keep him away from music and singing. Despite that, the young boy's talent soon revealed itself, that too in a strange way.

One day, when he was relaxing at home, he heard a voice singing a soulful song—a song in praise of Allah. Unable to stop himself, Pheeko ran out to see the person with such a mellifluous voice. Passing by his house was a dishevelled man in a patched, shabby black gown. The long unkempt hair and the rugged face, largely hidden by an overflowing beard, would perhaps have scared any child, but not Pheeko. The man's full-throated beautiful voice, accompanied by the *ektara* (one-stringed musical instrument) in one hand, had Pheeko rooted to the spot. The *fakir* (a religious ascetic living solely on alms) walked away, lost in his song, leaving his rapt listener awestruck. The young boy wondered if he would ever see the *fakir* again.

To his sheer joy, this became a daily routine. The *fakir* would pass by, playing his *ektara* and singing, and then walk down the lane and sit under a mango tree. Pheeko would follow the mendicant, as if he was being pulled by an invisible string, hypnotised by the magic in his voice. The *fakir* was not a beggar. But villagers passing by often offered him food or dropped a few *sikka*s before him, more out of compassion than in praise of his song. Pheeko would just sit at a distance and listen to him spellbound.

One morning, the *fakir* unknowingly sat on the verandah of his young listener's house and began singing, 'Khedan Dey Din Chaar Ni Maaye, Khedan Dey Din Chaar' (The days of fun and play are but few). As always, Pheeko got immersed in his *naat* (Muslim religious song). And as he finished singing, Pheeko requested his brother Siddique to get the *fakir* some food and alms. Just as the man was leaving, Pheeko asked his brother to call him back. The latter ran after the *fakir* and led him back home. For the first time Pheeko stood face to face with the man whose renditions he had admired all these days. He asked the *fakir* to sing again and the mendicant was perplexed; no one had ever asked him to repeat his songs.

'What is so special about it?' He asked with a puzzled look and his eyes seemed to pierce the soul of the young boy.

Pheeko humbly replied, '*Khaasiyat gaane mein nahin aapki awaaz mein hai. Jitni sachchai se aapne gaaya, mere dil ko chhoo liya.* (It is not the song that is special. It's your voice. The sincerity with which you sang has touched my heart.)'

The *fakir* looked at Pheeko intently. He understood that there was something special about this boy who could get to the depth of a song at such a tender age. With a smile on his lips, the *fakir* proceeded towards the mango tree, with Pheeko closely following him.

Both sat under the shade of the tree and encouraged by the *fakir*, the young boy sang 'Khaidan Dey Din Chaar.' The only background music for the song was the rustling of the mango leaves and the occasional chirping of the birds. His only audience was the shabbily clad *fakir*, who, by now, was riveted.

By the time the song was over, the *fakir*'s eyes were dancing with joy. Enthralled by the perfection of the rendition, he showered the boy with blessings and said, '*Tumhari awaaz kayenaat par hukumat karegi.* (Your voice will rule the world.)' A prophetic blessing indeed!

Music soon became the very essence of young Pheeko's life.

'It was unusual for a child of his age to have such a profound sense of music,' said his younger brother, Mohammed Siddique, now an octogenarian, and the only living sibling. He had spent the maximum time with his brother. One of their favourite haunts was the much revered shrine of Hazrat Data Ganj Buksh, located just behind their house.

Siddique still lives in the same house, full of memories of their childhood; the laughter, the pranks, the singing and the simple ways of life.

Although Pheeko was training to be a barber, music was in his soul. Even while doing his work, he used to sing Punjabi folk songs. The customers would find this quite amusing and would not mind his tardiness. Some of the customers even gave him tips for his singing. Pheeko revelled in their appreciation.

His elder brother, Mohammed Deen, noticed this prodigy's unusual talent and encouraged him wholeheartedly. Of course, this was without the knowledge of their father. Young Pheeko was often invited to *mehfils* (music gatherings) and people who knew him often requested him to sing. Mohammed Deen would always make sure that his young brother never missed an opportunity to do what he loved best.

In 1938, two years after coming to Lahore, Rafi made a short trip to Kotla Sultan Singh. This time, he went with a *baraat* (group of friends and relatives accompanying the bridegroom) to get married to his cousin (uncle's daughter), Basheera Bibi. He was just 14 years old and Basheera, all of 13. She was the eldest daughter of Deen Mohammed, the younger brother of Rafi's father. He had two other daughters and so was under pressure to get Basheera married off at the earliest. A teenaged Pheeko was the first choice. The wedding had been organised at short notice.

Back in Lahore, one day, as was his wont, he was singing a soulful hymn as he went about his work. Little did he know then that his life was about to change forever.

Lost in his own thoughts, Jiwan Lal Mattoo was passing through Noor Mohalla, and past the salon where Pheeko worked. This Programme Executive of music at All India Radio, Lahore, was captivated by a sweet, enchanting voice. He had rarely come across such range and tonal quality, even in the professional singers he met on a daily basis at All India Radio. He paused for a while, listening intently, the pristine quality of the voice touching his heart.

Mattoo entered the salon to take a look at the person with such an extraordinary voice. He was surprised to see it coming from an unassuming young boy giving a shave to a customer. Mattoo, who was known for his forthrightness, simply asked Pheeko if he was interested in becoming a radio singer. Exhilarated at this sudden offer, the young singer looked up and closed his eyes in gratitude to the Almighty before telling Mattoo an enthusiastic 'Yes'.

In March 1943, Pheeko appeared for an audition at the studios of All India Radio, Lahore, and passed the test with flying colours. He did not realise that this was his first definite step towards a four decade long, trailblazing career as a singer.

There was another person, apart from the elder brother Deen, who believed in Pheeko's extraordinary talent. Hameed, Deen's good friend, was to become the young singer's strongest support during his early years of struggle in Bombay. Although he lived in another locality—Hakima Bazaar—Hameed used to spend most of his time with Deen. Convinced that Pheeko was no ordinary singer, the two decided that he must get some formal training in classical music.

Bade Ghulam Ali and Chhote Ghulam Ali were two great *ustaad*s (expert, expecially in music) of that period in Lahore, under whose guidance young Rafi was introduced to the fundamentals of classical music, albeit for a short while. He also obtained *taalim* (training) from Barkat Ali Khan and Abdul Wahid Khan. He used to sing in *mehfil*s and fairs, where he would get unstinted praise. Among those who greatly admired his vocal skills was a man who had heard Rafi on All India Radio.

Shyam Sunder, who had recently begun his career as a music composer, was looking for a fresh voice for his upcoming Punjabi film, *Gul Baloch*. Filmmakers of that era had begun to notice his compositions. He approached Rafi. For the young man, it was another golden opportunity. He jumped at the offer, and went on to record his first playback song—a duet with Zeenat Begum. As Shyam Sunder had expected, the composition, 'Goriye Ni Heeriye Ni' sounded even more beautiful with Rafi adding his own nuances. Though the recording was completed in 1942, the film was released in 1944, around the time when Rafi was leaving Lahore.

By now, Hameed, who had become Rafi's mentor, was convinced that Rafi had a very limited future in Lahore. He had once visited Bombay and knew that this was the city where Rafi could really make his mark. Deen also agreed wholeheartedly.

Hajji Ali, Rafi's father, was livid when he heard of his elder son's plan. He was adamant that his young son would not be allowed to go anywhere and that too to pursue his interest in music. But thanks to Deen and Hameed's dogged determination, he finally relented, albeit half-heartedly.

Deen requested Hameed to accompany Rafi to Bombay, saying, 'My brother is not educated, but he is gifted. If he stays in Lahore his talent will be wasted. It is your responsibility to establish him in Bombay.' Then with misty eyes, he turned to Rafi, 'Do not return without earning name and fame.'

Meanwhile, by now it was evident that Rafi and Basheera were together just to fulfil the desire of their respective parents. When Rafi mentioned his plans to shift to Bombay, in search of a serious career as a singer, Basheera refused to accompany him, saying that she wanted to stay on in Lahore. The marriage lasted four years and they had a son, Saeed. Rafi now bid adieu to this part of his life and to his days in Lahore.

With a pillow case full of *chana* (Bengal gram) to stave off hunger, Rafi and Hameed left Lahore.

In those days, there were no direct trains from Lahore to Bombay. They left for Peshawar and then boarded the Frontier Mail to Bombay. Deen, Siddique and their friends were at the station to wish them good luck and see them off.

3

In the City of Dreams, Bombay

Intimidated by the sheer magnitude of Bombay, Rafi was also captivated by the city's beauty and the professionalism of its people. The immediate concern was to find a place to stay in? With their available resources, they found it difficult to afford even a rent of Rs 5.

After a desperate search, they were finally directed to Bhendi Bazaar, where they saw a place they could rent—in a 100-year-old *chawl* (cluster house) right in the middle of a teeming neighbourhood. They were guided up the steep staircase to a tiny flat on the second floor. The two newcomers now had an address: 259, Alka Mansion, 2nd Floor, Ibrahim Rahmatulla Road, Near Mandvi PO, Opp. Nawab Masjid, Bhendi Bazaar, Bombay.

Although it was tiny compared to their house in the village, they were happy to have found a place they could afford. They could see the Nawab Masjid from a window, something that gave them a positive feeling about the tenement. The narrow balcony on the rear was one spot that Rafi took an instant liking to. This, he decided, would be the perfect place to indulge in his favourite pastime—flying kites!

Rafi regularly visited the Nawab Masjid near his house for his *namaaz* (prayers). With an unfailing smile, he would greet everyone with an '*Adaab.*' His amicable demeanour earned him many local friends. He loved spending hours with them, along with Hameed, at the nearby restaurants like Zabbari Hotel or Nazari Hotel, enjoying tea and snacks, discussing films and singing a variety of songs. There was another famous eatery, Zam Zam Hotel, which Rafi frequented. Owned by Hajji Syed Haroon, it exists even today and specialises in Konkani food. Both Rafi and Hameed would never miss out on ordering *shaahi tukda* (dessert made of bread and condensed milk) at the end of their meal.

Rafi's favourite pastime, even as a young man, was flying kites. He preferred kites that were black in colour. A jet black kite flying high in the sky was an indication to the locals that Rafi was flying kites from his terrace. Usually soft-spoken, he was really competitive as far as his favourite game was concerned; he never took it kindly if his beloved kite got cut by an opponent!

Hameed, the dogged mentor, made a firm decision too. They would not leave this house until Rafi fulfilled his dream of becoming a successful professional singer. However, he also realised that such a thing was easier said than done. They were absolutely certain about one thing. They had to make things happen soon or they would not be able to survive in this city.

Since Rafi had already made a name singing in *mehfil*s in Lahore, it was logical to try the same route in Bombay. The first thing they did was start collecting information about the city's *mehfils*. After some enquiries, Hameed learnt that a big *mehfil* was being organised not far from their neighbourhood. It was no ordinary gathering, for the main performing artiste was none other than the greatest singing superstar of that era, Kundan Lal Saigal.

KL Saigal, the actor-singer, was an inspiration for many during that time. Such was the impact of his voice that almost all aspiring singers wanted to imitate his style. Rafi was no exception. He could not believe his ears when Hameed told him that he would probably get to share the same stage as his idol.

But Hameed did not know how he would be able to fulfil this dream of Rafi's. Scouting for information, he approached a shopkeeper in their locality. As providence would have it, the man happened to know the person who was organising the event—a Sikh, who was simply known as Sardar*ji*. The shopkeeper also told them the exact location of the *mehfil*.

That was all that Hameed and Rafi needed. They left for the venue on the evening of the event.

Rafi still found it hard to register that he was actually watching KL Saigal live. As expected, the singer left his audience spellbound. The sound of the thunderous applause made Rafi's heart soar. If only he could sing in front of this gathering, he thought, as he looked at Hameed. The pragmatic mentor was already looking for a chance to speak to Sardar*ji*.

Another popular singer in such *mehfils*, Khan Sahab, had now begun to perform. He presented a few *ghazals* (a lyrical poem in verse set to music), which were also well-received. Just as he finished his song, Hameed got his chance to talk to Sardar*ji*.

'Papa*ji*, this is my brother. He is a good singer. Could you please request Khan Sahab to give him permission to sing just one song?' Hameed pleaded with all earnestness.

When the request was passed onto Khan Sahab, the latter looked at Rafi for some time, as if trying to gauge his potential. Then he slowly nodded in acquiescence.

Hameed immediately announced that his younger brother would now be singing before them. If they appreciated his song, then they must give him their blessings but not any monetary reward. Hameed understood that it was more important for the people present to accept Rafi as a singer.

After an initial murmur of approval, the crowd fell expectantly silent. Rafi's talent, his elder brother's faith and Hameed's relentless efforts had finally created an opportunity. Rafi asked the *tabla* (percussion) player to play the *jhaaptal* (a 10-beat intonation). The musician did not know how to play this. Unperturbed, Rafi calmly asked him to play *Raaga Darbari* (a *raaga* is each of the six basic musical modes which express different moods in certain characteristic progressions). Then he presented a classical number to the audience.

Khan Sahab was stunned!

He had expected Rafi to sing a film song, just like every other young singer. He was not prepared to hear a seemingly immature young boy present a classical number so brilliantly, with his velvet voice caressing each note so perfectly. The audience, comprising discerning music lovers, whole-heartedly applauded. They realised that this young boy was no ordinary crooner. Instead, his understanding of music went far beyond his years.

As a spontaneous token of appreciation, one gentleman from the audience passed on a Rs 10 note towards the stage. It was a huge amount for the two strugglers in the city. But Hameed politely thanked the gentleman and refused it as the *mehfil* belonged to Khan Sahab. So along with the resounding applause for his classical recital, Rafi also earned their immense respect.

Delighted by the warm reception, Rafi now decided to present a *ghazal*. By now, the crowd was in raptures, and expressed their admiration with a standing ovation. Overwhelmed, Rafi found himself fighting back tears. Within no time, the appreciation turned into a profuse flow of monetary tokens, with the audience insisting that Rafi accept them. Sardar*ji*, pleasantly surprised at the overwhelming response from the audience, walked through the crowd, collecting the money in two cloth bags. He finally came to Hameed. Once again, Hameed politely refused saying that Khan Sahab was the one entitled to the token. He expressed gratitude for the opportunity given to his young ward and did not change his mind about accepting the monetary appreciation despite Khan Sahab's insistence.

Little did Khan Sahab know that even as Hameed was refusing to accept the small fortune, he was wondering how Rafi and he would return. They did not have enough money to go home. After thanking Khan Sahab once again, the two quietly walked a distance of five and a half kilometres to the nearest local train station.

Rafi's talent had completely bowled over the man who had agreed to share the stage with him. Khan Sahab had never come across a performer who could refuse a monetary reward for his performance, so nonchalantly. The sheer strength of character that Hameed and Rafi had displayed had moved him deeply. He now felt guilty for being unable to give them their due.

After a long, sleepless night, Khan Sahab arrived at their Bhendi Bazaar residence early next morning, with the bags of money. But Hameed was still unrelenting. Once again, Khan Sahab left feeling helpless.

Rafi's performance at the *mehfil* had apparently left its impression on somebody else too. Even as Hameed and Rafi were discussing the event, there was a knock on the door. Standing before them was a stranger. He revealed that his boss, a film producer, was among the audience at the *mehfil*. He wanted to meet Rafi. Sensing another opportunity, the two immediately agreed to accompany the stranger to the producer's studio. It was located in Dadar, several kilometres away from their house.

The producer greeted them warmly, once again congratulating Rafi for his incredible singing prowess. He then came straight to the point.

'Could you repeat the *ghazal* you sang at the *mehfil*?' He asked.

With a serene, humble smile, Rafi began to sing, immersing himself in its verses and the musical nuances. Once again, the song left the producer spellbound. 'You will be singing a duet for me,' he declared.

Rafi left no stone unturned to make the best of this enormous opportunity and the recording was flawless. The producer was all praise for the young singer. He was promised a payment after three days—an amount of Rs 30. It was far less compared to the amount Khan Sahab desperately wanted to give them. But for Rafi and Hameed, it was a princely sum that they had earned by the dint of their labour.

They soon learnt that it was the magnanimous Khan Sahab who had actually facilitated this opportunity.

Encouraged by their initial success, Rafi and Hameed now began to look for more work. However, they soon realised that in spite of the optimism, the real picture was far from rosy. Repeated rounds of studios yielded no response. Those were frustrating times. But despite the endless disappointments, Rafi kept his faith in the Almighty. Also, he had the unflinching support of Hameed.

Despite difficult times, Rafi would never miss his morning *riyaaz* (practice). He would sit by the seaside at Marine Drive and diligently practise for hours, so as not to disturb his neighbours in his *chawl*, who literally stayed across the wall.

On one such morning, it is believed that well-known singer-actress Suraiya, while on her morning walk, noticed him, absorbed in his singing. Within minutes, she was captivated by his voice. She walked up to Rafi and inquired why he was practising here by the sea rather than at home. The sincerity of his purpose made her offer her residence at Marine Lines for *riyaaz*, if he so wished.

Even as their struggle continued, Hameed felt it was time that he got married, perhaps to create a more stable home for the two bachelors in the city. A suitable match was found in their very locality. Hameed married Meherunisa Begum. Despite the added responsibility, Hameed diligently kept struggling to find work for Rafi, just as he had promised Mohammed Deen.

4

Meeting Naushad

Rafi's arrival in Bombay to try his luck as a singer could not have been better timed.

While the '30s saw a number of actor-singers rule the roost, things became quite different in the next decade. In the '40s, the balancing act of singing and acting could not go hand in hand anymore. The film industry was in dire need of trained singers. However, it was becoming increasingly difficult to find talented actors who were equally proficient with their vocals. The accomplished music directors were now creating compositions that could only be sung by trained professional singers. This created opportunities for playback singers.

There was a sudden rise in the number of talented female playback singers around the mid '40s. Noorjehan and Suraiya were already superstars, who not only acted well but could sing with equal felicity. It was almost as if formidable singers like Rajkumari, Zohrabai Ambalewali, Zeenat Begum, Amirbai Karnataki, Noorjehan, Suraiya and Shamshad Begum were just waiting in the wings for glory.

Rafi was in awe of these famous names. Little did he know that he would soon be singing some of his best duets with some of them. Rafi was also aware of the established and upcoming male playback singers of that era—Hemanta Kumar, Talat Mehmood, Manna Dey, and Mukesh.

In those days, music composer Naushad was a name to reckon with. Hameed knew that he had to take Rafi to the great composer. He learnt that Wahid Ali Sahab, Naushad's father, was a *munshi* (accountant) in the court of Lucknow. Hameed travelled all the way to Lucknow, along with Rafi, to meet Wahid Sahab and managed to get a letter of recommendation from him.

'It must have been quite a challenge to get a letter of recommendation from my grandfather, as he was totally against music,' said Rahman Naushad, the legendary composer's elder son. This was because Naushad had run away from home and come to Bombay, at the age of 14, much against his father's wishes, to pursue his dreams.

With the letter in hand, Hameed and Rafi went to visit Naushad at Kardar Studio. The letter contained just a single sentence which read, 'Naushad, if you find this boy worthy please give him a chance.'

The ploy worked! In 1944, Naushad gave Rafi a break in *Pehle Aap* (1944) with the song, 'Hindustan Ke Hum Hain, Hindustan Hamaara.' Rafi sang the song, with Shyam Sunder and Alauddin as the accompanying voices. The song had to be recorded with the chorus troupe striding up and down the recording area to simulate the scene on-screen, which depicted a group of soldiers marching; Naushad wanted to record the sound of their footsteps. After the recording Naushad appreciated Rafi with a *Shaabaash!* He gave him Rs 10. The young man was ecstatic.

Naushad suddenly noticed that Rafi's feet were bleeding and asked, '*Kya hua bhai? Aap ke paaon se toh khoon nikal raha hai.* (What happened? Your feet are bleeding.)'

Rafi replied, '*Hameed bhai* (brother) *ne naye joote lekar diye hain. Woh kuch zyaada tight hai.* (Hameed *bhai* has bought me this new pair of shoes. They are too tight for me.)'

Naushad said, '*Par aapne kuch bola nahin.* (But you did not say anything.)'

With a smile Rafi replied, '*Woh hum gaana joh gaa rahe the.* (It was just that I was singing.)'

Rafi's dedication left its mark.

'I had noticed a high level of confidence in Rafi on that first day. His sincerity was incomparable. Something about him told me that he would make enough space for himself in the industry,' Naushad had told his son. The composer would often narrate this anecdote to motivate newcomers even several decades after that eventful meeting.

Naushad and Rafi did not work together for almost two years after their first association, but a *connection* had been established.

Rahman Naushad said, '*Abba* advised him to try in other studios as well and continue his *riyaaz*. Yet he would invariably come to the studio to rehearse with *Abba*'s chorus group. Later, Rafi Sahab confided in *Abba* that he was afraid of being dropped if he did not show up for regular rehearsals.'

It had become a daily routine for Rafi and Hameed to visit the different studios and wait expectantly at the gate, till late evening, with the hope of getting noticed by a music director or a film producer. They were often disappointed, but Hameed would not let their hope evaporate.

Rafi's perseverance finally paid off. In 1946, Naushad and Rafi teamed up again for *Anmol Ghadi*. The song, 'Tera Khilona Toota Balak' became a hit. Naushad followed it up with another opportunity for this newcomer. This time, Rafi had to sing in a chorus with none other than the illustrious actor-singer KL Saigal. The film was *Shahjehan* (1946). It was a montage sequence and the song was 'Mere Sapnon Ki Raani, Ruhi, Ruhi, Ruhi.' The line 'Ruhi, Ruhi, Ruhi' was sung by Rafi. Though it was just a line, Rafi was over the moon for being able to sing a playback song with his idol.

This happened to be the only song that Rafi sang with KL Saigal.

As the years went by, it was clear that the Naushad-Rafi combination was destined to create wonders for music lovers.

Naushad had a special place for Rafi in his heart and it is best expressed in the couplet the great poet and music director composed for Rafi…

Meri sargam mein tera zikr hai,
Mere saazon mein teri awaaz hai.
(My music sings your praises,
My musical instruments have your voice in them.)

Naushad had been an integral part of the evolution of Hindi cinema since his debut in *Premnagar* (1940). One of the greatest gifts that Naushad gave to Indian cinema was to introduce Rafi to playback singing and bring out his versatility. His *Lucknawi* (associated with Lucknow) roots are well-reflected in his musical creativity; the literary richness found a perfect match with Rafi's Urdu diction. Rafi went on to become the blue-eyed boy of composers in the four decades of his career. The charisma of Rafi's voice had a magical hold on the box-office during a time when songs formed the backbone of films.

5

Making His Presence Felt

As things started shaping up professionally in the '40s, Rafi's personal life too added in another milestone—his marriage. It was facilitated by Hameed's wife, Meherunisa.

As Rafi and Hameed were out of the house most of the time looking for opportunities and meeting people, back home, Hameed's wife Meherunisa felt very lonely during the day. She often called over her younger stepsister, 13-year-old Bilquis, to her home for company. She was then studying in the sixth standard. Their brother, Zaheer, was also a regular visitor at Rafi and Hameed's house.

It was during this time that an idea struck Zaheer. With one sister married to Hameed, why not arrange a marriage between Bilquis and Rafi? Stunned by the sudden proposal, Rafi refused, saying that he was struggling to make ends meet, and hence, marriage was out of the question. Soon, even Hameed and Meherunisa joined in to convince Rafi till he finally conceded. The two families were immediately informed and the marriage preparations began in earnest. The only person who did not have a clue about the goings on was Bilquis, Rafi's 13-year-old would-be bride.

One day, as she returned home after school, she found the women in her house applying *mehendi* (the art or practice of applying temporary henna tattoos) on their palms. Meherunisa told her that she was to get married the next day! Young Bilquis was excited as she would now get to dress up in bridal finery.

In 1945, at a venue near JJ Hospital, Bilquis was married to Rafi. Bilquis happily embraced every aspect of his life including accepting Saeed, Rafi's child from his first marriage, as her own.

The initial years of marriage were tough. Although Rafi used to sing *ghazal*s and songs for Punjabi films, it was difficult to make ends meet. He gradually started singing in the chorus for Hindi films.

Marrying an ordinary man whose only possession at the time of marriage was his honest aspiration to become a successful singer, to being the wife of the most sought after singer and a bountiful man, Bilquis walked alongside Rafi unhesitatingly and supported him right through his rise to popularity, living through times both good and not so good.

'"Abhi Na Jaao Chhod Kar, Ke Dil Abhi Bhara Nahin…" Whenever *Ammi* (mother) heard this song she would walk down memory lane, way back to her *nikaah* (marriage) with *Abba* (father),' said Nasreen, Rafi's daughter. From being a daughter brought up in a conservative Muslim family to travelling the world as *Baji* (as she was fondly referred to by most of Rafi's acquaintances) Bilquis Rafi was his soulmate in every sense of the word.

~

The '40s tested Rafi's tenacity and desire to become a successful singer. During this decade, he sang in nine out of the top 30 box-office earners.

In spite of this, Rafi took time to establish himself in this rapidly evolving, highly competitive world of playback singing. It is true that the success of a film depends on many other attributes apart from its music. However, it must be noted that in the '40s, each film had an average of nearly nine songs. This means that about a third of the film's story was told in the form of songs. The songs had become as important as the film's script and its stars, if not more.

Music director Shyam Sundar, who had given Rafi his first playback song, was an unabashed admirer of his singing. When Sundar was offered another film, *Gaon Ki Gori* (1945), he immediately contacted Rafi. And just as he had expected, the duet with GM Durrani, 'Aji Dil Ho Qaabu Mein Toh Dildar Ki Aisi Taisi,' was a hit.

Meanwhile, thanks to his growing popularity in the *mehfil* circuit and his song from *Gaon Ki Gori*, Rafi had already started getting offers from many other music directors of that time. He sang for Pandit Govind Ram in *Hamaara Sansar* (1945), for Feroze Nizami in *Sharbati Aankhen* (1945) and *Amar Raj* (1946), for Hafeez Khan in *Zeenat* (1945), among some others.

But it was composer Feroze Nizami who gave Rafi a dream opportunity that took his career to new heights. He gave him a full-fledged duet with the inimitable Noorjehan, the reigning female actor-singer whose voice and face ruled the hearts of millions of music lovers of that generation. The film was *Jugnu* (1947) and the song was the unforgettable 'Yahaan Badlaa Wafaa Ka.' It became a superhit.

The year 1947 proved to be watershed year for Rafi, just like it did for the nation. He once again caught the attention of listeners with a solo 'Duniya Mein Aaj Mere Andheraa Hi Andheraa Hai' under the baton of SD Burman in *Do Bhai* (1947). He followed it up with 'Humko Tumhaara Hi Aasraa' (*Saajan,* 1947), a C Ramchandra composition. Both were hits and obviously, did not escape the attention of the other established composers.

Friday, January 30, 1948, left the country stunned; just when India was recovering from the trauma of Partition, it lost the father of the nation, Mahatma Gandhi, to an assassin's bullets. The nation went into mourning. Like several other artistes of that time, the music director duo of Husanlal-Bhagatram gave vent to this loss with a moving composition, penned by Rajinder Krishan. According to Nirmala, wife of Husanlal, her husband and Bhagatram were quite excited about this composition and her husband was clear that only Rafi could do justice to the song.

The song, 'Suno Suno Aye Duniyaan Waalon, Bapu Ki Yeh Amar Kahaani,' was finally sung by Rafi and described the brutal assassination of Gandhi. Rafi was invited personally by the then Indian Prime Minister, Jawaharlal Nehru, to his residence to sing the song. The rendition moved

Nehru to tears. Rafi received a silver medal from the Prime Minister on the first anniversary of India's Independence. For the 24-year-old, it was an honour beyond his dreams. The song took the nation by storm and Rafi's life was never the same again.

Between 1944 and 1948, he sang 100 songs. He continued his brilliant singing spree in films like *Pyar Ki Jeet* (1948), *Badi Behen* (1949), *Barsaat* (1949), *Chandni Raat* (1949), *Dillagi* (1949), *Jal Tarang* (1949), and *Zevrat* (1949).

~

The '50s was when India had just emerged as a new nation. This period was marked with a sentiment of social and political exuberance. This held sway over the subject of films too.

While there were films being made on serious subjects, it was also the time when the industry was discovering its lighter side. There were films like *Baazi* (1951), a crime thriller; *Baiju Bawra* (1952), the story of an unknown singer from the days of the Mughal Emperor, Akbar; *Mother India* (1957), the post-Independence struggle of a poverty-stricken matriarch who fights against all odds to support her family, and humour surfaced as an important element in films like *Awaara* (1951), *Shree 420* (1955), *C.I.D.* (1956), and *Chalti Ka Naam Gaadi* (1958). Besides depicting the social or political scenario of the period, these films had a distinctly high entertainment quotient.

Singers like Kishore Kumar, and to an extent even Mukesh and Talat Mehmood, were preoccupied with their acting careers. The vocals of Talat Mehmood and Hemanta Kumar were at times not suitable for the characters that were being conceptualised for the screen.

Rafi, on the other hand, could blend his voice with the character and sound as though it was the on-screen actor singing. He was also blessed with a mind-boggling range—cruising along effortlessly through the three octaves without faltering on a single note. It was hard to find a match for his veritable repertoire of musical skills.

Rafi played an important role in the career of Badruddin Jamaluddin Kazi, who adopted the screen name of Johnny Walker. Guru Dutt gave him the name after the famous Scotch whisky, after he acted brilliantly as a drunkard during his first screen test for *Baazi*. Since then, he became a permanent feature in Guru Dutt's films.

When one watches an inebriated Johnny Walker performing his antics, while he attempts to climb a tree and lip-sync to Rafi's 'Jungle Mein Mor Nacha Kisine Na Dekha' (*Madhumati*, 1958), one feels it is the comedian himself singing. It is almost impossible to believe that in the same film, Rafi could sing another gem, full of pathos, for Dilip Kumar; the song in question being 'Toote Huye Khwaabon Ne.' One instantaneously notices the difference in rendition as Rafi sang for the two diametrically opposite characters on-screen—that of Johnny Walker and Dilip Kumar.

It was not easy to lend a voice to a formidable comedian like Johnny Walker and match his expressions and gestures that were so full of frolic. One song that immediately strikes a chord when Johnny Walker and Rafi are remembered is 'Sar Jo Tera Chakraaye' (*Pyaasa*, 1957). Rafi perfectly matched his voice to the antics of Johnny Walker on-screen, in the act of giving a head-massage.

Johnny Walker's name gradually became synonymous with comedy, so much so that people who went to see his films expected at least one frolicking song. And it was invariably in the voice of Rafi. However, unlike the other purely fun-filled songs of Johnny Walker, 'Ae Dil Hai Mushkil Jeena Yahaan' (*C.I.D.* 1956) dealt with the vagaries of urban life.

The fact that songs enacted by a comedian became popular spoke of Rafi's versatility and his ability to create magic with his voice. Though Manna Dey has lent his voice on many occasions for Mehmood, also a great comedian, Rafi holds the credit for singing the maximum number of songs for a comic actor—155 for Johnny Walker. How the gentle Rafi managed to mimic the effervescent actor's performance on-screen is something that continues to mystify music lovers even today.

Some other unforgettable scores include 'Na Na Na Tauba Tauba' (*Aar Paar*, 1954; a Rafi-Geeta (Dutt) duet), 'Jaane Kahaan Mera Jigar Gaya Ji' (*Mr. and Mrs. 55*, 1955, a Rafi-Geeta duet), 'Haseeno Sambhaalo Apni Yeh Duniya' (*Khota Paisa*, 1958), 'Nashe Mein Hum Nashe Mein Tum'

(*Black Cat*, 1959; a Rafi-Suman duet), 'Suno Suno Miss Chatterjee, Meri Dil Ka Matter Ji' (*Bahaarein Phir Bhi Aayengi*, 1966).

Johnny Walker owed his immense popularity to two men—Guru Dutt and Rafi. They gave him a distinct identity. And going beyond professional camaraderie, they became really good friends.

~

The trickle of singing offers of the '40s now turned into a flood. Rafi now had an average of 183 songs a year, which was like recording a song almost every two days, round the year. Of the 1411 songs he sang in the '50s, 915 songs were recorded in the last five years (1956-1960) of the decade. Rafi was marching towards the peak of his career as the playback voice of almost every actor of the decade.

Rafi did more than justice to the wide array of songs he sung in *Pyaasa*. He rendered to perfection the lyrics of Sahir Ludhianvi, in a composition by SD Burman, to portray actor Guru Dutt's angst against discrimination and injustice in 'Yeh Duniya Agar Mil Bhi Jaaye To Kya Hai.' The frustration with society is evident in the poignant '*Yeh kooche ye nilaam ghar dilkashi ke, yeh lut-te hue karvaan zindagi ke*.' There is also a poetic recitation in the voice of Rafi, delivered in the style of *khudkalaami* (monologue) which sets a romantic mood in, 'Yeh Hanste Huye Phool, Yeh Mehka Hua Gulshan.' The same Rafi lent his voice to Johnny Walker, in this very film, for the effervescent 'Sar Jo Tera Chakraaye.' With *Pyaasa,* Rafi left all his critics speechless with his ability to render each genre to perfection.

Music composers, connoisseurs as well as the masses found it difficult to imagine a film without Rafi's voice enriching it. Rafi sang in nearly 50 per cent of the box-office releases during the '50s. From 164 in the '40s, the number of films with his songs rose to 594 in the '50s.

He had, by now, become the blue-eyed boy of almost all music directors and film producers of the period.

There were films during this period that saw the singer at his unique best. For instance, he brought to life two very different manifestations of the emotion of love; fun and frolicky romance in 'Ramaiyaa Vastaa Vaiyaa' (*Shree 420*, 1955) and an intense soulful love in the title track, 'Chaudhvin

Ka Chand' (*Chaudhvin Ka Chand,* 1960).' The latter got him his first Filmfare Award.

Rafi was the lead voice in 17 of the top 30 box-office earners during the '50s. This included eight blockbusters which generated revenue of more than Rs 1.25 crores each. This decade also marked two all-time blockbusters, *Mother India* (1957) and *Mughal-E-Azam* (1960) where Rafi sang 'Dukh Bhare Din Beete Re Bhaiya,' 'Na Main Bhagwan Hoon,' and 'Ae Mohabbat Zindabad' respectively—songs that took the industry by storm.

6

The Winning Combinations

Many music directors and lyricists, of the Golden Era of music, were deeply possessive about Rafi's voice. Rafi had a tonal range like no other and music directors created compositions especially for him. Lyricists believed their words created magic only when sung by Rafi.

Some of Rafi's associations with his colleagues from the film fraternity often resulted in great personal camaraderie.

Music Directors

Naushad

The early '50s were also the formative years of the Naushad-Shakeel-Rafi team. The trio stormed the industry with films such as *Deedar* (1951), *Aan* (1952) and *Baiju Bawra* (1952). It was the remarkable success of *Baiju Bawra* that made them a success formula; one that gave the industry 96 songs in 41 films, over the next two decades, before Shakeel Badayuni passed away in 1970. Rafi's versatility was what the composer kept in mind when he was composing for *Baiju Bawra*. The song 'O Duniya Ke Rakhwaale' illustrates Rafi's ability to modulate his voice aptly.

Rahman Naushad (the composer's son) recollected, 'After recording the song, *Abba* was very happy and he came home, all praises for this newfound talent. The next morning, at 6 o'clock, he found Rafi Sahab sitting in one corner of the verandah. The singer told him that he had not done justice to the song and would like to sing it again. Naushad Sahab reassured him that he was very happy with his rendition. Rafi Sahab held *Abba*'s hand and said, 'Let's do the recording again. I will bear the expenses for the shift.' *Abba* sternly said, 'I am the music director and I think you have done a fantastic job.' Such was Rafi Sahab's quest for perfection.

'This score of *Baiju Bawra* was a superhit. The masses went euphoric on this song. A rumour doing the rounds was that Naushad Sahab had made Rafi Sahab sing at such a high pitch that his throat had bled while recording the song. When he was being congratulated by *Abba* for the success of the song, he humbly told him, "*Sahab, yeh sab aap hi ka kamaal hain.* (Sir, all the credit goes to you.)"'

Naushad was innovative and a trendsetter. He was the first composer to bring folk music into films such as *Mother India* ('Gaadi Waale Gaadi Dheere Haaq Re,' a Rafi-Shamshad duet), *Ganga Jamuna* ('Nain Lad Jayi He,' with chorus), *Sangharsh* ('Mere Pairon Mein Ghungroo Bandh De') among others. He was instrumental in improving recording techniques, modernising the orchestra and strongly believed in using a powerful chorus. With him, the chorus was not merely a filler, but an integral part of the song. The point is well-illustrated in the songs 'O Door Ke Musafir' (*Udan Khatola*, 1955), 'Dukh Bhare Din Beete Re Bhaiya' (*Mother India*, 1957), 'Aayi Hain Bahaarein' (*Ram Aur Shyam*, 1967).

Raju Naushad (the composer's younger son) clearly remembered those days when Rafi would arrive at least an hour before the appointed time at *Aashiana* (Naushad's residence) and sit and chat with his father; the discussions would range from films to music. Rafi's brother-in-law and manager, Zaheer, in the meantime would write down the song with a felt-pen, in Urdu script, so that Rafi could read it. Raju recollected, '*Abba* being a perfectionist would make Rafi Sahab practise for hours, but even when he would call it a day, saying, "*Ab hum aapki soorat dekhenge* studio *mein,* (Now I will see you only at the studio)," Rafi Sahab would continue to sit and would come up with something like, "*Yeh gandhaar nahin jam rahi hai.* (This stanza of the song is somehow lacking perfection.)"

Naushad Sahab on a lighter note would say, "Now go and practise other songs or you will never become rich."

'During the recording of the *bhajan* "Madhuban Mein Radhika" (*Kohinoor*, 1960) Rafi Sahab came dressed in complete white and sang it with immaculate devotion. The studio was transformed into a temple as his voice resonated.

'Sometime during the '40s, Rafi Sahab took a special liking to an outfit which almost became synonymous with his name in the later years of his life—*sherwani* (long embroidered coat) with white pyjamas. He complimented it with brown, closed-toe *Pathani* (associated with the Pathans) slippers bought from his friend Moinuddin Alimuddin's shop, on the ground floor of his own building.

'Rafi Sahab used to confide in *Abba* and seek his advice at every step of life, as he considered him his mentor. Even when he was getting married to Bilquis aunty, Rafi Sahab and Hameed uncle had come to *Abba*. In the later years, Rafi Sahab was a regular visitor to our house and would play badminton with *Abba*. They also used to have kite-flying competitions. The Naushad-Rafi team would compete against experts, who were specially invited for the occasion. This was a serious matter for Rafi Sahab and he would get special threads all the way from Punjab.'

Naushad in his career had composed for 65 Hindi films (*Habba Khatoon* remained unreleased). By the time Rafi stepped into the industry in 1944, Naushad had already composed for 11 Hindi films. Five of the films that Naushad had composed for were released after Rafi's demise. It is well-known that the Naushad-Rafi association began with *Pehle Aap* (1944) but *Anmol Ghadi* (1946) saw the real bonding between them.

It was a co-incidence that the two stalwarts celebrated their birthdays just a day apart; Rafi on December 24 (b. 1924) and Naushad on December 25 (b. 1919). Perhaps this extended to their personal bonding and musical careers as well.

SD Burman

'Din Dhal Jaaye, Haye, Raat Na Jaaye,' the evergreen romantic composition, immediately brings to mind the unprecedented chemistry of Rafi and SD Burman; one that left music lovers spellbound every time they came together.

SD Burman, though senior to Rafi by 18 years, made his debut as a composer in Hindi films a couple of years after Rafi. Within a year of his entry in the Bombay film industry, in 1947, he gave Rafi the opportunity to sing one of his compositions; 'Duniya Mein Meri Aaj Andheraa Hi Andheraa' (*Do Bhai*).

However, there was a gap of almost eight years before the music director harnessed Rafi's voice again, this time for the poignant 'Manzil Ki Chah Mein,' for Bimal Roy's epic *Devdas* (1955). Surprisingly, SD Burman gave Rafi a miss as the primary male playback voice for Dilip Kumar, in *Devdas*, despite him being the already established voice of Dilip Kumar in films like *Deedar* (1951), *Hulchul* (1951), *Aan* (1952). Finally, it was Talat Mahmood who sang for the actor in *Devdas.*

In 1957, SD Burman found Rafi's voice suited to the agony of a struggling poet, Guru Dutt, in *Pyaasa* (1957), in the soul-stirring composition, 'Yeh Mahalon, Yeh Takhton, Yeh Tajon Ki Duniya' and used the dulcet voice again for his slow-paced grieving composition, 'Bichde Sabhi Baari Baari' (*Kaagaz Ke Phool*, 1959). This was the beginning of a memorable musical association.

SD Burman is credited for having brought out two of the best prodigious male singers the industry has ever seen—Rafi and Kishore Kumar. In his career, SD Burman had composed 46 Rafi solos and 53 Kishore Kumar solos, with a wider variety apparent in the SD Burman-Rafi repertoire.

In the '50s, SD Burman gave a fillip to Kishore Kumar's singing career. During those years, he was more accepted as a singer-actor who primarily sang the songs picturised on himself but it was SD Burman who established Kishore Kumar as an alternate voice of Dev Anand. In fact, SD Burman intelligently juggled between the top singers of his period and successfully got the best out of all of them.

Some of the best SD Burman-Rafi combinations include compositions for *Kaala Paani* (1958). 'Hum Bekhudi Mein Tumko Pukaare Chale Gaye,' a slow, rhythmic composition and 'Achcha Ji Main Haari Chalo Maan Jaao Na,' a playful Rafi-Asha duet.

Khayyam

Khayyam composed 'Ek Dil Ne Kaha, Ek Dil Ne Suna, Ek Dard Bhara Afsana' (*Parda*, 1949) under the pseudonym Sharma*ji*; it kickstarted his association with Rafi. During this time, another Khayyam composition rendered by Rafi was 'Akele Mein Woh Ghabrate To Honge' (*Biwi*, 1950), which reaped great success for the composer. 'Jis Pyar Mein Yeh Haal Hai,' a humorous duet by Mukesh and Rafi, highlights the composer's ability to blend orchestration and voice; the pace of the song shifts with the lyrical exchange between Rehman and Raj Kapoor on-screen. 'Sab Ki Ho Khair Baba Sabka Bhala' is a solo by Rafi in the film.

In the years that followed, Khayyam composed some of his best works with the singing maestro. 'Jeet Hi Lenge Baazi Hum Tum' (*Shola Aur Shabnam*, 1961), a Rafi-Lata duet, commences with only the notes from a piano. In the same way, Khayyam used the strings of a violin in the prelude to 'Jaane Kya Dhoondti Rehti Hai Yeh Aankhen,' a slow romantic solo in Rafi's voice. Though known for his style of using singular musical instruments, some of his compositions have heavy orchestration in the interludes like 'Parbaton Ke Pedon Par' (*Shagun*, 1964), which mellows down during the *antara*s (verses). The song, based on *Raaga Pahadi*, is an extremely melodic composition. 'Theheriye Hosh Mein Aa Loon' (*Mohabbat Isko Kehte Hai*, 1965), a Rafi-Suman Kalyanpur duet, is another classic by Khayyam, picturised on Shashi Kapoor and Nanda. In 1966, Khayyam experimented with folk music in 'Aur Thori Der Theher,' another gem in the voice of Rafi.

Khayyam is rightly considered the 'Genius of *Ghazals*' by the music fraternity. 'Ghazab Kiya Tere Wade Pe Aitbaar Kiya' and 'Yeh Na Thi Hamaari Kismet' (both Mirza Ghalib creations and sung by Rafi) illustrate how Khayyam would give *ghazal*s the requisite soft treatment with the use of musical instruments like *sitar*, *surbahar* (bass sitar, is a plucked string instrument) and flute.

Khayyam reminisced, 'The first song I recorded with Rafi Sahab was for *Biwi* (1950); "Akele Mein Woh Ghabrate Toh Honge." It was a melancholic song wherein the lovers depict a misunderstanding, which results in separation on-screen. This was the first time that a *ghazal* was tuned into a *tarannum* (the manner of reciting a poem in the form of a song), an easy style of rendering. I kept in mind that the character in the film was not a professional singer, but a common man. He could be what we call a bathroom singer, who is remembering his beloved. Rafi Sahab sang the song so well… *Kya kehnaa!* (I have no words.) The song became a hit.

'Then we did a song together which was written by Swami Dayananda, for *Parda* (1949): "Ek Dil Ne Kaha, Ek Dil Ne Suna, Ek Dard Bhara Afsaana." Then came *Lala Rukh* (1958), which literally means "Flower-like face," a film based on the *Arabian Nights*. We had a scene where a *rakasa* (court dancer) was dancing and the hero was a singer… "*Hai kali kali ke lab par, tere husn ka fasaana, mere gulistaan ka sab kuch, tera sirf muskuraana…*" Rafi Sahab wondrously delivered these words of Kaifi Azmi Sahab.

'I would like to share a very special experience. The period I am referring to is when Rafi Sahab was at the pinnacle of popularity. We had become good friends and I was often invited to his residence; something I looked forward to for the food used to be awesome. After being invited for the third time, within a week, I asked Hameed, "Why am I being invited so often?" Then Hameed told me, "Khayyam Sahab, actually Rafi Sahab wants something from you." I was perplexed and asked Hameed, "By the blessing of the Almighty, Rafi Sahab has achieved everything in life. What does he want from me?" Hameed then voiced Rafi Sahab's request, which I quote, "*Meri awaaz mein mithaas bhar deejiye.* (Please fill my voice with sweetness.)" Those days, Rafi Sahab was singing high-pitched, emotional songs. When I heard this request, I could not believe my ears. Just imagine such a great singer saying this to me. I told Rafi Sahab, it would be difficult to change the matured voice and style of singing but asked him if he was prepared to forget that he was a great singer. Rafi Sahab without hesitation said, "Yes." Then I laid down some conditions and the first was that whenever we rehearsed, there should not be anybody around, not even children. Secondly, he would not attend any phone calls during the rehearsals.

'Thus began the training...he did the rehearsals with great dedication and sincerity. He was like a sponge, would sit and listen attentively and then sing back the song with absolute finesse. How the efforts paid off can be gauged by the quality of the *ghazal* "Ghazab Kiya Tere Waade Par Aitbaar Kiya" and the *bhajan* "Tere Bharose Hey Nandlala" that Rafi Sahab sang for me right after the sessions we had together. Rafi Sahab got what he was in pursuit of...honey-like sweetness in his voice.'

In 1954 an album named *This is Mohammed Rafi* was released. The popularity of the album showed that people loved his new style of singing. Asha Bhosle was his co-singer in the album. During the making, each song was rehearsed nearly 18 times.

Khayyam explains, 'Every nuance, every word was worked upon to achieve that perfection. Rafi Sahab was very intelligent, highly adaptive and non-compromising. My humble contribution to this great legend's career was adding some *sweetness* to his already God-gifted voice.'

OP Nayyar

Nayyar and Rafi worked together for the first time in *Baaz* (1953). The song 'Ghata Mein Chup Kar Bhi Jo Dil Ki Baat Hoti Hai' has a flavour of *qawwali* (a style of Muslim devotional music now associated particularly with Sufis) though not in a typical set-up; that was quite unconventional for the era. It was only in 1954 that Guru Dutt signed him for *Aar Paar* which turned out to be a tremendous success! The three duets of Rafi with Geeta Dutt—'Sun Sun Sun Sun Zaalima,' 'Mohabbat Karlo Jee Bharlo' and 'Na Na Na Na Na Na Tauba Tauba'—were all hits. This gave Nayyar's career the much required push.

Nayyar brought with him the rustic robustness, exuberance and beats of Punjabi music. The folk tunes, with a distinct beat of *bhangra* (folk dance of Punjab), in the voice of Rafi and Balbir, 'Yeh Desh Hai Veer Jawaanon Ka' (*Naya Daur*, 1957) and again Rafi in 'Yeh Mere Haath Mein Tera Haath' (*Kashmir Ki Kali*, 1964) clearly illustrates the influence of folk music.

Another unique aspect of his compositions was the frequent use of the tonga-beat which can be traced in songs such as 'Aankhon Hi Aankhon

Mein Ishaara Ho Gayaa' (*C.I.D.* 1955), 'Yun Toh Humne Lakh Haseen Dekhen Hain' (*Tumsa Nahin Dekha*, 1957), and Rafi-Asha's 'Maang Ke Saath Tumhaara' (*Naya Daur*, 1957).

Nayyar was known for bringing out the unique aspect of the musical instruments he worked with. The point is well-illustrated in the three songs from *Kashmir Ki Kali* in the voice of Rafi and picturised on the flamboyant character played by Shammi Kapoor. 'Hai Duniya Usi Ki' where the bar scene was picturised on the actor depicts melancholy with a lingering touch of romance. The complex emotions of the moment are well brought out by the usage of saxophone, played by Manohari Singh. In the same film, the vibraphone played by Burjor Lord in 'Deewaana Hua Badal' created just the right amount of melodrama. Again in 'Kisi Na Kisi Se,' the harmonica, played as a prelude by Milon Gupta, sets the stage for the rhythmic yet romantic song.

Nayyar's brilliance as a composer also comes across in 'Ae Dil Hai Mushkil Jeena Yahaan' (*C.I.D.* 1956) where humour is used to communicate great philosophies of life; a song where Milon Gupta's harmonica added to the mood. 'Main Bambai Ka Babu Naam Mera Anjaana' (*Naya Daur*, 1957) is another comic tune by OP Nayyar in the voice of Rafi where one can easily trace his signature tonga-beat.

Madan Mohan

The musical association of Rafi and Madan Mohan began in 1950 when Madan Mohan made his debut with the film *Aankhen* and Rafi sang 'Hum Ishq Mein Barbad Hain Barbad Rahenge.' The golden association went on to give 164 songs, across 67 films, in 25 years. The fact that Rafi sang a staggering 56 per cent of the 165 male solos that Madan Mohan composed, shows the extent to which the duo complemented each other. While Madan Mohan was known to have composed more songs in female voices (342 female solos out of 681 songs) and preferred Lata Mangeshkar as the voice for his solo compositions, it is Asha Bhosle's voice that he leveraged for his duets. This is why Rafi has 40 duets with Asha as compared to only 11 with Lata, when it comes to Madan Mohan's creations.

Anil Biswas

Anil Biswas was often referred to as the 'Bhishma Pitamah' of the industry. The father of playback singing is known to have introduced great singers like Mukesh in *Pehli Nazar* (1945) and Talat Mehmood in *Arzoo* (1949) and encouraged their respective careers all through. He gifted the film industry with the concept of orchestration and raised the bar for Hindi film music. He is remembered for introducing Western orchestration, using indigenous instruments, both in the songs as well as in their melodic interludes.

One gets a glimpse of this association from Anil Biswas's daughter, Shikha vohra. 'My father once candidly mentioned that though Rafi Sahab was a great singer, his open-throated style of rendition, in high octave, was not suitable for the type of songs he composed, which were mostly in low or mid octave—songs characteristic of the '40s. If you listen to the songs of the '40s, every singer sang like the great Saigal Sahab. Besides, every music director had his own distinct techniques, which matched the voice of certain singers. The '40s to the '50s saw a major change in the trend of filmmaking. India was establishing herself as a free nation. The youth of the nation was getting out of the revolutionary mindset and romance was taking over. This was reflected in the kind of films and music being created; in the '50s, the songs were more rhythmic and fast-paced, apart from being romantic. This went very well with Rafi Sahab's effortless high octave style of singing.

'In *Do Raahen* (1954), my father got Rafi Sahab to sing all the tracks. The actor on-screen was Shekhar and unfortunately it was noted that when he lip-synced on Rafi Sahab's voice, the songs did not suit his docile and soft-spoken personality. The producers made the decision to have the songs re-recorded in the voice of Talat Sahab.'

Chitragupta

> *Rafi Sahab's voice could soar like a bird flying free in the open skies, limitless and boundless; one singer who would always put his soul in his singing.*
>
> —Chitragupta's personal diary

Rafi sang 248 compositions for Chitragupta, which is the third highest he sung for a composer, after Laxmikant-Pyarelal and Shankar-Jaikishan.

Their long association began with the film *Hamara Ghar* (1950). Chitragupta however got noticed for his compositions in *Sindbad the Sailor* (1952), where he gave a duet to Rafi and Shamshad Begum, 'Adaa Se Jhoomte Huye.' But the Chitragupta-Rafi combination achieved real stardom with *Bhabhi* (1957). The film celebrated its golden jubilee in many cities and all the five songs were superhits. The most popular song, 'Chal Ud Ja Re Panchi,' was sung in three parts by Rafi; one depicted a happy mood, the second was sad and the third had an even more sombre mood. 'This is quite a unique composition and an equally exceptional rendition by Rafi Sahab,' shared Sudha, Chitragupta's daughter.

'Chali Chali Re Patang,' another song from the same film, is remembered and hummed by music lovers and ardent kite flyers alike, a song in which Rafi's voice effortlessly soars high to match the kites floating in the sky. Another *patang* (kite) song that Chitragupta composed for Rafi is '*Yeh Duniya Patang, Nith Badle Yeh Rang, Koi Jaane Na Udaane Waala Kaun Hai*' (*Patang*, 1960)—a song that conveys the ever-changing colours of life. The Chitragupta-Rafi combination gave more than 100 songs between 1951 and 1960.

Lyricists

Rafi's singing career, from 1940-1980, saw the usage of Hindi, albeit with a heavy influence of Urdu. This impact was seen not only in dialogues but also in the songs that were being written. Rafi had some very talented lyricists writing for him. He left no stone unturned to bring out the essence of their words.

Rafi was as much a lyricist's delight as that of a music director. He sang for more than 300 lyricists (excluding around 50 songs for which the names of the lyricists are unknown). The clarity in Rafi's *talaffuz* (diction) and his fluency with Urdu, together with his *adaayegi* (mannerism) made him the preferred singer for many lyricists. For instance, the way he pronounced a word like *zindagi* (life; existence) with just the right amount of stress on the initial syllable *zah* (of Urdu), made the song sound better.

Dina Nath Madhok had written Rafi's first song, 'Hindustan Ke Hum Hain, Hindustan Hamaara' (chorus) in *Pehle Aap* (1944) with Naushad as the music director, little knowing that his lyrics were launching the career of a singer who would one day rule the music industry. Incidentally, he is also credited with helping Naushad get his first break in *Prem Nagar* (1940). In all, he wrote 35 songs for Rafi.

The laurel of penning the first solo for Rafi goes to Ramesh Gupta. The song was 'E-Dil-E-Nakaam Ab Jine Ki Tamanna Chhod De' (*Hamaara Sansar*, 1945) with music director Pandit Govindram. He wrote 14 songs for Rafi in the initial phase of the singer's career, which incidentally was the twilight of his own career as a lyricist.

Rafi gathered momentum in the industry with the solo 'Kehke Bhi Na Aaye Tum' (*Safar*, 1946), a creation of GS Nepali, to a tune by C Ramchandra. A few other songs that Rafi sang in the words of GS Nepali are 'Tu Baaghon Ki Morni' (*Insaaniyat*, 1955), 'Yeh Hasrat Thi Ki Is Duniya Mein' and the duet 'Bhool Jaaye Saare Gham' (both from *Nausherwan-E-Adil*, 1957). GS Nepali went on to write 50 songs for Rafi.

Raja Mehdi Ali Khan started his career in the Hindi film industry in 1946, almost the same time as Rafi. In 1947, SD Burman composed 'Duniya Mein Meri Aaj' (*Do Bhai*, 1947) written by the lyricist and voiced by Rafi. He is known for introducing the usage of '*Aap*' (most polite form of 'you') in his verses, 'Aap Yoon Hi Agar Humse Milte Rahe' (*Ek Musafir Ek Haseena*, 1962) and 'Aap Ke Pehloo Mein Aakar Ro Diye' (*Mera Saaya*, 1966), where Rafi brought out the anguish of a forlorn lover. In the same year, the team of Raja Mehdi Ali Khan and Rafi came together for 'Ek Haseen Sham Ko' (*Dulhan Ek Raat Ki*, 1966), a song in which the lyrics skilfully carve out a lovely evening where Dharmendra professes his love to Nutan. With his panache for poetry, this lyricist created 95 songs for Rafi.

Qamar Jalalabadi contributed 143 songs to Rafi's illustrious career. The lyricist is counted as amongst the most talented wordsmiths of his time. He wrote the popular song, 'Ik Dil Ke Tukde Hazaar Huye,' for Rafi, in *Pyar*

Ki Jeet (1948), composed by Husanlal-Bhagatram. 'Mohabbat Zinda Rehti Hai' (*Changez Khan*, 1957) is often referred to as a significant song in Rafi's career, marked for its intensity—especially in the line '*Chaali aa, chali aa, chali aa...*' which the singer has rendered with total vocal control to progressively reach a crescendo. It exemplifies how a song can sometimes surpass even the film and the actors involved in terms of success and recall value. 'Tu Hai Mera Prem Devta' (*Kalpana*, 1960), a classical duet by Rafi and Manna Dey, which begins with a *Shiva stuti* (prayer to Lord Shiva) in the voice of Manna Dey, spoke of the poet's genius in providing the right poetic expression to match the scene on-screen (a sequence of nine minutes and 35 seconds). The eloquent and popular, 'Ek Pardesi Mera Dil Le Gayaa' (*Phagun*, 1958), 'Eent Ki Dukki Paan Ka Ikkaa' (*Howrah Bridge*, 1958) demonstrate the talent of Jalalabadi.

Rajinder Krishan penned the landmark tribute to Gandhi*ji*, 'Suno Suno Ae Duniya Walo'. In films, his association with Rafi started in 1949 with the song 'Mohabbat Ke Dhoke Mein Koi Na Aaye' from the film *Badi Behen* (1949), a composition of Husanlal-Bhagatram. This prolific lyricist wrote an astounding 343 songs for Rafi. 'Chal Ud Ja Re Panchi' (*Bhabhi*, 1957), is probably the most defining film song of the duo; it brings out the agony of a well-settled family, which gets dispersed due to misunderstandings between the family members. Rafi's voice in the song reflected the pain and helplessness that the family goes through during separation.

Rajesh Duggal, Rajinder Krishan's son, added, 'My father wrote about 1400 songs and Rafi Sahab sang 343 of them. In fact, he has sung the maximum solos that were written by my father.'

It was in 1949 that the Indian film industry saw the entry of another legendary song writer. Hasrat Jaipuri came into the scene, alongside the young composer duo Shankar-Jaikishan who brought about a major change in film music. The song in question was 'Main Zindagi Main Har Dum Rota Hi Raha Hoon' (*Barsaat*, 1949), sung by Rafi. Like his contemporary Shakeel Badayuni, Hasrat Jaipuri was known for his proficiency at penning romantic lyrics. In fact, most of the romantic and breezy songs for Rafi, from the stable of Shankar-Jaikishan, have been written by Hasrat Jaipuri. He earned himself the moniker, 'King of

Romance' for his splendid articulation of the different aspects of love. The voice of Rafi did justice to the words of Hasrat Jaipuri on 290 instances.

Revolutionary poet Sahir Ludhianvi was also a major contributor to Rafi's musical career. In 1955, Rafi sang his first song penned by him; 'Manzil Ki Chaah Mein, Rahi Ke Vaaste' (*Devdas*), an SD Burman composition. This was followed by other musical gems like 'Yeh Desh Hai Veer Jawaanon Ka' (*Naya Daur*, 1957), 'Yeh Mahalon Yeh Takhton Yeh Taajon Ki Duniya' (*Pyaasa*, 1957), 'Rang Aur Noor Ki Baaraat' (*Ghazal*, 1964). Sahir and Rafi worked together for 186 songs.

Though Kaifi Azmi, the great Urdu poet made his debut in Hindi films with *Buzdil* in 1952, it was in 1955 that his words were rendered in Rafi's voice, under the baton of AR Qureshi (better known as the *tabla* maestro Allah Rakha and father of Zakir Hussain) for 'Ruke Na Raah Mein Kadam' (*Sakhi Hatim,*1955). The brilliance of his writing fetched him critical accolades for *Heer Ranjha* (1970) where the whole film was narrated in the form of verse—an outstanding feat indeed; 'Yeh Duniya Yeh Mehfil Mere Kaam Ki Nahin,' in the voice of Rafi, is believed to have left the audience in tears.

Each of the 73 songs that Kaifi Azmi worded for Rafi are remembered today as much for their melody as their eloquence. He is the wizard behind one of Rafi's most hummed patriotic songs; 'Kar Chale Hum Fida Jaan-O-Tan Saathiyon' (*Haqeeqat*, 1964) made a lasting impression on music lovers when it was first released. Even today, an Independence Day celebration is not complete without this heart-rending song playing in the backdrop.

Jan Nisar Akhtar, a notable poet and winner of the 1976 Sahitya Akademi Award, was an Urdu poet and lyricist of the Golden Era. His poetry reflected sentiments of freedom, dignity and the evils of economic exploitation. Romance was also an element he would portray quite adeptly in his verse. In 1956, he penned the playful number, 'Aankhon Hi Aankhon Mein Ishaaraa Ho Gayaa' for Guru Dutt's *C.I.D.*—a song that portrayed romance in a refreshing way through a bashful exchange of glances, in the voice of Rafi and Geeta Dutt. The lyricist wrote around 80 songs for Rafi.

7

The Chosen Voice for Yesteryear Legends

The vocalist could easily match his voice to the personality of the actor and the mood of the scene. That made him the ideal choice for most of the actors who ruled the silver screen during his time.

Dilip Kumar

Though Dilip Kumar made his debut in *Jwar Bhata* (1944), his real recognition came with his fourth film, *Jugnu* (1947) whose songs marked the beginning of his association with Rafi; it was to continue for 77 songs. In *Jugnu,* Rafi sang the memorable duet 'Yahaan Badla Wafaa Ka,' with Noorjehan, which is the only duet they sang together, for she migrated to Pakistan immediately after this film. Incidentally, Rafi even had a small role in the film. This was followed by another box-office hit *Mela* (1948) in which 'Yeh Zindagi Ke Mele,' a melancholic score in the voice of Rafi saw the perfection of this actor-singer combination. Naushad realised the potential of this combination and brought the two together again in *Deedar* (1951) with the evergreen, 'Huye Hum Jinke Liye Barbaad' and 'Meri Kahaani Bhoolne Waale.'

Dilip Kumar received overwhelming response from the masses for *Aan* (1952) and the songs 'Dil Mein Chhupaake Pyar Ka Toofan,' 'Maan

Mera Ehsaan,' 'Takra Gayaa Tumse' and 'Mohabbat Choome Jinke Haath' (Rafi's version), became very popular. In *Shikast* (1953), the Rafi-Lata duet, 'Nayi Zindagi Se Pyar Karke Dekh,' filmed on Dilip Kumar and Nalini Jaywant, also gained immense popularity. In 1954, *Udan Khatola* had some wonderful numbers of this actor-singer combination—'Mohabbat Ki Raahon Mein,' 'Na Toofan Se Khelon' and the haunting 'O Dur Ke Musafir.'

With a series of films on tragic themes, *Devdas* (1955), *Yahudi* (1958) and *Madhumati* (1958), the intense actor came to be identified with the mournful characters he played and earned the nickname, 'Tragedy King.' In all these films Rafi was his voice, though in *Devdas* and *Yahudi*, Rafi's voice is only heard in the background scores. 'Toote Huye Khwaabon Ne Humko Yeh Sikhaya Hai' (*Madhumati*) remains a timeless melancholic number.

Dilip Kumar then consciously took to acting in some lighter films in which he lip-synced to romantic numbers, again sung by Rafi. The year 1957 was the focal point of Dilip Kumar's career as well as that of Rafi with *Naya Daur*. This BR Chopra black-and-white *magnum opus* had memorable Rafi-Asha duets such as 'Maang Ke Saath Tumhaara,' 'Ude Jab Jab Zulfein Teri,' and 'Saathi Haath Badhaana.'

With *Kohinoor* in 1960, came 'Madhuban Mein Radhika Naache,' arguably one of Rafi's best songs to be filmed on Dilip Kumar. *Ganga Jamuna* (1961) again brought the duo together to offer music lovers the delightful folk song, 'Nain Lad Jayi He.' The music of both these films was composed by Naushad.

This was followed by *Leader* (1964) and *Dil Diya Dard Liya* (1966). Although these films did not do well at the box-office, it did not affect the popularity of the songs. 'Apni Aazaadi Ko Hum,' 'Tere Husn Ki Kya Taareef Karoon,' 'Mujhe Duniya Waalon Sharaabi Na Samjho' *(Leader)* and 'Dilruba Maine Tere Pyar Mein,' the lovelorn 'Guzre Hain Aaj Ishq Mein' and the semi-classical 'Saawan Aaye Ya Na Aaye,' (from *Dil Diya Dard Liya),* are enjoyed by music lovers even today.

The next three films, *Ram Aur Shyam* (1967), *Aadmi* (1968) and *Sangharsh* (1968) further strengthened the troika's (Naushad-Rafi-Dilip) claim as one of the best musical combinations of Hindi cinema.

SD Burman experimented with Kishore Kumar as the voice of Dilip Kumar for *Sagina* (1974), but that did not fare well at the box-office. The masses did not respond encouragingly either. Perhaps this was the reason why the singer and actor never got together again.

A couple of years later, Kalyan*ji*-Anand*ji* brought back Rafi to do playback for Dilip Kumar in *Bairaag* (1976). 'Saare Sheher Mein Aap Sa,' 'Peete Peete Kabhi Kabhi Yun Jam' (both with Asha) and 'Main Bairaagi Nachoon Gaaoon' (with Lata) are some of the duets that fetched instant popularity.

In an exclusive interview with Naushad, after the death of Rafi, Dilip Kumar's grief-stricken voice reached millions through *Jaimala Gold*, broadcast by Vividh Bharti, '*Rafi Sahab ko na koi ghamand tha, na ahankaar, kabhi bhi naaraaz nahin hote the, aur na hi kabhi unke baare mein maine aisi koi baat suni. Unka naam mousiki ki taareekh mein jagmagaata rahega.* (Rafi Sahab was devoid of any pride or ego. He would never get miffed and neither have I heard anything negative about him, ever. In the annals of music, his name will always shine in glory.)'

Guru Dutt

The first film where Guru Dutt appeared as the actor/director was *Baaz* (1953) opposite Geeta Roy. It was also the film in which Rafi became his voice for the song 'Jo Dilki Baat Hoti Hai.'

Aar Paar (1954) saw Guru Dutt donning the cap of actor/producer/director. He was known for going against the tide and this time had OP Nayyar aboard, who was yet to prove himself at the box-office as a music director. Crime thrillers were not popular in the '50s, yet he made this entertaining thriller with two actresses, Shyama and Shakila, who had no major successes to their credit. By taking Rafi, who by this time was an established singer, Guru Dutt ensured that he took no chances with his playback voice.

The film was followed by a series of brilliant cinematic treats on celluloid—*Mr. and Mrs. 55* (1955), *Pyaasa* (1957), *12 o'Clock* (1958), *Kaagaz Ke Phool* (1959), *Chaudhvin Ka Chand* (1960) and *Sahib Bibi Aur*

Ghulam (1962), amongst others. Rafi sang 36 of the total number of songs in these films, taken together.

Some of these songs, filmed on Guru Dutt, have gone down in the annals of Hindi film music history. 'Sun Sun Sun Sun Zaalima,' 'Mohabbat Kar Lo, Jee Bhar Lo,' (with Geeta Dutt) and 'Yeh Duniya Agar Mil Bhi Jaye,' 'Chaudhvin Ka Chand Ho,' 'Kahe Itna Ghumaan Chhoriye' (all with Asha).

Johnny Walker was a favourite of Guru Dutt. His gait, mannerisms and songs complemented Guru Dutt's style of filmmaking, especially in *Aar Paar*, *Mr. and Mrs. 55*, *C.I.D.* (1956), *Pyaasa*, *Kaagaz Ke Phool* and *Chaudhvin Ka Chand*.

When Guru Dutt passed away, many of his films were left incomplete. These included *Picnic* which had a Rafi-Asha duet 'Kitna Rangeen Hai Yeh Chand.' Guru Dutt's own venture *Bahaarein Phir Bhi Aayengi* was completed by his brother Atma Ram in 1966, by reshooting Dutt's portions with Dharmendra. The film had some wonderful songs in the voice of Rafi like, 'Aap Ke Haseen Rukh Pe.'

The last time Rafi sang for Guru Dutt was for Hrishikesh Mukherjee's *Sanjh Aur Savera* in 1964; the song was, 'Taqdeer Kahaan Le Jaayegi.'

Shammi Kapoor

The much talked about *twist* that Shammi Kapoor brought in was single-handedly voiced by Rafi. Energetic numbers, year after year, right from 'Chahe Koi Mujhe Junglee Kahe' (*Junglee*, 1961), 'Baar Baar Dekho' (*China Town*, 1962), 'Yeh Chand Sa Roshan Chehra' (*Kashmir Ki Kali*, 1964), 'Chakke Mein Chakka' (*Brahmachari*, 1968) to 'Badan Pe Sitaare' (*Prince*, 1969), all had Shammi Kapoor acting on-screen and Rafi emoting it in his rendition.

Speaking about the virtuosity of his favourite voice, actor Shammi Kapoor had said, 'The Macmillan dictionary defines a playback singer as a singer who sings songs in Indian films, which the actors pretend to sing. I would like to add to this definition—a playback singer is the one who not only sings but creates the on-screen aura with his voice. The untamed voice of Rafi Sahab could go *junglee* (boisterous) and then he could discipline his voice to sing "O Duniya Ke Rakhwale."'

Shammi Kapoor had developed a style of his own which gave him a massive fan-following. Films like *Tumsa Nahin Dekha* (1957) and *Dil Deke Dekho* (1959) established him as a youth icon with a gregarious personality. Mohammed Rafi effortlessly adapted his voice to reflect the unique style of acting that Shammi Kapoor developed. The chemistry between these legends was such that filmmakers and music directors naturally thought of them as a symbiotic duo.

Rafi sang 190 songs for Shammi Kapoor, which tops the number of songs he sang for any other actor. In Shammi Kapoor's brilliant career, he has emoted, danced and wooed his beautiful leading ladies, all in the voice of Rafi. On many occasions the star himself played an active role in creating, conceptualising and recording his songs.

In the '60s, the Shammi-Rafi duo brought in a trend that stayed on for the whole decade. OP Nayyar with his compositions for *Tumsa Nahin Dekha* (1957) gave birth to a unique musical era—a trend that continued with *Junglee* (1961) and *China Town* (1962) and reached its zenith with *Kashmir Ki Kali* (1964)—where the songs were remarkably romantic, pulsating and hummable.

The high energy of Shammi Kapoor on-screen, coupled with Rafi's lively renditions, created a huge fan following for the duo. Of all the music directors, it was Shankar-Jaikishan who caught onto this new trend.

This combination is best illustrated in 'Yahoo' (*Junglee*, 1961), 'Aji Aisa Mauka Phir Kahaan Milega' (*An Evening In Paris*, 1967), 'Badan Pe Sitaare' (*Prince*, 1969), title songs of *Rajkumar* (1964) and *Budtameez* (1966)—all these songs are distinctively different in tempo and in the usage of musical instruments, though they are all romantic songs. Rafi's electrifying declaration in *Junglee*—'Yahoo! Chaahe Koi Mujhe Junglee Kahe'—became the identity of Shammi Kapoor.

Arguably, many thought these numbers were less rhythmic and more boisterous in nature. However, this new, unconventional style went well with the youth. Shankar-Jaikishan also gave softer, melodious songs to the Shammi-Rafi combination, such as 'Khuli Palak Mein Jhootha Gussa' (*Professor*, 1964), a playful romantic song; 'Awaaz De Ke' (*Professor*), a soft love-duet of Rafi-Lata; and 'Janam Janam Ka Saath Hain' (*Tum Se Accha Kaun Hai*, 1969).

Junglee, which was Shammi Kapoor's first colour film, also had 'Ehsaan Tera Hoga Mujh Par' in the voice of Rafi; a romantic sublime solo where Shammi Kapoor's eyes convey his deep love for the nubile debutante Saira Banu. This number will always be remembered for the intensity with which it describes his *mohabbat* (love).

Shammi Kapoor acknowledged that no one could profess *love* more beautifully than Rafi; be it with passion, sensuousness, intoxication or a heady mix of all these elements. Shammi Kapoor had a huge female fan-following with his enchanting looks and his expressive eyes, empowered by the voice of Rafi.

One gets a peek into the vibrant aspect of Rafi's life through Shammi Kapoor's eyes. Although confined to a wheelchair, in the later stages of his life, Shammi Kapoor's unbeatable spirit took over the moment he began talking about Rafi.

'It is next to impossible to describe his greatness in words. He is an inseparable part of my life. The finesse with which he rendered songs picturised on me, it appeared as though Shammi Kapoor himself was singing…even to me when I used to hear those songs post recording. A lot of credit goes to the music composers and lyricists of our time, like OP Nayyar, Shankar-Jaikishan, Shailendra, Hasrat Jaipuri and many others, though I never got an opportunity to act in a Naushad composition in spite of Rafi being his favourite voice. But the connection Rafi Sahab and I shared was eternal and got reinforced with every song he sang for me. He was not only my voice, but a very dear friend as well.

'His voice had become a lucky charm for me, right from the songs of *Jeevan Jyoti* (1953) to "Jawaniya Yeh Mast Mast Bin Piye" and "Yoon To Humne Lakh Haseen Dekhe Hai" (*Tumsa Nahin Dekha*, 1957), "Hum Aur Tum Aur Yeh Samaa" and "Dil Deke Dekho" (*Dil Deke Dekho*, 1959), "Baar Baar Dekho" (*China Town*, 1962), "Govinda Aala Re Aala" (*Bluff Master*, 1963), "O Haseena Zulfon Waali" (*Teesri Manzil*, 1966), "Aaj Kal Tere Mere Pyar Ke Charche" (*Brahmachari*, 1968), "Badan Pe Sitaare" (*Prince*, 1969), "Tum Mujhe Yun Bhula Na Paaoge" (*Pagla Kahin Ka*, 1970) and many more that followed in the years to come.

'It was a long association. He sang for me in *Laila Majnu* (1953), *Rail Ka Dibba* (1953) and *Shama Parwaana* (1954), in my early days, but our real association started with *Tumsa Nahin Dekha* (1957) and the bond was strengthened in 1959 with *Dil Deke Dekho*. This was when I attended the recordings and developed not only a working rapport but a deep friendship with the beautiful human being that was Mohammed Rafi. And from there on, he became my singing voice by default and this was the beginning of the Mohammed Rafi-Shammi Kapoor phenomenon. It was Rafi Sahab's magical voice that accompanied me for over 25 years of my career.'

One of the memorable songs by this unbeatable combination is 'Taareef Karoon Kya Uski' (*Kashmir Ki Kali*, 1964). What is noteworthy about the song is the vocal expression of '*Taareef*' (praise) which was given a different treatment every time it was pronounced by Rafi. Shammi Kapoor too enacted it with gusto on-screen. Such versatility in teamwork would have been impossible but for the rapport the two shared offscreen.

Talking about the creation of this song, Shammi Kapoor recalled, 'I could not sleep the whole night prior to the recording, visualising the signature line, "Taareef Karoon Kya Uski" and wanted it to be repeated and then built up into a crescendo. The next day, while recording, when I told this to OP Nayyar*ji*, he didn't find the idea worth considering. I tried hard to convince him, but in vain. Seeing my disappointment Rafi Sahab told Nayyar Sahab, "Oh Papa*ji*, you are the composer, I am the singer, but he is going to act it out. If he wants it that way, why do you object? If you don't like it, we will do it again."

'Rafi Sahab rendered it exactly the way I had thought it to be. When Nayyar Sahab saw its first edited version, he held me in his arms and said, "God bless you." Rafi Sahab in his soft but mischievous voice said, "*Baat bani na abhi*? (See, all's well that ends well)." Rafi Sahab could win hearts in a jiffy.'

In a pensive mood, Shammi*ji* added, 'I am incomplete without Mohammed Rafi.'

Dev Anand

It was music director OP Nayyar who initiated the union of Rafi's voice with Dev Anand's urbane on-screen presence in the crime thriller *C.I.D.*

(1956). Rafi's duets 'Aankhon Hi Aankhon Mein Ishaara Ho Gaya' (with Geeta Dutt) and 'Leke Pehla Pehla Pyar' (with Shamshad Begum), and the perky solo 'Aye Dil Hai Mushkil Jeena Yahaan,' filmed on Johnny Walker, all claimed instant success. 'Aankhon Hi Aankhon Mein' became a brilliant teaser for what Rafi's voice could do for Dev Anand.

In 1957, senior Burman also experimented with Rafi's voice for Dev Anand in two of the duets he composed 'Aaja Panchi Akela Hai' and 'Kali Ke Roop Mein' with Asha in *Nau Do Gyarah*. The Dev Anand-Rafi equation further prospered in the tunes of SD Burman in the megahit *Kala Paani* (1958). In the iconic solo, 'Hum Bekhudi Mein Tumko Pukaare Chale Gaye,' Dev Anand can be seen immersed in the introspective *ghazal* sung with equal involvement by Rafi behind the scene. Dev Anand earned his first Filmfare Award as an actor and the film, the status of a classic. The film also earned credits for the team of music director, lyricist Majrooh Sultanpuri and the singers Rafi and Asha alike.

The duo of Shankar-Jaikishan was equally convinced about Rafi's versatility blending well with Dev Anand's on-screen portrayals. *Love Marriage* (1959) had some appealing songs such as 'Dheere Dheere Chal,' 'Dil Se Dil Takraaye' (with Geeta Dutt). The film set the stage for another musical blockbuster, Nasir Hussain's debut production, *Jab Pyar Kisi Se Hota Hai* (1961) where the composer duo of Shankar-Jaikishan cast a spell with engaging classics like 'Jiya O Jiya Kuchh Bol Do,' and the Rafi-Lata duets 'Sau Saal Pehle Humein Tumse Pyar Tha' and 'Yeh Aankhen Uff Yummaa.'

In 1960, the three Anand-brothers came together on the silver screen in their home production *Kaala Bazaar*. SD Burman was still continuing to compose brilliant music. By now, Rafi's voice was reaping huge rewards for Dev Anand. The partly-romantic, partly-devotional 'Apni To Har Aah Ek Toofan Hai' qualifies as one of the most unique *train songs* in a Hindi film; Rafi effortlessly brings out the playful mischief that the composition demanded. He also lived up to senior Burman's faith in the other songs of the film—be it the ethereal 'Khoya Khoya Chand' or the lively 'Teri Dhoom Har Kahin.'

Composers like Salil Chowdhury were also seen acknowledging Rafi's voice as apt for Dev Anand in *Maya* (1961). 'Tasveer Tere Dil Mein Jis

Din Se Utaari Hai,' a melodious Rafi-Lata duet, 'Zindagi Hai Kya Sun Meri Jaan,' a spirited Rafi solo and 'Koi Sone Ke Dilwaala,' the breezy piano song by Rafi, left music lovers wanting more from the Salil Chowdhury-Rafi melodious accord. The same year, Jaidev cast a spell with some of the most unforgettable tunes for the Dev Anand-starrer *Hum Dono* (1961); bringing for music lovers, a legion of songs like 'Kabhi Khud Pe Kabhi Haalat Pe Rona Aaya,' 'Main Zindagi Ka Saath Nibhaata Chala Gaya,' 'Abhi Na Jao Chhod Kar' (with Asha).

In the '60s, the SD Burman-Rafi-Dev Anand association became synonymous with success, resulting in a string of triumphs; *Tere Ghar Ke Saamne* (1963) had 'Dil Ka Bhanwar Kare Pukaar,' the playful romantic interlude on a stairway, between Dev Anand and Nutan, set in the Qutab Minar. The song was shot in the studio in a replica of the Qutab Minar and is remembered as a timeless romantic classic. The title song of the film, 'Ek Ghar Banaoonga' (Rafi-Lata duet) also hit the right notes along with its innovative visual of Nutan inside a wine glass; reflecting the imagination of the intoxicated character portrayed by Dev Anand.

Thereafter, Rafi was the obvious choice for the three solos of *Guide* (1965); 'Din Dhal Jaaye,' 'Tere Mere Sapne' and 'Kya Se Kya Ho Gayaa.' Two years later, in 1967, *Jewel Thief* was released, and it turned out to be another box-office hit for Navketan Films. The music played an important role in making the film the sixth highest grosser of the year, where senior Burman was seen juggling between both Rafi and Kishore Kumar's voice for Dev Anand. It was from this film that the odds seemed to favour Kishore as the playback voice for Dev Anand; Rafi had to be content with just one song in the film.

The song that saw the towering talents of Dev Anand and Rafi come together for the last time was a Rajesh Roshan composition, 'Logon Ka Dil Agar Haan Jeetna Tumko Hai' (*Mann Pasand*, 1980).

On February 3, 2011, at the premier show of the coloured version of *Hum Dono*, Dev Anand said, 'What a voice! Rafi Sahab could create moods on-screen with his voice and make acting easier. His voice was smooth as silk, serene as the morning dew and energetic like a fountain. The film *Hum Dono* made it to the Berlin Film Festival in 1967 and the songs were highly appreciated. We had sub-titles even for the songs and the Germans were very fascinated with the song, 'Main Zindagi Ka Sath Nibhata Chala Gaya.' They thought the song was sung by me and they complimented me for my beautiful voice. I did narrate this to Rafi Sahab and he replied with a smile, "If I sing this song in a live show in Berlin then the Germans will mistake me for Dev Anand..." We both had a good laugh.

'Rafi Sahab was an embodiment of melody. I owe the success of so many of my films to him. His voice stood by me from the time of 'Jiya O Jiya Kuch Bol Do' (*Jab Pyar Kisi Se Hota Hai*, 1961) to 'Logon Ka Dil' (*Mann Pasand*, 1980).'

8

A Versatile Singer Conquers Hearts

The '60s emerged as a period of major transition. India as a nation was undergoing social reforms and there were films like *Kala Bazaar* (1960), *Kanoon* (1960), and others, that portrayed this change and the related impact. The '60s also saw gregariousness and romance, in their rather bold avatars, replacing the sombre, pensive subjects of the films of the '40s and the '50s. The influence of Western music was another trend evident in the compositions of both newcomers and the established music directors in the '60s.

By now, Rafi had established himself as the default voice of lead actors like Dilip Kumar, Guru Dutt, Dev Anand and Shammi Kapoor. His charm was not limited to the high-spirited numbers. Rafi could easily juggle between the classical 'Madhuban Mein Radhika' (*Kohinoor*, 1960), a swinging 'Aaja Aaja, Main Hoon Pyaar Tera' (*Teesri Manzil*, 1966) and the fun-filled, light-hearted 'Aai Aai Yaa, Karoon Main Kya, Sukoo, Sukoo' (*Junglee*, 1961); all of which demonstrated his versatility.

There were other musical jewels from Rafi during this period—the soulful romance of 'Baharon Phool Barsaao' (*Suraj*, 1966), a father's heavy heart on his daughter's wedding in the award-winning song, 'Baabul Ki Duaayen Leti Jaa' (*Neel Kamal*, 1968), the saga of a crestfallen lover in 'Tum Mujhe Yun Bhula Naa Paaoge' (*Pagla Kahin Ka*, 1970)—to name a few.

Rafi's controlled slurring in songs like 'Chhalkaye Jaam' for *Mere Humdum Mere Dost* (1968) won him much appreciation. Though the singer had never consumed alcohol, he could create a mood of intoxication and sensuousness. Laxmikant-Pyarelal used Rafi's voice in *Do Raaste* (1969), the same year as the superhit Rajesh Khanna starrer *Aradhana*.

It was in the mid '60s that Zaheer, Rafi's brother-in-law became an active part of his singing career and Hameed took the backseat. Hameed and his family migrated to Canada in 1975.

Among the top 50 box-office grossers of the '60s, Rafi's contribution to the success of 90 per cent of the films remains undeniable. All the toil and labour of the last two decades was finally paying off. Rafi was now the choice of a majority of established music directors. Not only that, the new entrants in the industry, such as Kalyan*ji*-Anand*ji*, Usha Khanna, Laxmikant-Pyarelal, RD Burman, to name a few, also wanted to have his voice adorn their compositions.

This was the era that crowned him as the 'Emperor of Playback Singing.' Out of 11 blockbusters in the '60, Rafi lent his voice to 10.

Besides singing in 14 languages (Assamese, Konkani, Bhojpuri, Oriya, Punjabi, Bengali, Marathi, Sindhi, Kannada, Gujarati, Telugu, Maghi, Maithili and Urdu), Rafi recorded two songs in English which were released in 1968. The songs are, 'Although We Hail From Different Lands, Remember Friends We Are One,' an adaptation of the tune from the Hindi song 'Baharon Phool Barsaao' and 'The She I Love Is Beautiful,' English version of 'Hum Kaale Hain Toh Kya Hua Dilwaale Hain' (*Gumnaam,* 1965). He also sang a song in Creole when he visited Mauritius in the late '60s.

Rafi could add life to every poetic intonation. He made the effort to understand every inflection of poetry in songs like, 'Main Zindagi Ka Saath Nibhaata Chala Gayaa' (*Hum Dono,* 1961). Even though his formal training of classical music was short, Rafi could do great justice to some of the classical-based compositions of the period; his rendition of 'Aye Husn Zaraa Jaag' (*Mere Mehboob*, 1963), based on *Raaga Yaman,* has an overwhelming effect on the listener.

~

The '70s ushered in the trend of modern storytelling. The subjects shifted to the stress and struggle of the common man grappling with day-to-day issues like corruption, financial inequality and the social evils of smuggling, drug addiction and the like. These films were about the common man standing up for his rights and challenging his circumstances.

In the early '70s, post *Aradhana*'s success, when the Kishore Kumar wave engulfed the industry, some film producers and actors began to insist on having Kishore as their playback singer and Rafi had to be content sharing the space with him.

SD Burman composed the music for *Aradhana*. He had taken Rafi as the male playback voice for the first two recorded duets, 'Baaghon Mein Bahaar Hai' and 'Gunguna Rahe Hain Bhanwre.' After these two recordings, SD Burman fell ill and his son and assistant music director, took over the responsibility of completing the rest of the recordings for the film. The composer offered Kishore the solo numbers, 'Roop Tera Mastana' and 'Mere Sapnon Ki Rani.' Both these songs appealed to the younger generation, and gave a tremendous boost to the career of Kishore Kumar as a playback singer.

The '70s also saw the exit of actors from the previous decades for whom Rafi was an established voice. Also, music directors and lyricists, who had regularly teamed-up with Rafi to form a winning team, were also no longer active. Compared to the number of songs Rafi sang at the peak of his career, the same plummeted noticeably from 1973 to 1976, as a large number of playback opportunities went to Kishore Kumar.

A section of Rafi fans strongly believe that the death of Jaikishan in 1971 created space for RD Burman and the resultant effect was evident on Rafi's career. Even during this supposedly low period, the versatile maestro had lent his vocals to 28 of the top 50 box-office earners of the '70s, still making a mark in nearly 60 per cent of the top grossers.

Though he got to sing fewer numbers of songs in early '70s, some of these clearly stand out. 'Yeh Duniya Yeh Mehfil' (*Heer Raanjha*, 1970, composer Madan Mohan) and 'Tum Mujhe Yun Bhula Na Paaoge' (*Pagla Kahin Ka*, 1970, composer Shankar-Jaikishan) remain popular even today.

For the 18th Filmfare Awards, Rafi once again was a strong contender in the Best Male Playback Singer category for 'Khilona Jaan Kar' (*Khilona*, 1970). In an interview, Madan Mohan had revealed that he could not even dream of anyone else, but Rafi, singing 'Tum Jo Mil Gaye Ho' (*Hanste Zakhm*, 1973).

The average number of songs that Rafi sung in nine years and six months of the '70s was much behind Rafi's mindboggling average of 158 songs a year in the '60s. Many thought that the '70s started the decline of Rafi's towering career. However, the singer stunned his naysayers into silence in 1977, with his unforgettable *qawwali* 'Parda Hai Parda' (*Amar Akbar Anthony*). It still ranks as one of the most popular *qawwali*s in Hindi cinema. The other two songs from the same film, 'Tayyab Ali Pyaar Ka Dushman' and 'Shirdi Waale Sai Baba' are also outstanding in their rendition.

Rafi's voice seamlessly blended with Rishi Kapoor's youthful and audacious on-screen presence to give it the upswing it needed. Rafi gave memorable hits like 'Hum Kisi Se Kum Nahin,' 'Parda Hai Parda' and many more for Rishi Kapoor in box-office grossers like *Hum Kisise Kum Nahin* (1977) and *Amar Akbar Anthony* (1977) respectively.

Incidentally, *Amar Akbar Anthony* also had the rare distinction of having Rafi, Kishore, Mukesh and Lata singing for one composition, 'Humko Tumse Ho Gayaa Hai Pyaar'—the only time the four musical greats lent their voices for one song. After the stupendous success of this film, director Manmohan Desai declared, 'Rafi Sahab *ki awaaz Khuda ki awaaz hai*. (Rafi Sahab's voice is the voice of the Almighty.) '

The other chartbusters of Rafi in this period were for films like *Yaadon Ki Baaraat* (1973), *Laila Majnu* (1976), *Chacha Bhatija* (1977), *Jaani Dushman* (1979) and *Sargam* (1979).

During this time, Rafi's soulful song 'Kya Hua Tera Waada' (*Hum Kisise Kum Nahin*, 1977) achieved iconic status, fetching him the coveted National Award and what was to be his sixth and last Filmfare Award.

During a candid discussion, *ghazal* singer Jagjit Singh made an interesting statement about Rafi's adaptability, 'Rafi Sahab may not have been a great singer, but was an expert of cinema music.' The statement left one baffled. He elucidated, 'Rafi Sahab himself in an interview, to BBC, in

1977, had said that he had no formal training in singing but was inspired by a *fakir* in his early childhood. So, he cannot belong to an established school of singing or a *gharana* (any of the various specialist schools or methods of classical music or dance). Nonetheless, he had drama and a distinctive style in his voice, which made him an authority on cinema music. However, he was not someone from whom you could learn any specific form of Indian singing like classical, *ghazal*, *bhajan* or folk. This was primarily because he was not a formally trained singer. Though, I must admit, he has sung some wonderful non-*filmi ghazals* too.' On being asked to sing Rafi's 'Chahe Koi Mujhe Junglee Kahe' Jagjit Singh smiled and said this was a song only Rafi could do justice to.

It is interesting to note from Jagjit Singh's statement how musicians specialising in a particular genre consider film music as an altogether separate form of Indian music. Rafi had mastered this form to perfection. If one were to list out the various moods of film songs that Rafi has sung over the years, one can find scores of broad sets; no *raaga* was difficult, no song beyond his vocal talents.

Pandit Jasraj, maestro of Hindustani classical singing, had once affirmed Rafi's genius as an adaptable singer, 'The basic trait that distinguishes a playback singer from a classical vocalist is not the range or ability as a singer but the voice quality and its modulation.The ultimate strength of Rafi Sahab was the amalgamation of both these qualities that helped him reign supreme in the field of playback singing.'

In 1980, nobody could afford to ignore Rafi's performance in *Shaan*. The RD Burman-Rafi combination once again paid rich dividends in the form of the catchy 'Yamma Yamma' and 'Jaanu Meri Jaan.' Rafi's other song from the same film, 'Naam Abdul Hai Mera,' brought in immense recognition for Mazhar Khan, the actor on-screen.

Even after three decades as a playback singer, Rafi's voice was still fresh and young. And he proved it by lending his voice to the charming Rishi Kapoor in the hit film *Karz* (1980) with the outstanding 'Dard-E-Dil.' Rafi's other musical hit of the year was from the Amitabh Bachchan starrer *Dostana*, 'Mere Dost Kissa Yeh Kya Ho Gaya,' which again had the pathos which only Rafi could impart to the notes. That year too Rafi earned three Filmfare nominations.

The force with which Rafi came back in 1977 is shown clearly by the numbers: 100 songs in 1977 whilst 67 songs in 1976. He was recording a song every third day. It may be noted that this was also the decade when Rafi toured extensively for domestic and international live shows. He had never done so many stage performances before.

This juggling of dates therefore was by no means an easy task, as in those days rehearsal meant perfect synchronisation between a singer and musicians; a song was rehearsed to perfection, over days, before it was recorded live.

The Backgrounders

Often, the background song sets the tone for a film and at times is a more effective means of communicating the emotion of a scene rather than actors lip-syncing to it. On this front, Rafi's role requires special mention. He has the distinction of having sung 170 songs that were used as background tracks.

Guru Dutt's film, *Chaudhvin Ka Chand*, was a musical blockbuster of the year 1960, where each song was more lyrical than the other. As the opening credits rolled on the screen, Rafi's voice with 'Yeh Lucknow Ki Sar-Zameen, Yeh Rang Roop Ka Chaman' contextualises the story in Lucknow, a city known for its rich cultural heritage, warmth and traditions. The song closes with some more beautiful poetic expressions for the city

Har ek shaakh par yahaan,
Hai bulbulon ke chehchahen...
Gali-gali mein zindagi,
Kadam-kadam pe kehkahen...
Har ik nazaaraa dilnasheen,
Yeh Lucknow ki sar-zameen...
(On every stem of this garden,

There is the chirping of nightingales...
There is life in every lane here,
On every step there is laughter...
Every sight here evinces beauty
The homeland of Lucknow...)

The song enthrals the viewer, only to unfold into a beautiful drama of love, friendship and sacrifice.

In another instance, for the film *Cha Cha Cha* (1964), with actor Chandrashekhar and Helen as the lead pair, the background song signifies the power of true love... 'Subah Na Aai, Sham Na Aai, Jis Din Teri Yaad Na Aai' was filmed on Helen who is physically challenged but the yearning of her beloved (expressed through the song without the protagonist being shown on-screen) helps her to leave behind her crutches and rush out of her bed, to be united with him.The lyrics of Neeraj beautifully elaborate that love is beyond materialistic needs and has the power to create miracles. But it is the intensity of Rafi's voice that truly moves the movie-goer in this heart-wrenching number composed by Iqbal Qureshi.

In *Waqt* (1965), music director Ravi conceptualised a song, 'Waqt Se Din Aur Raat' as the background score for a juncture in the film where a close-knit family, of mother-father and three sons, is torn apart by an earthquake. The lyrics of Sahir Ludhianvi and Rafi's voice connect the audience with the grim situation in the story; highlighting the philosophy that joy and sorrow are two inevitable aspects of life and neither is permanent.

The song 'Na Tu Zameen Ke Liye Hai Na Aasmaan Ke Liye' (*Dastaan*, 1972) delineates the mental agony of a man, who has been cheated by his wife and best friend. The background song in the voice of Rafi conveys Dilip Kumar's dejection on his unexpected discovery of his wife's extra-marital affair. Dilip Kumar, without a word, communicates his dismay while Rafi paints the state of his mind through the background score. Laxmikant-Pyarelal used the orchestra very intelligently in the prelude to match the state of Dilip Kumar's mind; that of a shattered man. Rafi did the rest. And the song became unforgettable!

'Do Din Ginati Ke Umariya Beeti Jaaye' (*Do Dil*, 1947), 'Chandaa Kaa Dil Tootaa' (*Khoj*, 1953), 'Aana Hai To Aa Raah Mein' (*Naya Daur*, 1954), 'Chal Ud Ja Re Panchi' (*Bhabhi*, 1957), 'Raat Bhar Ka Hai Mehmaan Andheraa' (*Sone Ki Chidiya*, 1958), 'Dekhi Zamaane Ki Yaari Bichade Sabhi Baari Baari' (*Kaagaz Ke Phool*, 1959), 'Meri Awaaz Suno' (*Naunihal*, 1967) are some of the the other memorable songs sung by Rafi that were used as background scores.

9

Old Bonds Grow Strong; New Bonds Are Forged

Rafi's voice was unanimously acknowledged as having the Midas touch; whatever he touched would turn into gold. The songs that he got associated with set the box-office and the cash registers ringing.

While composers like Laxmikant-Pyarelal, Kalyan*ji*-Anand*ji* and Shankar-Jaikishan continued to churn out a stunning variety of compositions, RD Burman took the baton from his father SD Burman and unleashed a unique brand of youthful, vigorous, pulsating music, completely in sync with the demand of the sizzling '70s. While the established music directors continued with Rafi as their first choice, RD Burman's unconventional compositions found Kishore Kumar the more suitable voice.

Music Directors

Naushad

Rafi was to playback singing what Naushad was to music composing and their brilliant combination meticulously built a catalogue of 149 songs. Naushad has to his credit 26 silver jubilees, eight golden jubilees and four diamond jubilees—Rafi's contribution to this record is significant. The two all-time blockbusters *Mughal-E-Azam* (1960) and *Mother India* (1957) are a product of this unbeatable collaboration; the former grossed a little over Rs 5 crore and the latter Rs 4 crore at the box-office—a remarkable feat for that era. Besides these, Naushad-Rafi together gave superhits like *Anmol Ghadi* (1946), *Aan* (1952), *Baiju Bawra* (1952), *Kohinoor* (1960), *Ganga Jamuna* (1961), *Mere Mehboob* (1963), *Ram Aur Shyam* (1967) and *Pakeezah* (1972).

Naushad had composed the following *shayari* (recitation of Urdu poetry) for his favourite singer…

> *Abhi saaz-e-dil mein taraane bahut hai,*
> *Abhi zindagi ke bahaane bahut hai,*
> *Dar-e-ghair par bheekh maangon na fann ki,*
> *Jab apne hi ghar mein khazaane bahut hai.*
> (There are still so many melodies within my heart,
> There are still many excuses to live,
> Let's not beg for talent from anyone,
> When there is vast treasure in our own house.)

Rahman Naushad relates an incident that occurred during a song recording for *Habba Khatoon* (unreleased film)…

When Naushad presented the *ghazal* to Rafi, he started crying. The composer asked him the reason. Rafi responded, 'I really like what you have composed. The songs that I am singing these days only reach my throat; none of them reach the heart.' Chastising Rafi for getting too emotional, the composer urged him to rehearse which he did to perfection.

After the final recording, he embraced Naushad and cried incessantly, refusing to accept any fee for the song and left saying, '*Main paise nahin loonga, main paise nahin loonga.* (I will not take any money for this.)' Incidentally, this was the last *ghazal* the composer created for Rafi.

In the '70s, Naushad was asked to comment on Rafi's career. Raju Naushad recollected what his father had then said, '*Maine bade se bade* singer *ko suron se hat te huye dekha hai. Ek tanha Mohammed Rafi hai jinko kabhi sooron se hat te huye nahin dekha.* (I have seen many great singers miss their notes but I have never seen Rafi making any such mistake.)'

The Rafi-Naushad association translated into the duo working together in 41 films till *Love And God* (recorded earlier, released 1986). Naushad only composed for four Hindi films after 1980, the fateful year Rafi passed away.

In the '90s, once Naushad was asked in a radio interview... 'If you were to compose the best music of your life today, what would you do?' The composer had replied, 'Rafi and I were one. Since he passed away, only 50 per cent of me has remained! I will pray to Allah to send Rafi for an hour, to create my best composition.'

SD Burman

The '60s saw the bond between Rafi and SD Burman growing stronger. 'Naache Mann Mora' (*Meri Soorat Teri Aankhen*, 1963) was a song that epitomised the composer's brilliance; he created a classical song based on *Raaga Bhairavi* in *Kaherava Taal* (a *taal* is a traditional rhythmic pattern in classical Indian music) that Rafi opens with an *alaap* (overture), immediately followed by *tabla* (percussion instrument), played by Pandit Samta Prasad which added a classical splendour to the song.

SD Burman continued to divide his compositions between his favourite voices; for instance, for a particular film, he would record two songs in the voice of Rafi and the remaining in the voice of Kishore. This trend was seen in films such as *Nau Do Gyarah* (1957) and *Teen Deviyaan* (1965), right up till *Aradhana* (1969). In some of his films, senior Burman could be seen breaking accepted conventions like an actor's bonding with a certain singer's voice.

In *Tere Ghar Ke Saamne* (1963), SD Burman extensively leveraged Rafi's talent for the title song as well as 'Dil Ka Bhanwar Kare Pukaar,' for the romantic, refreshing on-screen pair of Dev Anand and Nutan. For the iconic film *Guide* (1965), SD Burman composed a variety of songs in Rafi's voice, which contributed in making the film an epic in the history of Indian cinema. The year 1965 saw another musical hit *Teen Deviyaan* where Rafi's voice mellifluously flows on SD Burman's compositions, 'Aise To Na Dekho' and 'Kahin Bekhayaal Ho Kar.' The last offering of this golden association was *Uss Paar* (1974) where Rafi sang 'Ae Mere Mann Main Hoon Magan.'

Khayyam

The Rafi-Khayyam association, though brief with only 26 songs, is a fusion of some extraordinary film and non-film compositions that music lovers cherish till today. Khayyam said, 'Sher Ka Husn Ho, Naghme Ki Jawaani Ho Tum' (*Chambal Ki Kasam*, 1980) was Rafi's last song with the unconventional music composer.

Their combination went on to achieve something remarkable... In 1968, on the 100th anniversary of Mirza Ghalib's death, HMV came out with an album named *Ghalib: Portrait of a Genius*. The poetry was written by Kaifi Azmi and the songs were sung by Rafi and Begum Akthar. Khayyam considers this to be one of his most treasured works.

OP Nayyar

OP Nayyar had also composed some fusion scores by amalgamating Western music with that of the East. He uses the versatile voice of Rafi in 'Naazni Bada Rangeen Hai Waada Tera' (*Phir Wohi Dil Laaya Hoon*, 1963) to create one such score. The song starts off with the traditional folk sequence with a Punjabi flavour, whereas the *antara* (the equivalent of a verse in Hindustani classical music)—'*Humdum mere naam na janu*'—has a Western influence, beautifully brought out by a guitar. Nayyar uses Rafi's voice for many such romantic songs with a Western influence. 'Humne To Dilko Aap Ke Kadmon Mein Rakh Diya' (*Mere Sanam*, 1965), 'Phir Miloge Kabhi Is Baat Ka Waada Karlo' (*Yeh Raat Phir Na Aayegi*, 1966). In these songs, *sarangi* (a stringed instrument originating in Rajasthan) and *santoor* (a stringed instrument native to the state of Jammu and Kashmir) have been very well utilised by Nayyar to accentuate Rafi's dynamic voice. Nayyar can be credited to have made optimum use of string instruments.

Nayyar and Rafi had a showdown while recording for *Sawan Ki Ghata* (1966). Two songs had already been recorded with Rafi. 'Zulfon Ko Hataa

De Chehre Se' and a duet with Asha, 'Honthon Pe Hansi Aankhon Mein Nasha,' but after the tiff, Rafi was replaced by Mahendra Kapoor for 'Meri Jaan Tum Pe Sadke.'

Kishan Sharma, a former announcer at All India Radio, who accompanied Rafi for a few live events, gave an account of this discord between the two talented giants. 'Nayyar was a very punctual man. So was Rafi. Nayyar used to close the door of the recording studio at 9:10 a.m. and nobody was allowed to enter after that. Rafi was usually very punctual and arrived before time but that particular day he was late by an hour. The musicians were all set and waiting. Rafi walked in and apologised, saying he had got stuck at Shankar-Jaikishan's recording. OP Nayyar reacted sharply, "You have time for Shankar-Jaikishan and not for OP Nayyar. Now onwards, OP Nayyar will not have time for Rafi." The recording was cancelled and the accountant was asked to settle the bills. After this incident a journalist interviewing Rafi, tried to sensationalise the incident by asking him how OP Nayyar could treat him with such disrespect. Rafi politely replied, "I was wrong and Nayyar Sahab was correct."

'Three years later, Rafi came to Nayyar's residence. The composer was overwhelmed. He respectfully said to his favourite singer, "Rafi, by coming here today you have proved that you are much superior to OP Nayyar. You could overcome your ego. I could not!"'

The bonding between the two can be inferred from the fact that Rafi would often sing, '*Yun to humne lakh sangeetkaar dekhe hain,* OP Nayyar *sa nahin dekha!* (Though I have seen many composers, I have never seen one like OP Nayyar!)'

By the late '60s, Rafi's teaming with OP Nayyar had cast a spell on music lovers. The third dimension of this new trio was Asha Bhosle, whose refreshing voice complemented that of Rafi. This association culminated in innumerable hits and evergreen melodies. Till today, the Rafi-OP Nayyar duo is remembered for its uniqueness and the Rafi-Asha confluence, for the highest number of duets.

Nayyar and Rafi worked together for 197 songs in 55 films, out of the 70 films that he composed for in his whole career.

'Kitna Bada Sitam Hai Yeh Do Jahaan Waale' (*Bin Maa Ke Bache*, 1979) is the last composition they did together.

OP Nayyar is believed to have told a group of young composers once, 'You people are unlucky as you do not have a Mohammed Rafi to record your songs.'

Madan Mohan

In 1964, Madan Mohan composed 'Meri Awaaz Suno' as a tribute to Pandit Jawaharlal Nehru—the impassioned voice of Rafi reflected the emotions of the bereaved nation. Later, this popular song was used in *Naunihal* (1967).

'Kar Chale Hum Fida Jaan-O-Tan Saathiyon' (*Haqeeqat*, 1965) from the stable of Madan Mohan, is outstanding for its patriotic fervour. This film also has the soulful song, 'Main Ye Soch Kar Uske Dar Se Utha Tha,' with very little musical support, except the soulful violin strings.

Madan Mohan had great regard for Rafi and when he won the National Award for his score in *Dastak* (1971), which had a Rafi solo, 'Tumse Kahoon Ek Baat Paron Se,' he called Rafi to express his gratitude, thus acknowledging the singer's contribution to this success.

Ustaad Rais Khan, one of Madan Mohan's favourite musicians, spoke of the enchanting music this composer-singer duo could effortlessly produce. He recollected that his *sitar* (a large, long-necked Indian lute with movable frets, played with a wire pick) pieces were an integral part of many of Madan Mohan's compositions, the finest of them being the Rafi songs, specially, 'Meri Duniya Mein Tum Aaye, Kya Kya Apne Saath Liye' (*Heer Ranjha*, 1970), a duet by Rafi and Lata—an unusual composition where the song opens with Rafi's voice, sans any instrumentation till the first interlude, from where it breaks into a reverberation of *sitar* by Ustaad Rais Khan. Some of the other memorable creations from this combination were from the films *Dil Ki Raahein* (1973) and *Hanste Zakhm* (1973), amongst others.

The last couple of songs that Madan Mohan and Rafi recorded were the two chartbusters 'Tere Dar Pe Aaya Hoon' and 'Barbaad-E-Mohabbat

Ki Duaa' (both from *Laila Majnu*, 1976). The film turned out to be the highest grosser that year, during the supposed slack years of Rafi; it was Madan Mohan who brought him back with a bang as the voice of the young Rishi Kapoor.

Madan Mohan's elder son, Sanjeev Kohli, who has worked with leading music labels like Polydor, HMV and Yashraj Music, spoke about Rafi's association with his father.

'Rafi Sahab was extremely versatile and Madan*ji* got him to sing different types of songs in several *raaga*s which ranged from the soulful, to the sombre, to the more playful numbers. Keeping Rafi Sahab in mind he composed *ghazal*s like "Humsafar Saath Apna Chhod Chale" (*Aakhri Daao*, 1958) in *Raaga Gara*; "Rang Aur Noor Ki Baaraat Kise Pesh Karoon" (*Ghazal*, 1964) based on *Raaga Puriya Dhanashree*; "Main Nigaahen Tere Chehre Se Hataaun Kaise" (*Aap Ki Parchhaaiyan*, 1964) in *Raaga Darbari Kanada;* "Aap Ke Pehloo Main Aakar Ro Diye" (*Mera Saaya*, 1966) in *Raaga Bhim Palashri*; "Teri Aakhon Ke Siwa Duniya Mein Rakha Kya Hain" (*Chiraag*, 1969) in *Raaga Jhinjhoti*.

'As I grew up and started looking more closely at the music industry, about which I had heard innumerable anecdotes from my father, I realised the iconic status Rafi Sahab had in the industry. Many times, if a music director composed a song for Rafi Sahab and he was not available, the recording would be cancelled till the next date that worked for him.'

Kohli explained Rafi's popularity as a brand, from the perspective of a marketing person, 'Say a music album is to be launched for top 10 songs from the '60s. This was the time when many hits songs were composed by Shankar-Jaikishan, sung by Rafi for Shammi Kapoor, songs like "Yahoo!" "Badan Pe Sitaare" and others. I can brand the album in three ways—*Yahoo-Mohammed Rafi* or *Yahoo-Shankar-Jaikishan* or *Yahoo-Hasrat Jaipuri* or *Yahoo-Shammi Kapoor*. Undoubtedly, *Yahoo-Mohammed Rafi* is the most saleable. The brand perception and fan-following of Rafi Sahab is beyond imagination.

'The "Rafi-Lata" combination, due to its versatility had a great demand both amongst the masses and the music directors. But from 1963 to 1967 these two legends were not singing together. If Rafi Sahab was regarded as the "Emperor of playback singing," Lata*ji* was the "Queen of playback singing." They were the formula for success. The period of rift between the two was certainly a loss to most of the music directors, except OP Nayyar Sahab (The composer primarily had Asha Bhosle sing his compositions). Madan*ji* worked out a solution; some songs that were envisioned as duets were made into tandem songs, where there would be a female and male version of the same song. For duets where Rafi Sahab's voice was considered necessary, a replacement for Lata*ji*'s voice was found in other female voices like Suman Kalyanpur. Similarly, when composers necessarily wanted Lata*ji* in a duet song, they chose other singers like Mahendra Kapoor*ji*, Manna*da* and Mukesh*ji* as male voices. Still the music composers were not content with the loss of their choicest combination and many would request them to come together.

'It was Burman*da* who finally brought the two legends back together. Even Nargis*ji* played a critical role in this. It was at an SD Burman Night organised at Shanmukhananda Hall in 1967. Nargis*ji* and Madan*ji* were the hosts for the evening. The show was planned in such a way that all the maestros, Lata*ji*, Asha*ji*, Mukesh*ji*, Rafi Sahab, Manna*da* were to sing solos. A moment came after these performances, when the two hosts announced, "Now there is a great surprise for all of you." Then Lata*ji* entered the stage from one side and Rafi Sahab from the other. The applause that followed cannot be put into words. After a silence that prevailed between the two for four years, it was "Dil Pukaare, Aa Re, Aa Re" (*Jewel Thief*, 1967) that broke this silence.

'My father was fastidious about his compositions. He was working on *Jahan Ara* in 1962-63—the same time when *Junglee* was being made. He told Rafi Sahab frankly that after singing "Chahe Koi Mujhe Junglee Kahein" he would need some time before he could sing a serious classical number. That's how my father thought of Talat Mehmood for *Jahan Ara*, even against the wish of producer Om Prakash, as the era belonged to Rafi, who was the first preference for every filmmaker.

'Ten years later, in 1973-74 during the making of *Laila Majnu* (released in 1976), the same Madan*ji* strongly insisted on having the voice of Rafi for the young Rishi Kapoor. That was the time when many thought that Rafi Sahab belonged to the yesteryears. Moreover, Kishore*da* had gained immense popularity and Shailendra Singh had already sung for Rishi Kapoor in *Bobby* (1973), hence Rafi was obviously not the producer's choice. Madan*ji* however persisted that he wanted only Rafi or else he would leave the film. One of the probable reasons for this conviction was that Rafi Sahab had exceeded Madan*ji*'s expectations in one of his prior compositions, "Tum Jo Mil Gaye Ho," *Hanste Zakhm* (1973). Ultimately, the producer and the director had to give in to Madan*ji*'s decision and that's how Rafi Sahab became the voice of Rishi Kapoor. It almost became a success formula and Rishi Kapoor wholeheartedly accepted Rafi as his voice in his forthcoming films. This also gave back Rafi Sahab his *number one* position in 1976 and he maintained that till the last day of his life.

'On Eid, I still remember mutton and *kheer* (Indian dessert) used to come from his home... We eagerly waited for this. If we got even an inkling that Rafi Sahab was coming over for a rehearsal, we would sit in the music room all through the rehearsal. I would get up early and make excuses to skip school to be able to accompany Madan*ji* for the recording. At the recording studio, I would sit in the room where the music director used to sit and observe Rafi Sahab—the way he sang, his gestures and his hand movements. Rafi Sahab would enter the studio, quietly smiling; but once he was in front of the mike, his magic was unparalleled. Those who were witness to this, would wonder how he could transform so drastically when in front of the mike.

'I remember when the song "Yeh Duniya Yeh Mehfil" (*Heer Raanjha*, 1970) was being recorded; it was a long song (seven-eight minutes). Madan*ji* asked for several retakes to get the desired results and Rafi Sahab was smiling at every instance.

'July 14, 1975, was a sad day for us... Madan Mohan*ji* passed away. I vividly remember seeing Rafi Sahab cry on my father's death. That day, perhaps Rafi Sahab's tears silently sang, "*Kaise kategi zindagi tere bagair tere bagair... paaoonga har shay mein kami, tere bagair, tere bagair...*" a song Madan*ji* had composed keeping Rafi's soulful voice in mind.

'On July 29, 1980, two days prior to Rafi's death, I was at his residence, taking his pictures for the upcoming album to be released by Polydor. We took many shots of him—like Rafi Sahab playing the harmonium, or simply smiling before the camera. It was my sheer good fortune that I got to meet and interact with him so closely. He looked absolutely fine. Though honestly, I feel guilty somewhere that we may have over-stressed him, but then who could imagine that this was to be his last photo session…his smile was so deceiving. Imagine a person who was singing, literally, till he breathed his last. But he left all of us too soon, at the age of 56. So did Madan*ji* at the age of 55.'

Chitragupta

For duets, Chitragupta specialised in creating unusual twists of rhythm with the two voices. He utilised the whole range of Rafi's voice, with the energetic and multifaceted voice of Lata, to create perfect numbers. An example is 'Chand Jaane Kahaan Kho Gayaa' (*Main Chup Rahungi*, 1962). Here the two voices came together to create a magical spell, with minimal use of music in the background.

Chitragupta is also known for his fascination with the saxophone. Daughter Sudha emphasises, 'Why only the saxophone, he also used to love the guitar, mandolin and flute. But he preferred to keep the use of instruments to a minimum. I remember one song from *Toofan Mein Pyar Kahaan* (1963), "Itni Badi Duniya, Jahaan Itna Bada Mela." If you listen carefully, you will find that the song has only three instruments. But what a song it turned out to be!'

Chitragupta was himself an ardent Rafi-fan. He would say, 'Rafi Sahab sings the best for me.' Indeed, he could extract the best from Rafi in compositions like 'Akhiyaan Sang Akhiyaan Lage Aaj' and 'Agar Dil Kisise Lagaaya Na Hota' (both from *Bada Aadmi,* 1961), 'Mujhe Dard-E-Dil Ka Pata Na Tha' and 'Jaag Dil-E-Diwaana Rutt Jaagi' from *Akashdeep* (1965).

Through her childhood, Sudha had heard her father appreciating the nuances of Rafi's vocal talents. He would particularly commend how Rafi would end his line smoothly to ensure that it blended with the music seamlessly, without making it obvious as to when the orchestra picked it up.

This seamless transition was no easy task. She recollected another anecdote when Chitragupta, in his early days as a chorus singer, had once gone for a song recording. Amongst his fellow chorus singers was a thin young man. He was none other than Rafi. Years later, during a practice session, when Rafi Sahab had become famous and gained weight, Chitragupta narrated the incident to him and the two shared a hearty laugh.

The rehearsal sessions often brought Rafi to Chitragupta's home. Once he had arrived a bit earlier than the scheduled time. He spent the time strolling outside. At 8:00 a.m. he knocked on the door! That was very unconventional for an established singer like him. During these sessions, they would rehearse with Dilip Dholakia, assistant to Chitragupta. Sometimes Anand, his younger son, would accompany them on *tabla* or *khanjari* (an instrument of the tambourine family).

'In *Mahabharat* (1965), there was a long song in chaste Hindi, "Ye Mahabharat Ki Katha." Rafi found the *shuddh* (pure) Hindi and few Sanskrit words a little difficult to pronounce. Papa corrected him several times and each time he would repeat with a smile. Later Papa came home and told us that he was amazed to see Rafi Sahab's dedication,' narrates Sudha fondly.

Chitragupta and Rafi continued the musical association till Rafi passed away in 1980, taking the total number of Chitragupta-Rafi songs to 211, spread across 100 films.

Hemanta Mukherjee

Hemanta (Kumar) Mukherjee was a multifaceted talent who was not only a prolific singer of the '50s and '60s but also a brilliant composer. He also produced films. This accomplished composer from Bengal had added to Hindi film music his interpretations of Rabindra Sangeet. One of the singer's compositions, in the voice of Rafi, that shows this influence is 'Hum Laaye Hain Toofan Se Kashti Nikal Ke' (*Jagriti*, 1954).

In 1966, Rafi and Hemanta Kumar sang the duet, 'Dushmano Savdhaan, Shatruo Savdhaan' (*Netaji Subashchandra Bose*, 1966). Incidentally this happens to be the only duet sung by these two legends besides the two group songs 'Is Vishal Dharti Par Chahe Rahein Kahin Hum Saathi' (*Love in Canada*, 1979) and 'Rahega Jahaan Mein Tera Naam' (*Love And God*, released 1986).

Hemanta Kumar's first composition for Rafi was 'Hum Laaye Hai Toofan Se Kashti Nikal Ke' (*Jagruti*, 1954) while 'Jaaney Kahan Dekha Hai' (*Biwi Aur Makaan*, 1966) saw the two legends converge for the last time. Out of the 55 films Hemanta Kumar composed for, Rafi had sung in 19 films; 31 solos and duets.

Roshan

Roshanlal Nagrath made it to Bombay in 1948 and in the very next year composed songs for *Neki Aur Badi*, a Kidar Sharma film. Though the film was a box-office disaster, Kidar Sharma gave young Roshan another opportunity in *Baawre Nain* (1950). The film had most of its songs in the voice of Mukesh and Rajkumari, but also had a Rafi-Asha duet, 'Mohabbat Ke Maaron Ka Haal.' The first solo that Rafi sang for Roshan was 'Zameen Bhi Wohi Hai Wohi Hai Aasmaan' (*Chandni Chowk*, 1954).

Roshan was enamoured with the *dilruba* (a bow instrument). He also used other musical instruments proficiently, like the *sarangi*, violin, flute, Spanish guitar and the accordion, to give his compositions a distinctive character.

The efficient use of *sarangi* can be heard in 'Maine Shayad Tumhe Pehle Bhi Kabhi Dekha Hai' (*Barsaat Ki Raat*, 1960) in the prelude, just before the melodious voice of Rafi effectively brings out actor Bharat Bhushan's emotions for his screen love Madhubala. The skilful use of the same musical instrument complimenting the enchanting voice of Rafi in 'Zindagi Bhar Nahin Bhoolegi' in *Raaga Yaman*, from the same film, is mesmerising.

Though Rafi had been the voice of Pradeep Kumar since 1956 it was *Aarti* (1962) that established the long association between Roshan, Rafi and Pradeep Kumar. The composition of Roshan and lyrics of Majrooh Sultanpuri in the film, with Rafi singing for Pradeep Kumar, won over the masses. 'Ab Kya Misaal Doon' is the only solo by Rafi in the film, a song that flawlessly describes the beauty of a woman. There were three duets of Rafi with Lata. 'Baar Baar Tohe Kya Samjhaaye,' 'Tere Bin Lage Na Jiya,' and 'Aapne Yaad Dilaya' and two duets with Asha, 'Na Bhanwara Na Koi Gul' and 'Woh Teer Dil Pe Chala.' All became popular, but 'Aapne Yaad Dilaya To Mujhe Yaad Aaya' in the voice of Rafi stood out with its sadness, and is said to have left the audience in tears in the theatre.

Taj Mahal (1963), a historical film based on the immortal love story of Shah Jahan and Mumtaz, won two Filmfare awards: Roshan for Best Music Composer and Sahir Ludhianvi for Best Lyricist. The composer could not have made a better choice than Rafi to render the songs especially the Rafi-Lata duet, 'Jo Waada Kiya Woh Nibhaana Padega,' in *Raaga Pahadi.*

Bheegi Raat in 1965 again saw the winning combination of Rafi, Roshan, Majrooh Sultanpuri and Pradeep Kumar. Rafi's songs, 'Dil Jo Na Keh Saka' (solo), 'Aise To Na Dekho' (Rafi-Suman duet), 'Jaane Wo Kaun Hai Kya Naam Hai' (solo) and 'Mohabbat Se Dekha' (solo) were all masterpieces.

The other gem from this hit quartet was *Bahu Begum* (1967) with the popular song 'Hum Intezaar Karenge Tera Qayamat Tak.' Interestingly, the same tune has been extended to express two different emotions in two different situations in this love story—this tandem song in the voice of Rafi depicts pain of separation whereas the one in Asha's voice depicts faith and anticipation. 'Waqif Hoon Khoob Ishq Ke' and 'Dhoond Ke Laaoon Kahaan Se' from the same film are two *qawwalis* in which Roshan once again leveraged the voices of Rafi and Manna Dey effectively. Rafi's voice repeated its miracle for Pradeep Kumar and the film did well at the box-office, and was particularly recognised for its superhit songs.

The year 1967 also saw the film *Noorjehan* where Roshan had Rafi singing 'Woh Mohabbat Woh Wafayein' and 'Aap Jab Se Kareeb Aye Hain' (Rafi-Asha duet). Here Roshan chose to have the lyrics by Shakeel Badayuni for the romantic songs picturised on Pradeep Kumar. Roshan established Rafi as the voice of Pradeep Kumar with these six successive films, just the way OP Nayyar was instrumental in making Rafi the energetic voice of Shammi Kapoor. Rafi with his supple voice proved that he could do equal justice to both actors on-screen.

Roshan and Rafi worked together in 32 films and had 88 songs to their credit. 'Mile Na Phool To Kanton Se Dosti Kar Li,' (*Anokhi Raat*, 1968) was the last time they worked together.

Ravi Shankar Sharma

As a composer Ravi Shankar Sharma made his debut in *Vachan* (1955). The association with Rafi that began with the song, 'Babu O Jaane Waale Babu Ek Paisa De De,' lasted for over two decades. Their collaboration resulted in 235 songs in 79 films.

The title song of *Chaudvin Ka Chand* (1960) gave instant recognition to Ravi as a composer. This was followed by *Gharana* (1961) in which the songs 'Husnwaale Tera Jawaab Nahin' and 'Jab Se Tumhe Dekha Hai' established the Ravi-Rafi magic. He won the Filmfare Award for this film's compositions. Another success for the duo came in 1961; 'Mujhe Pyar Ki Zindagi Denewaale,' from the film *Pyar Ka Saagar*, became a hit with the masses. In the following year, 'Baar Baar Dekho' (*China Town*, 1962), an energetic composition for Shammi Kapoor, had the audience clapping. 'Na Jhatko Zulf Se Paani' (*Shehnai*, 1964), 'Choo Lene Do Nazuk Hoton Ko' (*Kajal*, 1965), 'Badi Der Bhai Nandlaala' (*Khandaan*, 1964), 'Bhari Duniya Mein' (*Do Badan*, 1966), 'Tujhko Pukaare Mera Pyar' (*Neel Kamal* 1968), 'O Nanhe Se Farishte' (*Ek Phool Do Mali*, 1969) are some of the other songs that the music lovers loved in the '60s. Ravi won his second Filmfare Award for *Khandaan*.

Rafi's last song with Ravi was 'Koi Kaam Nahin Hai Mushkil' (*Admi Sadak Ka*, 1977).

Music director Ravi recollected an episode during the rehearsals for 'Aaja Tujko Pukare Mera Pyar' (*Neel Kamal*, 1968) when he had praised Rafi for his vast repertoire. In his characteristic humility Rafi had responded, 'Playback singing *toh dariya hai music ka. Yeh toh kabhi khatam hota nahin. Jitna is mein leen ho jao utna hi sukh milta hai. Har ganey se mujhe nayi seekh milti hai.* (Playback singing is an ocean of music. It is endless. The more you immerse yourself in it the more joy you derive. I get to learn something new from every song.)'

Ravi reminisced, 'I met Rafi Sahab in 1947, in my hometown, Delhi. This was right after independence when Mukesh and he came for a live show at the Lal Quila. I was a diehard fan of Rafi and asked my friends to help me meet my icon. My friend and I went all the way to the Coronation Hotel to meet him. Though my dream was to become a playback singer, I told my friend to introduce me as an aspiring music director to Rafi Sahab. This was because if I said that I wanted to be a singer, he could have asked me to sing. I would be too nervous to sing in front of such a perfect singer. In this meeting, he gave me some valuable advice on how to become a music director.

'A few years later, I came to Bombay and struggled in my initial days. Finally, the prolific singer and music director, Hemanta Kumar, gave me an opportunity to be his assistant. So my modest lie to Rafi Sahab came true and my desire to become a playback singer just faded away.

'In 1954, I met Rafi Sahab again; I wanted him to sing my composition for *Vachan*—"O Babu O Jaane Waale Babu Ek Paisa De De." The Rafi-Asha duet "Jab Liye Hath Mein Hath," from the same film, also became very popular. Every time I met him I wanted to tell him that the Delhi boy has now become a music director, with your blessings. But I just could not tell him the Delhi episode.

'The Ravi-Rafi-Shakeel combination was often referred to as one made in heaven. I would always imagine Rafi's voice while composing and set the notes and the pitch accordingly. Although I must add that Rafi was one singer who could sing any kind of song.

'The differences between BR Chopra Sahab and Rafi Sahab made things difficult for me. It all started during the making of *Dharmputra* (1962). Rafi Sahab was offered the *qawwali* "Yeh Masjid Hai Woh Butkhaana," as a duet with Mahendra Kapoor, which Rafi Sahab refused on the grounds that Mahendra Kapoor and he had similar voices and hence the song would not sound good. Chopra Sahab disagreed and it led to a misunderstanding.

'For *Gumraah* (1963) I had composed the songs keeping Rafi in mind. But being a BR Chopra film, I was told to take Mahendra Kapoor. The song won a Filmfare for the Best Male Playback Singer. After all Rafi was Mahendra's *guru*!

'When I was composing the music for *Waqt* (1965), again a BR Chopra production, I insisted that the title song be sung by Rafi Sahab as he was the only one who could do justice to it. Chopra Sahab was hesitant but agreed. I personally requested Rafi Sahab saying that I would give up music if he did not sing it. Rafi Sahab could not say no and sang "Waqt Se Din Aur Raat."

'Rafi Sahab was a perfectionist. Sometimes it meant long hours of practice and several takes. During the recording of "Zindagi Kya Hai Gham Ka Dariya Hai" (*Pyar Kiya To Darna Kya*, 1963), I made him repeat the song six times before the final take. After the sixth time, I was hesitant to ask him to sing once more. He just smiled and said, "I will sing it as many times as it takes to ensure that it is perfect." A great singer like him could be so unassuming. After the final take, everyone in the studio applauded and he came rushing to embrace me. That was Rafi Sahab!

'Once, many years later, he came to meet me after his London tour. He reminded me of this particular song and said, "You made me sing this song so many times that I have fallen in love with it; I inevitably sing this song for all my stage performances and many times, the audience demand this song the moment I step onto the stage. Ravi Sahab, I am so grateful to you."

'Can you believe that Rafi Sahab has sung for actors like Radhakrishan? It was easier said than done as his voice was very different and hoarse. Once I thought of playing a prank and asked Rafi to sing a song for Radhakrishan for *Devar Bhabi* (1958). I was expecting Rafi Sahab to say no, but to my surprise he took on the challenge sportingly. He sang an offbeat number like "Tasveer Teri, Dil Mera Behla Na Sakegi," so well. No one could have matched Radhakrishan's voice better. Despite being a non-conventional song, it made its mark.

'During the recording of the evergreen romantic song "Yeh Zulf Agar Khul Ke Bikhar Jaaye Toh Achchha" (*Kaajal*, 1965), I wanted the word '*achchha*' (ok; good) to be said by the actor Raj Kumar. Somehow, after several takes, I was still not satisfied. In this song, Sahir Ludhianvi had used the word several times and it was challenging to repeat it each time in a different way and yet maintain the poetic rhythm. Seeing the struggle that I was going through, Rafi Sahab, who was singing the song, came and said in a soft voice, "Ravi Sahab, can I say '*achchha*' in my own way." He presented the word "*achchha*" in three different ways. I just wondered as to why I had not thought of this earlier? He could effortlessly emulate every actor's voice. In the same film, the song, "Chhoo Lene Do Naazuk Honthon Ko" demanded the rendition of an inebriated lover. Knowing that Rafi Sahab was a teetotaller and shy by nature, I had my doubts whether he could bring out the drunken man's mood. He left me stunned with his rendition.

'There is another interesting episode that I must mention… It was in the mid '80s when I went to London. One evening we, my host, who was a great Rafi fan, and I, went out in a taxi to look around London. The driver was an Indian and was playing songs from a cassette. He commented, "In Hindustan, there are only two talented men, Ravi and Rafi." I was thrilled to know that people in this part of the world also knew my name. My friend got excited and told the driver, "Ravi is right inside your cab." The driver did not believe him and responded, "Sir, I am not so lucky that I will ever get an opportunity to see my favourite music director in person. And you are saying that he is sitting in my car." I was enjoying this conversation and finally confirmed my identity. The young man was so moved that on reaching our destination he touched my feet and refused to accept the fare. I realised that my music had become popular and successful to a large extent because of Rafi.'

The composer cited a beautiful verse written for Rafi and him by a music lover long ago…

Rafi aur Ravi, yeh do fankaar,
Ek gayak, ek mousikar,
Amar rahenge inke naghme,
Jab tak hai saara sansaar.
(Rafi and Ravi, these two talents,
One a singer, the other a composer,
Their songs shall remain immortal,
As long as humans exist on this earth.)

Shankar-Jaikishan

Shankar-Jaikishan was a towering musical duo of the '50s and '60s, who contributed 341 songs to Rafi's career. Their offerings are masterpieces of their creativity—'Yahoo' (*Junglee*, 1961), 'Jiya-O-Jiya' (*Jab Pyar Kisi Se Hota Hai*, 1961), 'Bahaaron Phool Barsaao' (*Suraj*, 1966) are just few of their many compositions that have been registered forever in the mind of music lovers.

Coming from different backgrounds, it was music that brought Shankar and Jaikishan together. They assisted music composers, Husanlal-Bhagatram before launching their independent career as a music duo for Raj Kapoor's *Barsaat* (1949). 'Main Zindagi Mein Har Dum Rota Hi Raha Hoon' marked the beginning of their long innings with Rafi. Of the two, Shankar's speciality was dance-based compositions (he had learnt Kathak in his early days), whereas Jaikishan was adept at composing background scores.

The duo was always keen on innovating—reversing *taals*, introducing the saxophone in unusual interludes, placing the accordion differently, introducing yells and yodels by changing chords, using multiple *raagas* in one composition or by simply, yet skilfully, combining the musical instruments like violin and the mandolin with the chorus. Shankar-Jaikishan stood out for their distinctive approach of leveraging the orchestra to heighten the effects of their compositions.

Innumerable films for which they composed music celebrated silver jubilees. The masses were bowled over by their compositions; be it the evergreen duets 'Tujhe Jeewan Ki Dor Se' (*Asli Naqli*, 1962); 'Sau Saal Pehle Mujhe Tumse Pyar Tha' (*Jab Pyar Kisi Se Hota Hai*, 1961) by Rafi and Lata; a lullaby 'Main Gaaoon Tum So Jaao' (*Brahmachari*,1968); one of the most poetic expression of love inside an elevator, 'Main Kahin Kavi Na Bann Jaoon' (*Pyar Hi Pyar*, 1969), where the rhythm gets enhanced by the optimum use of *dholak* (a percussion instrument shaped like a barrel) in the verses and flute in the interludes; the despondent song, 'Yaad Na Jaaye Beete Dinon Ki' (*Dil Ek Mandir*, 1963) where Shankar-Jaikishan made Rafi lay emphasis on '...*unhe dil kyooo bulaaye*' for the desired effect of desperation and pain.

Making Rafi sing 'Humein Bhi De Do Saharaa' (*Seema*, 1955), that begins with no instrumentation and finally merges into a fast-paced chorus, along with harmonium and *dholak*, was an exemplary stroke of innovation. They also delivered an offbeat romantic number 'Aaa Gale Lag Jaa' (*April Fool*, 1964), a song that starts at a soft pace in Rafi's voice and as it proceeds, he throws his voice across high and low octaves.

Two of the most remembered songs featuring the role a love letter plays in a budding romance, are also the brainchild of Shankar-Jaikishan. 'Yeh Mera Prempatra Padh Kar' (*Sangam*, 1964) and 'Likhe Jo Khat Tujhe' (*Kanyadaan*, 1969).

The light-hearted 'Teri Pyaari Pyaari Soorat Ko' (*Sasuraal,* 1961) is one that Rafi loved to perform on stage; it was one of the most frequently requested songs by any audience. Usha Timothy recalled that Bilquis (Rafi's wife), who had accompanied him for a show, once requested him to sing 'Teri Pyaari Pyaari Soorat Ko' for her at a show.

Rafi lending his voice to Shankar-Jaikishan became a guarantee for success, especially from 1960 to 1967. Such was the charisma of their association that films would turn into blockbusters just riding on the popularity of the songs. The team gave a fillip to the career of many actors.

Shankar-Jaikishan compositions, with Rafi as the playback voice for Shammi Kapoor, were another proven success formula in the '60s. The personal bond amongst them was well brought out by the late actor, 'Rafi Sahab had sung a duet for the film *Suraj* (1966). The song was to be pictured on the hero, Rajendra Kumar, but he said that the song did not go well with his character and was not needed in the film. The composers were very disappointed. Jaikishan narrated this to Shammi Kapoor and regretted that the song was going waste. Shammi Kapoor recalled, 'I told him that I wanted to listen to the song, so he fetched it from his car and played it for me. I instantly said, "Jai this song is mine and anyway Rafi Sahab is my voice." I included the song in *Brahmachari* (1968); it was "Aaj Kal Tere Mere Pyar Ke Charche Har Zubaan Par." It turned out to be a great success.'

The heydey of the composer duo, between 1961 and 1967, showcases incredible melodies. 'Jiya O… Jiya O Jiya Kuch Bol Do' (*Jab Pyar Kisi Se*

Hota Hai, 1961), 'Yahoo!' (*Junglee*, 1961), 'Nazar Bacha Kar Chale Gaye' (*Dil Tera Diwaana*, 1962), 'Ae Gulbadan Phoolon Ki Mehak' (*Professor*, 1962). 'Yaad Na Jaye Beete Dino Ki' (*Dil Ek Mandir*, 1963), 'Ey Phoolon Ki Rani, Bahaaron Ki Mallika' (*Arzoo*, 1965), 'Bahaaron Phool Barsaao' (*Suraj*, 1966), 'Akele Akele Kahaan Ja Rahe Ho' (*An Evening in Paris*, 1967).

The prolific duo hit a rough patch because of personal differences. It is believed that Rafi was the one who intervened to help prevent the fallout, thus ensuring many more years of wonderful music. Between the two, they fully recognised each other's forte: if Shankar excelled at dance numbers, Jaikishan's forte was the romantic compositions. The success and popularity that this music composer duo was enjoying abruptly came to an end with the death of Jaikishan in 1971.

The last song that Rafi sang for Shankar-Jaikishan (the banner name they retained, as a pact between the two, even after Jaikishan's demise) was from the film *The Gold Medal* (1979); the song was 'Aazaadi Aayi Bhi To Kya.'

The eternal quality of the music of this composer duo and Rafi's golden voice is apparent in the way they continue to be a part of the music milieu of today's generation; 'Yahoo!' as a song redefined the whole notion of *masti* (fun) songs, thus creating a distinct genre. Their song 'Jan Pehchaan Ho, Jeena Aasaan Ho' (*Gumnaam*, 1965), with its rock-n-roll feel, continues to create a buzz not only in India but in Hollywood too for its foot-tapping feel. More than 35 years after its conception, it was featured in the opening credits of *Ghost World* (2001; American comedy-drama film) and also in the 2011 commercial, *The Date*, for Heineken... timelessness exemplified!

Shankar-Jaikishan won the Filmfare nine times. This was also the combination which brought Filmfare Awards for Rafi for *Sasuraal* (1961), *Suraj* (1966) and *Brahmachari* (1968).

Kalyan*ji*-Anand*ji*

'Rafi's unique style of singing had drama accompanied by melody,' said Anand*ji*.

Young Anand*ji* was yet to join hands with Kalyan*ji*, when the latter got a breakthrough to compose songs for *Samrat Chandragupta* in 1958. This was the film which lay the foundation for a 169-song association with Mohammed Rafi. The rhythmic compositions 'Chaahe Paas Ho Chaahe Door Ho,' and 'Bhar Bhar Aaye Akhiyaan' are some memorable duets in the voice of Lata and Rafi from this film.

Haseena Maan Jaayegi (1968) continued the spell and the combination of composers Kalyan*ji*-Anand*ji*, singer Rafi, and actor Shashi Kapoor translated into some great romantic songs like 'Bekhudi Mein Sanam,' 'Chale They Saath Milke,' 'O Dilbar Janiye' and 'Dilbar Dilbar Kehte Kehte Hua Diwaana.'

All through their long melodious innings, the cadence of their music was always simple, yet capable of completely engaging music lovers. The duo excelled in using the right musical instruments for their compositions; for instance, opening the song with xylophone in the prelude of 'Ek Tha Gul Aur Ek Thi Bulbul' (*Jab Jab Phool Khile*, 1965) gave it the needed fairytale appeal to depict the unusual romance between a boatman and a wealthy city girl.

The intelligent blend of singers, contributed to the success of the 1967 film *Upkaar* that brought great acclaim to the talented music directors. Every composition in the film, right from 'Kasme Wade' by Manna Dey and 'Mere Desh Ki Dharti' by Mahendra Kapoor, to 'Gulaabi Raat Gulaabi,' a Rafi-Asha duet, was impeccable and spoke of their creative brilliance.

In 'Main Tujhse Milne' (*Heera*, 1973), a Rafi-Lata duet, the composer duo applied an unusual folk instrument called *ravan hattha* (bowed, string instrument) to add to the rural texture that the song demanded and 'Rehne Do Gile Shikwe, Chhodo Bhi Takraar Ki Baatein' (*Rakhwala*, 1971), a Rafi-Asha duet, is an excellent example of the adeptness in unifying classical and contemporary music in the same song. An optimum blend of percussion and piano can be seen in their composition 'Kuch Log Yahan Par Aise Hai' (*Vardaan*, 1974), a song with a tinge of pain, soulfully sung by Rafi.

Their creative ideation is further evident from the fact that they conceptualised the title song of *Muqaddar Ka Sikander* (1978) in the voices of both Kishore and Rafi, where Kishore renders the spirited version for Amitabh Bachchan zooming through the city on a bike and Rafi sings the doleful version emoted by Vinod Khanna on the death of his friend in the climax.

'Kya Dekhte Ho Soorat Tumhaari,' a duet by Rafi and Asha, from *Qurbani* (1980), is one of the last compositions that Kalyan*ji*-Anand*ji* could embellish in the voice of their favourite singer Rafi.

Anand*ji* reminisced, 'Anyone who has sung for four decades and delivered quality work has to be not just good but fantastic! The most difficult songs are the folk songs but he sang folk compositions in so many languages. For "Humko Hone Laga Hai Pyar Tumse" (*Dil Ne Pukara*, 1967), he came home and rehearsed in Carnatic style. "Govinda Aala Re" is another folk-based film song sung by him. Rafi Sahab was such a devoted singer that he never recorded a song without a rehearsal. He used to understand the meaning and nuances of every composition and most importantly who it was going to be picturised on. Initially, he would sing in half tempo to understand the sections he would need to lay stress on. Then he would record the song in the required tempo. His knowledge of Urdu helped him immensely. Urdu, essentially a mix of Hindi and Persian has slight variations in the pronunciation of some words. Urdu is like Hindi with an overdose of sugar (*laughs*). After each recording, he would listen to the song and politely ask, "*Jaaoon* Sir? (Sir, may I leave?)" He believed in the dictum that a singer must give the composer exactly what the latter wants.

'Every music director had his own technique of composing. It must have been an uphill task to live up to the expectations of so many music directors. Moreover, each of them belonged to a different state, with their tunes reflecting this different cultural affinity—for instance, Burman*da* was from the East, Naushad Sahab from the North and we were from the West of India. Rafi Sahab had grasped the music sense and style of every music director. His musical intonations were immaculate; he understood the technique of breathing while rendering a song, like no other.

'Singers of today's era also appreciate and respect him and deep in their hearts, they know that very few can scale the height of Rafi Sahab's talent.'

Usha Khanna

'Rafi Sahab's humility remains exemplary and this was his key to success. Talent alone can't create a legend as monumental as Mohammed Rafi,' said Usha Khanna emphatically.

After Saraswati Devi (in real life Khorshed Minocher-Homji), who composed music for Bombay Talkies (a music studio founded in 1934), Usha Khanna is the only female composer in the history of Hindi film music, who has the distinction of having a successful career for almost three decades (1960-1990).

She joined the league of Hindi film music composers in 1959 with her upbeat and promising compositions for the Shammi Kapoor starrer *Dil Deke Dekho* (1959). The musical scores rendered by Rafi panned the entire gamut of romantic moods, created by the clever interplay of instruments like the mandolin and violin.

She has also sung 13 duets with Rafi, 10 of which were her own compositions—'Sham Dekho Dhal Rahi Hai' (*Anjaan Hai Koi*, 1969), 'Dost Banke Aaye Ho, Dost Banke Hi Rehna' (*Bin Phere Hum Tere*, 1979), 'Kahe Karta Hai Tu Itna Shor' (*Ek Paheli*, 1971) and 'Thehar Zaraa O Jaan-E-Mann' (*Ladki Bholi Bhali*, 1976) are a perennial source of joy.

Her last song for Rafi was 'Aise Na They Hum Jaise Hamaari Ki Ruswai' (*Saajan Ki Saheli*, 1980).

Rafi and Usha Khanna have worked together in 61 films, creating a portfolio of 114 songs in Rafi's voice, of which 69 were solos.

'In 1959, Mukherjee*da* (Sashadhar Mukherjee) gave me an opportunity to compose for his film *Dil Deke Dekho*. I remember my first interaction with Rafi Sahab. He walked into the studio and smiled, "Namaste Usha*ji*, what should I sing?" I fumbled with my words and sat down with the harmonium. Rafi Sahab sat beside me and said, "You are the music director and I shall sing exactly the way you ask me to." The title song, "Dil Deke Dekho" became a huge hit. Mukherjee*da* was very impressed with the outcome. I was given the opportunity to compose for his next film *Hum Hindustani* (1961) and the song "Hum Jab Chale Toh," in the voice of Rafi Sahab, was very well-received by the masses.

'My style of composing matched Asha Bhosle's voice and there are many duets where I have paired her with Rafi Sahab. In my first film, there were five duets by these two singers. Some of their duets, "Pyaar Ki Qasam Hai, Na Dekh Aise Pyar Se" (*Dil Deke Dekho*), "Rupaiya Jahaan Hain Wahaan Hai Roop" (*Roop Rupaiya,* 1968), became quite popular,' she shared about her association with Rafi.

One of the composer's innovative creations was 'Aao Neele Gagan Ke Baadlon Mein Jhoolen' (*Gumraah*, 1977), a song where Rafi, Suman Kalyanpur and even actor, Danny Denzongpa lent their voices.

Usha Khanna said, 'Another favourite composition of mine is "Khudaa Hi Judaa Kare To Kare" (*Aap To Aise Na The,* 1980) where I had the privilege of having the two great talents, Rafi and Kishore Kumar, sing the duet, though they had contrasting personalities. Rafi Sahab, quiet and reserved by nature, had a good sense of humour and enjoyed the playfulness of Kishore Kumar.

'Rafi Sahab's sudden death in 1980 shook the Indian film industry. His incredible voice, which is so often heard even today, makes it impossible to accept the fact that he is no more.'

RD Burman

> *Main samajhta hoon ki Bharatvarsh mein jitne bhi gaanewaale the, aur jitne bhi aayenge, unmein Rafi Sahab jaise bahut kum hi honge.*
> (I believe that among all the past and present singers in India, and the ones to come, it is unlikely that anyone would be as great as Rafi Sahab.)
>
> —RD Burman (July 31, 1980, 'Jaimala Gold', Vividh Bharti)

RD Burman, fondly known in the industry as Pancham (literally, master of the fifth note of music), got his first break in actor Mehmood's production *Chhote Nawaab* in 1961. He had assisted his father SD Burman in his orchestras before taking the plunge as an independent composer. The influence of SD Burman's style was somewhat evident in RD Burman's debut compositions for *Chhote Nawaab* where he composed for the two vocal legends, Rafi and Lata. A memorable solo rendition in the film was Rafi's 'Ilahi Tu Sunn Le Hamaari Dua.' Another noteworthy song from the film is 'Matwaali Aankhon Waale,' a Rafi-Lata duet, which was a rhythmic Spanish-music based composition. Though the film did not make it big at the box-office, it earned the young composer critical acclaim in a period that was dominated by the likes of Naushad, SD Burman, Salil Chowdhury, OP Nayyar, Shankar-Jaikishan, Madan Mohan and many others.

Incidentally, it took RD Burman five years before he surfaced with his signature élan in *Teesri Manzil* (1966).

This Nasir Hussain production had all the ingredients of a superhit—direction by Vijay Anand, Shammi Kapoor and Asha Parekh in the lead and Rafi and Asha's voice to back some romantic, dramatic and peppy compositions. From the racy 'Aaja Aaja Main Hoon Pyar Tera,' a Rafi-Asha duet; the romantic, 'Tumne Mujhe Dekha Hokar Meherbaan,' a solo by Rafi; to 'O Haseena Zulfon Waali,' where RD Burman pioneered the use of the electric organ to give an extra edge to this high-spirited number, each composition was as good as the other, leaving music lovers mesmerised with the unconventional interplay of tunes with traces of Western influence. It is no surprise therefore that the modern generation can identify with the melodies from the RD Burman banner.

RD Burman utilised Rafi's voice in 73 films, which is almost half of the films that he worked in till Rafi was alive. In these 73 films, Rafi sang 40 solos, 65 duets and 14 group songs. The decade 1961-70, the formative years of RD Burman's career, show a clear leaning on Rafi. In this period, he composed for 17 films, and leveraged Rafi's voice in 12 of them. Out of the 75 male songs that he composed in these 17 films, he had Rafi's voice in 36 of them, Manna Dey's in 14 and Kishore's in 13 songs. It is a clear indication of RD Burman hedging his bets by mostly taking Rafi, who was a successful voice of almost every lead actor of that period. The rest were being shared between Manna Dey and Kishore Kumar, a trend established by senior Burman to distribute the songs in a film among multiple established singers.

The adherence between RD Burman and Kishore post *Aradhana* (1969) translated into 314 songs in 118 films between 1971 and 1980, against Rafi singing just 68 songs in 44 films. Interestingly, Kishore Kumar sang almost three times the compositions of Pancham*da* as against the combined total of Rafi (68 songs) and Manna Dey (31 songs) put together. The patronage of Kishore Kumar by RD Burman in the '70s however did have an effect on Rafi's career. But the composer relied on Rafi's voice for gems such as 'Chand Mera Dil,' 'Kya Hua Tera Waada' and the title track of the 1977 award-winning film *Hum Kisise Kum Nahin*, and the iconic *qawwali* 'Pal Do Pal Ka Saath Hamaara' (*The Burning Train*, 1980) and so on.

In the '70s, the Rafi-RD Burman combination intermittently gave music lovers offbeat melodies like 'Gulaabi Aankhen Jo Teri Dekhi' and 'Ni Soniye' (Rafi-Asha duet) in *The Train* (1970); 'Kitna Pyaara Waada Hai' and 'Chadhti Jawaani Meri' (both Rafi-Lata duets) in *Caravan* (1971).

After Laxmikant-Pyarelal acknowledged Rafi's voice for young Rishi Kapoor's on-screen persona in *Amar Akbar Anthony* (1977), RD Burman too was seen reaffirming this fact. The *qawwali* title track of *Hum Kisise Kum Nahin* (1977) fetched Rafi incessant praise from music lovers. Another unusual composition that saw Rafi voicing an RD Burman tune was 'Aate Jaate Main Sab Pe Nazar Rakhta Hoon' (*Shaan,* 1980).

In fact, *Shaan*, a blockbuster, witnessed RD Burman and Rafi singing together an RD Burman composition, 'Yamma Yamma', with Rafi singing for Shashi Kapoor, and RD Burman for Amitabh Bachchan. In the trailing '80s, films featuring Rishi Kapoor had RD Burman selecting Rafi to sing 'Poochho Na Yaar Kya Hua' (*Zamaane Ko Dikhana Hai*, released 1981), which had the signature RD Burman touch of the West. Rafi earned the last Filmfare Award of his career for 'Kya Hua Tera Waada' (*Hum Kisise Kum Nahin*, 1977), an RD Burman composition.

Laxmikant-Pyarelal

> *Unhe hum sirf ek gaayak nahin, apna pita maante the. Unke chale janey se* Laxmikant-Pyarelal *ke gaano se jaan hi chali gayi hai.*
> (For us, he was not only a singer, but our father. With him gone, the songs of Laxmikant-Pyarelal have lost their soul.)

This was Laxmikant's bereaved statement on Rafi's death, in an interview broadcast by Vividh Bharti.

Like many others, the duo made their debut with Rafi giving voice to their composition. The first film which featured them as music directors was *Parasmani* (1963) with Rafi, who was at the peak of his career then. The song 'Roshan Tumhi Se Duniya' was a dulcet melody which became quite popular. The duo never failed to thank Rafi for his support in the initial stages of their career.

If one were to give a quantitative measure of this association, then it can be seen that Laxmikant-Pyarelal composed 369 songs for Rafi in 173 films; out of the 242 films that the duo worked in till 1980. In fact it was a Laxmikant-Pyarelal composition that Rafi recorded as his life's last song, 'Tere Aane Ki Aas Hai Dost, Shaam Kyu Phir Udaas Hai Dost' (*Aas Paas,* 1980).

They were masters at division of work. Laxmikant excelled at tuning the melody, while the other critical responsibility, of arrangement and orchestration, was shouldered by Pyarelal. Their combined strength made them retain their number one position among music composers for a long time. A 35-year career studded with success calls for not only talent but the virtue of adaptability.

Pyarelal had many prized memories to share. 'Laxmi*ji* and I became music directors after a long period of struggle in the industry. But we had known Rafi Sahab because we had been musicians for many years even before we entered the industry.' Pyarelal had been a violinist in the film industry before Laxmikant and he launched their independent career as a music director duo. 'He was our lucky charm.'

'My father had once taken me to Rafi Sahab's house for some monetary help as we were passing through bad times, with the hope that once things improved, he would be able to repay. Rafi Sahab had given my father Rs 500 which was a lot in those days. Similar help came from Lata*ji* as well. At that time, these amounts meant a lot. Later, when I became a composer and was doing moderately well, I thought it was time to return the money to both of them. It was after the recording of the song "Yeh Dil Tum Bin Kahin Lagta Nahin" (*Izzat*, 1968) that I offered the sum to Rafi Sahab.

He didn't even recall that he had once lent some money to my father and simply refused to take it—the very fact that Rafi Sahab had forgotten having helped my father with a substantial amount, spoke volumes of his benevolent nature.

'Rafi Sahab used to talk less but would laugh a lot. He would rarely attend social gatherings but twice he came over for my birthday parties. His life was centred on two things, practice and prayer.

'He had a distinct style of nodding his head while talking. For him, everybody was equal and he would talk to everybody in the same composed manner. Our first composition, with him on the vocals, was "Tere Pyar Ne Mujhe Gham Diya" for *Chhaila Babu* (1967). We recorded the song in 1961, but the film was released six years after the recording. (Meanwhile, our composition for *Parasmani,* recorded much later, had already been released). I remember we paid Rafi Sahab Rs 1000 as his fee for this song. Rafi Sahab, instead of keeping the fee, offered Rs 500 each to Laxmi*ji* and to me as his blessings. Rafi Sahab loved this song and said in his usual composed disposition, "You will go a long way."

'In 1963 "Woh Jab Yaad Aaye" and "Roshan Tumhi Se Duniya" from *Parasmani* received a tremendous response from the listeners. After that we worked with Rafi Sahab in compositions like "Chahoonga Main Tujhe," "Jaane Waalon Zaraa" and "Raahi Manva Dukh Ki Chinta" (*Dosti*, 1964). What is not known is that the song "Chahoonga Main Tujhe," that won the Filmfare Award that year, was about to get scrapped from the film. It was Rafi Sahab who insisted on retaining the song…and the rest is history. Rafi Sahab was so pleased with this composition that he only accepted Rs 1 as his fee.

'People are often curious why we chose Rafi Sahab as the voice of young Rishi Kapoor in *Amar Akbar Anthony* (1977). We were absolutely confident that Rafi Sahab was versatile and would be able to relate to these songs and were glad that it worked as his comeback.

'Every song that had the imprint of Rafi Sahab's voice on it would become extremely popular. Even "John Jani Janardhan" (*Naseeb*, released in 1981) was received very well. He always considered his work supreme. He used to practise so diligently that even the most difficult composition would appear easy. I don't remember him cancelling a single recording, even if he was running a high fever. It is a matter of pride that Rafi Sahab has sung the maximum number of songs for us.'

Omi-Sonik

Omi-Sonik started their voyage in the industry as chorus singers for music director Roshan and later worked as assistants with him and Madan Mohan. During their eight years with Roshan, they worked with Rafi in several films such as *Barsaat Ki Raat* (1960), *Wallah Kya Baat Hai* (1962), *Aarti* (1962), *Taj Mahal* (1963) and *Chitralekha* (1964). The Omi-Sonik duo is among the few composers who recorded a song with Rafi few days prior to his death.

Dil Ne Phir Yaad Kiya (1966), *Saawan Bhadon* (1970), *Dharma* (1973), *Raftaar* (1975) are among the many memorable films in which their compositions were voiced by Rafi. The *qawwali* 'Raaz Ki Baat Keh Doon Toh' from *Dharma* is a popular composition by Omi-Sonik, rendered impeccably by Rafi and Asha, and equally well-emoted on-screen by Pran and Bindu.

In 1966, the uncle-nephew duo, took off as independent music directors for *Dil Ne Phir Yaad Kiya*. Rafi was the first choice for their debut compositions. They approached him with apprehension. To their surprise, Rafi agreed, saying, 'You got a chance; it is a very prestigious thing! My prayers are with you.' The title song was recorded in the voices of Rafi, Mukesh and Suman Kalyanpur. The three solos 'Kaliyon Ne Ghunghat Khole,' 'Lo Chehra Surkh Sharab Hua' and 'Yun Chaal Chalo Na Matwaali,' sung by Rafi and the Rafi-Asha duet 'Main Suraj Hoon Tu Meri Kiran,' became hits. The film became a musical blockbuster and successive hits such as *Aabroo* (1968), *Mahua* (1969) and *Saawan Bhadon* (1970) followed.

Omi-Sonik continued to compose for Rafi even in the so-called lean period of his career. Omi reminisced about the singer, 'Rafi Sahab went to Mecca… He was deeply affected by the admonitions of some elders he met there, who told him that singing as a profession was against his religion. He took it to heart and this impacted his career to an extent in the early '70s. The industry was also seeing a change in trend brought about by RD Burman and Kishore Kumar. Some of the actors too got carried away by this wave. I remember an incident, when actor Jeetendra insisted that Kishore Kumar should be his voice in *Bhai Ho To Aisa* (1972) to ensure the success of the film. I received a call from Manmohan Desai, the director, expressing Jeetendra's wish. I rang up Jeetendra, as I was the music director of the film, and explained that the song "Ae Phuljhadi, Ae Guljhadi" would be more suitable in the voice of Rafi Sahab. Finally it was sung by Rafi Sahab. But the duet, from the same film, "Bol Meri Gudiya," was recorded in the voice of Kishore*da* and Lata*ji*.'

Omi mentions that Rafi had once got annoyed with him, something unheard of for a man of gentle demeanour. The composer smiles as he recollected, 'It was during the recording of *Dharma* in 1973. Our affinity was not limited to our profession alone, but could be traced back to our origins in Punjab. We were recording the *qawwali*, "Raaz Ki Baat Keh Doon Toh," with Rafi Sahab and Asha*ji*. I wanted a retake. Rafi Sahab got a bit edgy and said, "What are you saying?" This was unexpected from the otherwise soft-spoken perfectionist. I also said in a firm tone, "Fine, let's pack up." Rafi Sahab walked out without a word. The next morning my doorbell rang at 6:00 a.m. It was Rafi Sahab! He said in Punjabi, "Did I offend you? Let's listen to the *qawwali* that we recorded yesterday." Zaheer was standing behind him with a pair of huge speakers. Rafi Sahab said, "Let us listen to the *qawwali* on these speakers, I got them from America." We heard it together and then Rafi Sahab politely asked, "Do we need to re-record?" I could not evade that conquering smile. I embraced him and said, "Take your speakers Khan." I used to call him Khan because in Punjab, Khan is used for great singers. Rafi Sahab said, "These are for you." His fee was Rs 3000 and the speakers were for Rs 20,000. I was so touched that I could not look him in the eyes. That was Rafi Sahab. The song became a superhit.'

There were other notable songs from the composer duo. 'Kaliyon Ne Ghunghat Khole' (*Dil Ne Phir Yaad Kiya*, 1966) or 'Dono Ne Kiya Tha Pyar Magar Mujhe Yaad Raha Tu Bhool Gayi' (*Mahua*, 1969).

Just a fortnight before Rafi's demise, Omi-Sonik had recorded 'Allah Ka Naam Paak Hai, Paak Rahega,' with him, for an SK Kapoor production, *Maan Gaye Ustaad* (released in 1981).

Omi continued, 'Late night on July 31, I was woken up from my sleep with a call from a close associate saying Rafi Sahab was no more! I couldn't believe my ears and rushed to Rafi Villa. The bungalow that always gleamed with Rafi Sahab's beaming smile stood dark and desolate. I understood that his family hadn't yet got his mortal remains home.

'I couldn't sleep that night and returned to Rafi Villa the next morning. There, I met the grief-stricken Zaheer, crying like an orphan. He embraced me and sobbed, as he whispered, "*Laale, ab tu kisko Khan bolega? Tera Khan te gaya.* (Brother, who will you now refer to as Khan? Your Khan has gone.)"

'A few days later, when I met Zaheer, he was still trying to recover from the loss. He just said, "When God asks Rafi something, he wouldn't be able to answer. I will have to go reply for him," implying how strongly Rafi depended on him. True to his utterance, he passed away within a few months of Rafi Sahab's death.'

As a homage, Omi recited:

Har ik buraai se tu door tha,
Saare zamaane mein mash-hoor tha,
Aawaaz mein teri woh noor tha,
Amar hai, amar hai, ye kehte sabhi,
Mohammed Rafi, Mohammed Rafi…
Ikatees julaai ki woh raat thi,
Falak ro pada aisi barsaat thi,
Gamgheen saari yeh kaayanaat thi,
Awaaz aayi yeh tha wali,
Mohammed Rafi, Mohammed Rafi…
(You were away from all worldly vices,
You were popular in the entire world,
Your voice had such grace,
It is eternal, everybody said,

Mohammed Rafi, Mohammed Rafi…
It was the night of July 31,
The heavens above cried in the form of rain,
The entire universe was drenched in pain,
A sound said, 'He was the custodian,'
Mohammed Rafi, Mohammed Rafi…)

Ravindra Jain

'*Mera rishta* Rafi Sahab *ke saath ek Bargad ke darakht aur uski jadon jaisa tha.*' Ravindra Jain likens his association with Rafi to that of a Banyan tree with its roots. In his benevolent way, Rafi used to look after those under his care. His music also had the innate ability of *Bargad* (the Banyan tree), known for its ability to survive for centuries.

'For one of my initial compositions in the film *Lori* (unreleased), which was a *qawwali*, Rafi Sahab took 14 days to rehearse, which was his way of inching towards perfection. He would not be satisfied till he could flawlessly render a tune. Rafi Sahab sang for my first release, *Kaanch Aur Heera* (1972). The song was 'Nazar Aati Nahin Manzil.' Our association picked up momentum with 'Tota Maina Ki Kahaani' and 'Paaon Mein Dori, Dori Mein Ghunghroo' *(Chor Machaye Shor,* 1974).

'I have penned down the immense loss in few lines…

Peshaani pe shams, aankh mein taron ki ziya thi,
Woh kaise bujha, jisko zamaane ki dua thi?
Nakhush hai khuda apne farishton se,
Nahin toh dharti ke farishte ki zaroorat kya thi?
Hajji tha, namaazi tha, bada nek tha banda,
Kya iske alava bhi koi iski khata thi?
Naghmein to tere phir bhi sune jaayange,
Lekin kuch teri zaroorat humein iske sivaa bhi thi…
(The forehead was resplendent as the sun, the eyes shone with the brilliance of the stars,
How could he be extinguished who had the blessings of the world?

God is displeased with his own angels,
Otherwise, what was the need for recalling an angel from earth?
He was a pilgrim, he used to render *namaaz*, and he was a great person,
Was there any fault of his other than this?
Your songs will no doubt be heard,
But we needed you also somewhat besides this…)

Anu Malik

The eminent music director of the '90s, Anu Malik has known Rafi through his father, Sardar Malik. He shared that, as a child, he often heard praise for Rafi in his father's unfeigned words, 'There is no greater singer than Rafi Sahab.' Anu Malik recalled some compositions that his father had composed for Rafi such as 'Mujhe Tum Se Mohabbat Hai' (*Bachpan*, 1963), 'Na Ja, Mere Saathi Na Ja' (*Saaranga*, 1960), that are popular even today.

Anu Malik is also one of the few composers of this era who can take pride in the fact that Rafi sang some of his initial compositions. The films were *Poonam* (released in 1981) and *Pagal Premee* (recorded in 1977, released in 1985). He recollected the morning of his first recording session with Rafi for *Pagal Premee*. Excitement and anxiety made him reach Rafi Villa at 6 a.m. when he suddenly realised that it was too early. He found Rafi in his lawn feeding the birds amidst absolute tranquillity. The warmth with which he was received, even though he was a novice composer, left an indelible imprint on his mind.

He has never been able to forget the sincerity of the towering legend, who even during the month of Ramadan, recorded with full fervour, a high-pitched composition, 'Aa Zara Mere Humnashi' for *Poonam* (released in 1981). 'Rafi Sahab had tears in his eyes after the recording. It wasn't easy to sing at that pitch after fasting the whole day,' acknowledges Anu Malik.

Incidentally, this was his last meeting with Rafi; six days later Rafi passed away.

Lyricists

Poet Shakeel Badayuni started his career with Naushad, and in the years that followed, gave lyrical expression to a majority of the gifted composer's compositions. Badayuni won the sobriquet '*Geetkaar-E-Azam*' from the Indian government. The film *Dulaari* (1949) is remembered for one of the finest songs of Rafi's career; 'Suhaani Raat Dhal Chuki,' again penned by Shakeel Badayuni and set to tune by Naushad. His songs in *Baiju Bawra* (1952) have of course become legendary in the annals of Hindi cinema.

Known for giving brilliant expression to the emotion of love, Shakeel Badayuni has created jewels such as 'Pyar Kiya To Darna Kya,' 'Zindabad, Zindabad' (*Mughal-E-Azam*, 1960). The much-hummed romantic title song of *Chaudhvin Ka Chand* (1960) is the result of Badayuni's proficiency in Urdu combined with Ravi's soul-touching music and Rafi's velvet voice; it won Badayuni the Filmfare Award for Best Lyricist in 1961. The lyricist, in the company of composers like Naushad, Ravi and others, penned 235 songs for Rafi.

Javed Badayuni, son of this noted lyricist, recalled, 'Not many know that my father, Shakeel Badayuni, holds the record of being the first lyricist to score a hattrick of winning Filmfare Awards; for *Chaudhvin Ka Chand* (1960), *Gharana* (1961) and *Bees Saal Baad* (1962).

'The mystical association of the three legends, Naushad Sahab, Rafi Sahab and my father, started in 1949 with "Suhaani Raat Dhal Chuki" (*Dulari*). It was one of the songs he would often sing for his stage shows. With the prolific success of this song, the trio actually became a team to reckon with and worked together in 30 films. They were like three strings of a musical instrument. I distinctly remember how much time Shakeel Sahab and Naushad Sahab would spend on a song or even on a line of a song. Often this meant working all night and sheets of discarded papers—for instance "Pyar Kiya To Darna Kya" (*Mughul-E-Azam*) took many days and nights. It is a timeless romantic classic and has outlived its creators. Similarly, the way Rafi Sahab sang "Zindabad, Zindabad," he has elevated Naushad Sahab and my father's toil to another level. It makes one wonder how the man, who otherwise would never be heard speaking loudly, went on to sing such an evocative song. For this particular song, Naushad Sahab had used a 100-member chorus to attain the desired effect. And Rafi Sahab, with his voice, captured the spirit of the entire film in four minutes and 47 seconds.'

The professional bonding of Naushad-Shakeel-Rafi also brought their families closer. Javed added, 'All of us would often go for picnics to Mahabaleshwar, Panchgani or Lonavala. I have some black and white pictures of those moments that are highly treasured today. In his leisure time, Rafi Sahab was very fond of flying kites. I still vividly remember that Naushad Sahab would organise *patangbaazi* (kite-flying) competition on his terrace. Johnny Walker Sahab would also join in in the amusement—a break from their hectic lives woven around recordings.

'Rafi Sahab also enjoyed fishing. The same comrades, Naushad Sahab, my father, Johnny Walker Sahab and Rafi Sahab would head to Powai in pursuit of a catch, which would then be cooked for a feast in one of the houses.'

On April 20, 1970, the day Shakeel Badayuni passed away, Rafi reached the Badayuni residence and was seen crying copiously next to the gifted lyricist's mortal remains.

Shailendra was the other lyricist who worked with Shankar-Jaikishan to create magical songs for Rafi. It began with *Awaara* (1951), 'Naiyya Teri Majdhaar, Hoshiyar, Hoshiyar,' a boatman's song and the only one in the film in the voice of Rafi. This is one of the three songs picturised one after the other to form the nine-minute dream sequence featuring Raj Kapoor and Nargis, which took three months to shoot. This film gave birth to the concept of dream sequences in Hindi films.

Unlike the well-known lyricists of the period, Shailendra's strength lay in his usage of simple Hindi for narrating emotions from everyday life; the reason why he could find a direct connect with the masses.

Dinesh, Shailendra's son, said, '*Brahmachari* was released in 1968. Soon after that, Baba's run abruptly came to an end. The songs, "Chakke Mein Chakka, Chakke Pe Gaadi" and "Main Gaaoon Tum So Jaao," in the voice of Rafi Sahab, were well-received by the masses and Baba was conferred the Filmfare Award, for the third time. Shankar-Jaikishan and

Mohammed Rafi too received the Filmfare Award for *Brahmachari*, in their respective categories. Had Baba been alive on that day, to receive the award along with Rafi Sahab and Shankar-Jaikishan, it would have been a great day for them to celebrate and cherish. More so, as it came as recognition of the excellence of the team that repeatedly gave the industry prolific music.

'Talking about *Brahmachari* reminds me of Baba's ingenious ways of writing lyrics. One day, early in the morning, Shammi*ji*, who was in the lead role and Bhappi Soni, the director of the film, came to meet Baba. He had gone to Juhu beach for his morning walk. They went there looking for him. They found him sitting on a rock and smoking. They approached him and requested him to complete the lyrics of the song, to be filmed on Shammi Kapoor and the children featured in the film. While this was being discussed, Baba looked over his shoulder, saw a car passing by and said the song would be "Chakke Mein Chakka, Chakke Pe Gaadi." (*Smiles)* Interestingly, the song has names like Chunnu, Gattu etc. which were the names of some of the children in our neighbourhood.

'Once, late evening, he returned from a party where he had had a few extra drinks. Seeing Baba take unsteady steps, as he got off the car, our neighbours—Hemanta*da*'s wife and sister-in-law—could not help laughing. This did not go unnoticed by Baba. He came home and instantly wrote the song, "*Jungle mein mor naacha kisine na dekha, hum jo thodi si pikey zaraa jhoome haay re sab ne dekha*." This was sung by Rafi Sahab and filmed on Johnny Walker in *Madhumati* (1958) to a tune by Salil Chowdhury.

'My father's poems portrayed his sensitive mind, in contrast to the breezy romantic songs he often wrote. "Nanhe Munhe Bache Teri Mutthi Mein Kya Hai," a Rafi-Asha duet, captured the dreams of innocent underprivileged children for a future, bright and free from poverty. The song was composed by Shankar-Jaikishan, for *Boot Polish* (1953). Some of the other unforgettable gems he created were for films like *Kaala Bazaar* (1960) and *Guide* (1965), regarded as all-time classics.'

Shailendra wrote 145 songs for Rafi.

The other lyricist who made a significant contribution to Rafi's musical repertoire was Majrooh Sultanpuri. The duo collaborated for the first time for 'Jo Dil Ki Baat Hoti Hai' (*Baaz*, 1953) under the aegis of OP Nayyar. Rafi's voice added life to every word that came from this genius poet. 'Tujhe Kya Sunaau Main Dilruba' (*Akhri Daao*, 1958) or 'Kahin Bekhayaal Hoke' (*Teen Deviyaan*, 1965) illustrates the point.

One of the reasons for Majrooh's professional longevity was his ability to adapt to the changing times. 'Kya Hua Tera Waada' (*Hum Kisise Kum Nahin*, 1977) from his pen got Rafi his sixth Filmfare Award and also a National Award. Majrooh has the distinction of having written the highest number of Rafi's renditions; a staggering 374 songs.

Andalib, Majrooh Sultanpuri's son, spoke, 'Earlier, lyricists used to write the songs and then the tune was composed. But in the case of Majrooh Sahab, it was the reverse. For instance, "Dekhiye Sahibaan Woh Koi Aur Thi" from the blockbuster *Teesri Manzil* (1966) is one such song where RD Burman, influenced by Western music, had formed the tune and my father fitted in the meaningful words.

'Another instance was during the making of *Yaadon Ki Baaraat* in 1973. Film producer Nasir Hussain explained the storyline to music director RD Burman and just like before, "Chura Liya Hai Tumne Jo Dil Ko," happened.

'During the rehearsals, Rafi Sahab would often ask my father to help him with the exact pronunciation, though he himself was quite good at it. Most singers would never bother to talk to the lyricist and would only practise with the music director. It was a great honour that in the majority of musical programmes organised for Rafi Sahab, at least 50 per cent of the songs were from the pen of Majrooh Sahab.

'Rafi Sahab's passing away was a big loss, a loss that shook my father. I remember my father saying, "*Ismein koi shaq nahin ki Rafi Sahab poore aan-o-baan ke saath aaye aur usi aan-o-baan ke saath is duniya se gaye. Marta to har koi hai, par woh jis aan-o-baan se gaye wohi unki mahaanta ka saboot hai*. (There is no doubt that Rafi Sahab came with a lot of dignity and also departed with pride. Death is the ultimate reality for everyone, but the way he came and left, is a testimony to his greatness.)"'

Anand Bakshi, the unconventional poet and an ardent movie buff, came together with Rafi for the first time in S Mohinder's 'De Deedar O Dildaar' (*Sun To Le Haseena*, 1958). *Jab Jab Phool Khile* and *Himalay Ki God Mein*, both films released in 1965, provided the much-awaited break for the poet/lyricist and earned him immense acclaim. A bond that started in the late '50s continued till Rafi's last days. During this period, Anand Bakshi wrote nearly 369 songs and many of these were super hits—the iconic song that continues to be the universal birthday song for Hindi music lovers, 'Baar Baar Din Yeh Aaye' (*Farz*, 1967), was Anand Bakshi's brainchild in Rafi's voice. He mastered the art of writing simple, but meaningful, lyrics which ensured his popularity with the masses for over four decades. Some of the notable pieces of work by Anand Bakshi, in the voice of Rafi, are 'Pardesiyon Se Na Akhiyaan Milaana' (*Jab Jab Phool Khile*, 1965), 'Mere Dushman Tu Meri Dosti Ko Tarse' (*Aaye Din Bahaar Ke*, 1966), 'Aaja Tujhko Pukaare Mere Geet Re' (*Geet*, 1970), 'Yeh Jo Chilman Hai Dushman Hai' (*Mehboob Ki Mehndi*, 1971) and 'Shirdi Waale Sai Baba' (*Amar Akbar Anthony*, 1977).

The last song that Anand Bakshi penned for Rafi was 'Tu Kahin Aas Paas Hai Dost' (*Aas Paas*, 1980). Shortly after recording this song, Rafi departed from this world.

~

A career of four decades with many illustrious achievements has as many lyricists to talk about, some of who were eclipsed by the sheer brilliance of the singer, yet they were unconditionally happy to be a part of Rafi's universe—'Sau Baar Janam Lenge' (*Ustaadon Ke Ustaad*, 1963, lyrics by Asad Bhopali), 'Chal Chal Re Naujawaan' (*Ek Phool Do Mali*, 1969, lyricist Prem Dhawan), 'Ek Pardesi Mera Dil Le Gayaa' (*Phagun*, 1958, lyricist Qamar Jalalabadi), 'Hum Laaye Hain Toofan Se Kashti Nikal Ke' (*Jagriti*, 1954, lyricist Pradeep), 'Likhe Jo Khat Tujhe' (*Kanyadaan*, 1969, lyricist Neeraj) are counted amongst Rafi's most popular songs.

There are many such lyricists whose invaluable contribution added to Rafi's glorious career as a singer.

Lyricist Dev Kohli started his film journey with the song 'Geet Gaata Hoon Main' (*Lal Patthar*, 1971). Though his career is primarily rooted in modern music with Westernised accents, he had the privilege of working with some music giants of the yesteryear, including Mohammed Rafi. Dev Kohli had written around 10 songs for the singer. In fact, the first song of their association remains their best—'Maati Ke Jalte Deepak Ki Jot To Ek Din Bujh Jaani Hai' (*Khoon Khoon*, 1973).

He recollected, 'Once Rafi Sahab was rehearsing a song written by me for *Aakhri Kasam* (1979). The lyrics were "*Tera rang bada hai gora, nazar tennu lag jaye na, le bandh le kaala dora, nazar tennu lag jaye na* (Your complexion is very fair; I hope you don't get affected by the evil eye. Tie a black strand, lest you get affected by the evil eye.)" The lyrics were light-hearted, and every time Rafi Sahab would read it, he would chuckle. Later, after the recording, he walked up to me with a smile and praised me for creating exactly what the situation demanded, adding that he had truly enjoyed rendering the song; a compliment that I cherish as a blessing even today.'

There are many other lyricists—Asad Bhopali, Bharat Vyas, Farooq Qaiser, Gulshan Bawra, Indeevar, Naqsh Lyallpuri, Neeraj, PL Santoshi, Pradeep, Prem Dhawan and SH Bihari, amongst others, who can be mentioned here for their immense contribution to Rafi's rich musical repertoire.

Musicians

Sketching Rafi's career graph would be quite incomplete if one doesn't touch upon the contribution of the musicians in the more than 5000 songs he had sung in his lifetime. However, even as the songs they contributed to became chartbusters, these masters mostly remained in the shadows.

'*Abba* had great respect for musicians and used to spend a lot of time with them. He often used to say, "They are the invisible heroes of my songs,"' said Shahid Rafi.

The wizard behind many of Rafi's songs was Anthony Gonsalves. He is the first arranger in the history of Hindi films. 'He made a great contribution to Rafi songs,' revealed Pyarelal Sharma, of the legendary musical duo Laxmikant-Pyarelal. Few know that Pyarelal had learnt to play the violin from Anthony Gonsalves. It is believed that he composed the iconic song in *Amar Akbar Anthony*, 'My Name Is Anthony Gonsalves,' as a tribute to the legend.

Amongst the numerous chartbusters Anthony Gonsalves contributed to, were Rafi gems like 'Suhaani Raat Dhal Chuki' for Naushad (*Dulari*, 1949), 'Yeh Desh Hai Veer Jawaanon Ka' for OP Nayyar (*Naya Daur*, 1957), 'Jungle Mein Mor Naacha' for Salil Chowdhury (*Madhumati*, 1958), and many more. Incidentally, Pyarelal himself had played the violin in Rafi's soulful ditty 'Main Yeh Soch Kar Uske Dar Se Utha Tha' for Madan Mohan (*Haqeeqat*, 1964).

Another musician who played a big role in Rafi's songs was Vipin Reshammiya, an innovative musician and the father of the current music composer-singer Himesh Reshammiya. 'Rafi Sahab could fulfil the dreams of all the great music directors of his time as he gave superhits one after the other. A musician earns fame and establishes himself only when a song becomes popular. Rafi Sahab was the source of bread and butter for many in the industry, be it the music director, lyricist, co-singer or musician,' said Vipin Reshammiya.

He recollected having played musical instruments, in about 500 songs, with Rafi. 'The amount of respect and love I received from him is unforgettable. For the title song of *An Evening In Paris* (1967), composed by Shankar-Jaikishan, I played the latest reverb model of the clavioline (it was the talking point of that period). I must mention that Kalyan*ji bhai* had replicated the tunes of the *been* (instrument played by snake charmers), on the clavioline, in *Nagin* (1954) and I was very inspired by it. I had instantly bought this new musical instrument. The other song of that era where I played this instrument was 'Badan Pe Sitaare' (*Prince*, 1969). I was amazed to hear Rafi Sahab's rendition of the number. After the recording everyone present there said aloud, "*Wah* Rafi Sahab, *aap ne toh kamaal kar diya.* (Rafi Sahab, you have done a fabulous job.)" In his usual style, with a smile, he lifted up his hands towards the sky and said, "*Yeh Khuda ki marzi hai.* (It is what the Almighty wills.)"'

Amar Haldipur, a veteran musician, who began his career in 1966 as a violinist, had an anecdote to share. 'In those days, composers were hard taskmasters. During a recording in 1967-68, when composer C Ramchandra was recording a song with Rafi Sahab, the latter made repeated mistakes due to which the recording had to be done a couple of times. C Ramchandra was annoyed and said, "Rafi *miyan! Kya ho raha hai? Maine kya* music school *khol rakha hai? Jo gaana diya hai, yaad kijiye aur gaiye.* (Rafi *miyan*! What is happening? Have I started a music school? Memorise and sing the song given to you.)" Rafi Sahab said apologetically, "*Maaf kijiye. Ye gaana mere zehen main nahin baith raha hai. Main abhi kartaa hoon.* (Pardon me. I am unable to get a grasp on the song. I will do it.)" He repeated it over and over again till the music director was completely satisfied. He went and humbly apologised to the musicians for the several retakes. This admirable temperament made Rafi Sahab stand apart from the rest and he was a favourite amongst all.'

Manohari Singh, a saxophone wizard, is also an inseparable name from many of Rafi's chartbusters. At a live show in 2009, the then 80-year-old played Rafi's 'Gulaabi Aankhen Jo Teri Dekhi' (*The Train*, 1970). The great saxophonist could proficiently play the flute, the clarinet and the mandolin as well.

Singh, fondly known as Manohari*da*, played the mandolin in 'Achcha Ji Main Hari,' (*Kaala Paani*, 1958), a Rafi-Geeta duet, for SD Burman. The musician's proficiency with several musical instruments is evident in the following songs. 'Mujhe Duniyawaalon' for Naushad (*Leader*, 1964), 'Dil Jo Na Keh Saka' for Roshan (*Bheegi Raat*, 1965), 'Aye Phoolon Ki Rani' for Shankar-Jaikishan (*Arzoo*, 1965), 'Tere Mere Sapne' for SD Burman (*Guide*, 1965). The flute strain in 'Ek Haseen Shaam Ko' for Madan Mohan (*Dulhan Ek Raat Ki*, 1967) shows his finesse with the key flute (the instrument he started his career with), complimenting the romanticism of Rafi's voice.

A discussion on musicians in Hindi film songs and their contribution to Rafi's glorious career simply cannot be complete without mentioning the *Lords of film music*—Cawas Lord, the pioneer percussionist; Kersi

Lord, a multi-instrumentalist; Burjor Lord, also a percussionist and Hilla Lord, the pianist.

Burjor, fondly known in the music fraternity as Bujji, was a well-known drummer and a vibraphone player. Some songs where his rhythm and beats have accompanied Rafi's voice include, 'Gulaabi Aankhen Jo Teri Dekhi' (*The Train,* 1970), 'Chand Mera Dil' and 'Kya Hua Tera Waada' (*Hum Kisise Kum Nahin,* 1977) with drums; 'Laakhon Hain Nigaah Mein' (*Phir Wohi Dil Laaya Hoon,* 1963) and 'Ek Haseen Sham Ko' (*Dulhan Ek Raat Ki,* 1963) with wood blocks; 'Pukaarta Chalaa Hoon Main' (*Mere Sanam,* 1960), 'Deewaana Mujhsa Nahin Is Ambar Ke Neeche' (*Teesri Manzil,* 1966) with vibraphone and 'Ek Tha Gul Aur Ek Thi Bulbul' (*Jab Jab Phool Khile,* 1965) with the xylophone.

The vibraphone added to the aura of romance where Shammi Kapoor flatters gorgeous Sharmila Tagore in 'Deewana Hua Baadal' (*Kashmir Ki Kali*, 1964) in the charming voice of Rafi. In fact, most songs of Shammi Kapoor had the bongo as the prime instrument. The fingers at the bongo would mostly be of one of the Lord brothers.

Cawas Lord is credited with playing castanets, the Latin American instrument on Indian shores. He was the one playing the instrument for the melodious RD Burman composition, 'Matwaali Aankhon Waale' (*Chhote Nawaab*, 1961). The song opens with Rafi's *la la la la*...an Arabian-night feel, from where the guitar picks up, followed by the castanets, marking the entry of Helen as a flamenco dancer, with a pair of castanets in each hand. Composer RD Burman aptly used the instrument to accentuate the rhythm of the song.

Burjor Lord inherited the magical fingers, on the percussion, from father Cawas. Besides being an integral part of many Rafi-scores, Burjor, as the drummer, also accompanied Rafi on foreign trips for his stage performances. The Burjor-Rafi association in the studios was well-known, especially in the '60s. Burjor shared, 'On a personal level, we knew Rafi Sahab as our next door neighbour for a few years in Almeida Park. Rafi Sahab, though shy by nature, was close to Daddy. He would often come to him for advice, ask him to read his income tax slips and bills as he was not familiar with English. He also attended my wedding in 1970. Besides, I have played in many shows with Rafi Sahab; in fact my first international tour, to the West Indies, in 1966, happened with him. The show was a great success. The newspaper headlines on the next day of the show (he has meticulously preserved the clippings) read, "*It surpassed all other shows*." After my performance, the awestruck audience found it difficult to believe that I used my own arms and not some electric device to play the drums, since my hands were moving that fast.'

Kersi Lord, the multi-faceted musician had a long association with Rafi. He also happened to be the singer's next door neighbour. 'I remember once an Iranian couple had come to India and they wanted Rafi Sahab to sing an Iranian song. He called me home to play the synthesizer as he sang the song, with a fluency that made it seem as if it was his own mother tongue. The couple was left spellbound.

'I recall an incident from a recording, though I do not remember the song, when we were waiting for him to arrive at the studio. That day, he walked in a bit late and to our surprise, apologised not only to Chitragupta, the music director, but to every musician since he would have to cancel the recording for that day. He candidly said that he had eaten some *rasam* (soup) and *idli* (rice cake) the previous night and his voice was affected by the tamarind and hot spices. Rafi Sahab was fond of good food but normally it used to be mildly spiced. His professionalism was exemplary.

'During the month of Ramadan, we musicians used to wait for Rafi Sahab to break *roza* (fast), when dry fruits, *jalebi* and *halwa* (Indian sweets) would come from his home and all of us in the studio would enjoy the feast.' Kersi Lord, who was present at the hospital after Rafi had passed away, said misty-eyed, 'All night I stayed there in despair... I cannot forget that night at the Bombay Hospital.'

Sumit Mitra, an ace accordionist of the Indian film industry wistfully recalled, 'Those were the days when music directors had to use a full orchestra. For a Shankar-Jaikishan recording, there would be 10-12 violins, cellos, guitars and mandolin. To create the required effect, nearly 30-odd musicians would be required and most of the musicians would come every day to rehearse—Joe Menezes, Martin

Dourado and Jerry Fernandez with violins—everyone fondly called them the *Three Musketeers*, Albuquerque played the cello, Issac David the mandolin, D'Melo and Boney the guitar, Sumant Raj played the flute, Leslie Coutinho and Kersi Lord played the drums and percussion instruments and Robert Corea would be on the piano. Though Rafi Sahab was a reserved man, he would, with his radiant smile, connect with everyone present in those recording sessions, right to the musician in the last row.'

Mitra continued, 'Rafi Sahab used to travel a lot for his outstation musical concerts. Once it so happened that his regular accordion player, Dheeraj, could not accompany him, so I was selected to replace him. It was an opportunity to observe Rafi Sahab beyond the recording studios. All through the tour, he was very particular in briefing the organisers to take special care of all the musicians. He was always pleasant, constantly smiling and motivating people around him, irrespective of time, place or situation. He had a very positive aura.'

At this point, Sumit Mitra picked up his accordion (a customised one with his name inscribed on one side of the bellows in bold letters) and his fingers magically ran on the keys to play, 'Aji Aisa Mauka Phir Kahaan Milega' (*An Evening in Paris*, 1967) and 'Chhalkaaye Jaam, Aaiye Aapki Aankhon Ke Naam' *(Mere Humdum Mere Dost*, 1968). The veteran added, 'The accordion is such a beautiful instrument. Even though fewer musicians play it today, it will never go extinct. It is immortal, just as Rafi Sahab's voice is.'

Satish Gupta, an eminent sound recordist, who worked with Rafi in the last few years of the legend's career, recalled, 'A Punjabi song was being recorded, where Rafi Sahab, Asha*ji* and Dilraj Kaur were singing. I was doing my usual task of placing the mike. Unaware of protocols, I placed three mikes and beckoned Rafi Sahab to stand at the first mike for recording. Rafi Sahab walked up to me and asked where would Asha*ji* stand? I got quite nervous and told him that I had placed the second mike for her. He instructed me to place Asha*ji*'s mike in position one and his second. Though Rafi Sahab was quite senior, both in terms of age and experience, he showed great respect for Asha*ji*. His courteousness towards a colleague has stayed with me as a lesson for life.'

Rafi had great regard for the musicians and would often refer to them as the *precious jewels* of his team. During his tours for live shows, he would make sure that the musicians were given accommodation in the same hotel where he stayed. Some of his close associates, like Krishna Mukherjee, Usha Timothy and Kishan Sharma, who travelled extensively with him for the live shows, fondly remember these little gestures and relate how Rafi ensured that each member of the orchestra had their food before he had his own meal.

And there were others like sitar maestro Ustaad Rais Khan who was like family, being related to Rafi. Khan Sahab shared, 'Rafi was a 24-carat human being—pious, caring and efficacious; similar to pure gold. He undoubtedly was the greatest playback singer of all times. He was not a formally trained singer and if one has to analyse him from a purely classical angle, it would be doing him injustice.

'Let me also clarify that singing a film song requires a lot of expertise and dedication too. It is not necessary that every classical singer can become a great playback singer, unless he commits himself to learning playback singing as a separate genre. However, I would also like to assert that a classical base is essential to be a good singer of any category or style, especially, if you are not as gifted as Rafi was.'

10

Heroes Find Their Voice

Earlier, it was the film's success that largely influenced Rafi's career. But in the '60s and '70s, it was Rafi's voice that influenced the film's box-office returns. It was a belief among struggling film producers, music composers and actors that Rafi's songs in their films could save their careers.

The '70s launched a new generation of superstars; Rajesh Khanna, Amitabh Bachchan and Rishi Kapoor became sensations. Film music too followed the trend; to complement the modern style of storytelling, music directors were now creating songs which had a strong influence of popular Western music.

Just as music directors of that period needed him to do justice to their compositions, so did actors, to give their respective careers a boost, by lip-syncing to Rafi's vocal excellence. He poured his voice and the emotions into every word and made the actors look even better on-screen. Dharmendra, Rajendra Kumar, Joy Mukherjee, Biswajeet and Shashi Kapoor were among the many top stars whose on-screen presence seamlessly gelled with Rafi's voice.

Rajendra Kumar

Rajendra Kumar, popularly known as 'Jubilee Kumar,' shot to fame with the epic film *Mother India* (1957). However, Rajendra Kumar's first hit as a lead romantic hero was *Goonj Uthi Shehnai* (1959) where his co-star was Ameeta. The songs 'Maine Peena Seekh Liya' and 'Keh Do Koi Na Kare Yahaan Pyaar,' in the voice of Rafi, became instant hits. His *Dhool Ka Phool* (1959), Yash Chopra's first film as director, made its mark with the meaningful song 'Tu Hindu Banega Na Musalman Banega,' in the soulful voice of Rafi.

In the '60s, Rajendra Kumar left his contemporaries and fans stunned with successive silver jubilees—*Mere Mehboob* (1963), *Sangam* (1964), *Aayee Milan Ki Bela* (1964), *Zindagi* (1964), *Arzoo* (1965) and *Suraj* (1966). All these films had Rafi as Rajendra Kumar's playback voice and the songs were mega hits, thus contributing in making him a Jubilee star.

In *Mere Mehboob* (1963), the title song, 'Mere Mehboob Tujhe Meri Mohabbat Ki Kasam' was nominated for the Filmfare Award in three categories: Rafi for Best Male Playback Singer, Naushad for Best Music Director and Shakeel Badayuni for Best Lyricist of the year.

The association of Rafi, Rajendra Kumar and Shankar-Jaikishan, became a favourite with almost all big banners of the '60s. There are several films that illustrate this. *Sasuraal* (1961) with two solo songs by Rafi which included 'Teri Pyaari Pyaari Soorat Ko,' composed by Shankar-Jaikishan, won Rafi his second Filmfare Award and *Gharana* (1961), a superhit family drama had Rafi's 'Husnwaale Tera Jawaab Nahin' creating enthralling moments between the lead couple Rajendra Kumar and Asha Parekh, for which Rafi was nominated for a Filmfare Award.

In *Dil Ek Mandir* (1963), Shankar-Jaikishan used Rafi's voice for 'Yaad Na Jaye Beete Dinon Ki'—the touching score of this melodramatic love story became one of the chartbusters of the year. The lyrics of Shailendra, with Rafi's voice and Rajendra Kumar on-screen created the right pensive ambience that the storyline demanded.

The magic of the Rafi-Rajendra Kumar *jodi* (pairing) worked again in Raj Kapoor's *Sangam* (1964), in the evergreen song, 'Yeh Mera Prem Patra Padh Kar.' *Aayi Milan Ki Bela* (1964) and *Arzoo* (1965) saw Rajendra Kumar moving steadily up his career graph. An emotional love story, *Arzoo* was shot in the picturesque locations of Jammu and Kashmir and had Shankar-Jaikishan compositions in the dulcet voice of Rafi—'Aye

Phoolon Ki Rani Bahaaron Ki Mallika' and 'Chhalke Teri Aankhon Se Sharab.' Both added to the romantic aura on-screen.

Rajendra Kumar starrer *Suraj* (1966) won Rafi his third Filmfare Award for 'Baharon Phool Barsaao,' once again a Shankar-Jaikishan composition with lyrics by Shailendra.

In all, Rajendra Kumar lip-synced on 112 songs sung by Rafi and composed by the talented music directors of that era.

Manoj Kumar

Manoj Kumar made his debut with *Fashion* (1957) followed by five other films between 1957 and 1964. His image as the patriotic protagonist was established with *Shaheed* (1965), where he played the role of the martyr Bhagat Singh. 'Aye Watan Aye Watan' and 'O Mera Rang De Basanti Chola' are the two patriotic songs sung by Rafi for Manoj Kumar.

Upkaar (1967) too was special for Manoj Kumar in many ways. Besides being his directorial debut, the subject of the film was suggested to him by the then Prime Minister Lal Bahadur Shastri. With the Indo-Pakistani War of 1965 serving as the backdrop, it was an attempt to propagate the *Jai Jawaan Jai Kisaan* (hail the soldier, hail the farmer) slogan. The film was a huge success at the box-office, cementing Manoj Kumar's image as a patriot and also earning six Filmfare Awards in the bargain.

Rafi brought immense appreciation for Manoj Kumar in films like *Gumnaam* (1965), and *Himalay Ki God Mein* (1965). The solo 'Ek Ladki Hai Jisne Jeena Mushkil' and a duet with Sharda, 'Jane Chaman Shola Badan,' both from *Gumnaam,* became very popular with the masses. In *Himalay Ki God Mein,* Rafi sang the duet, 'Tu Raat Khadi Thi Chhat Pe, Ni Main Samjhaa Ki Chand Nikla' with Usha Timothy in a typical Punjabi style.

There were others that captured the hearts of music lovers of that generation; 'Naseeb Mein Jiske Jo Likha Tha' (*Do Badan*, 1966), 'Zulfon Ko Hataale Chehre Se' (*Sawan Ki Ghata*, 1966), title tracks of *Patthar Ke Sanam* (1967) and *Saajan* (1969), 'Door Rehkar Na Karo Baat' (*Amaanat*, 1977), to name a few.

The common background of this actor and singer, going back to the state of Punjab in the pre-Partition days, added a special quality to the songs they brought to the silver screen.

Even though Manoj Kumar's voice behind the screen was usually Mukesh, some of his on-screen portrayals are better remembered because of Rafi's renditions.

Manoj Kumar fondly remembered, 'Rafi Sahab had an aura of divinity around him. He was a righteous and simple man. Despite reaching dizzying heights of fame, he remained humble, totally disciplined and devoted to his art. Once, the notable writer and my friend Salim Khan, who is also related to the Rafi family, was visiting a religious shrine and co-incidentally met Rafi Sahab there. Salim Khan Sahab candidly told Rafi Sahab, "I have noticed that in many of your stage shows when you sing songs from *Deedar* (1951), *Baiju Bawra* (1952) and other classics, though you sing them brilliantly, you miss out on an extremely important aspect of establishing a *connect* with the audience present before you."

'Salim Khan suggested that he should memorise his lyrics; that way all his attention would be on the audience instead of reading the lyrics. Rafi accepted the advice graciously and the listeners were blessed with a more livewire Rafi on stage,' Manoj Kumar recollected with a smile.

'One of the songs of Rafi Sahab I love listening to, time and again, is "Matlab Nikal Gayaa Hai Toh Pehchaante Nahin" (*Amaanat*, 1977); the last time I emoted to a song in his voice.

'In the late '70s, we had organised a charity show for the film *Shirdi Ke Sai Baba* (1977). Satya Sai Baba had agreed to preside over the function and had asked me to invite Rafi Sahab. He said that he would surely come if time permitted. He not only came for the charity show, but sang 'Mann Tadpat Hari Darshan Ko Aaj' for over an hour. He created such an ambience with his singing that the audience was moved to a trance. Rafi Sahab would not differentiate between a rendition for Sai Baba or Garib Nawaz.

'As a young boy, I remember listening to his songs. Although I was too young to understand cinema then, I knew he was someone extraordinarily special. He lives on in my memories...'

Dharmendra

In one of his interviews in *Filmfare* (December 2000), Dharmendra was asked: 'Hemant Kumar, Mukesh, Mohammad Rafi, Kishore Kumar…all provided playback for you.Whose voice suited you the best?'

He responded, 'Mohammad Rafi's contribution to my career is immense. From numbers like 'Jaane Kya Dhoondti Rehti Hain Yeh Aankhen Mujh Mein' *(Shola Aur Shabnam,* 1961*)* till 'Main Jatt Yamla Pagla Deewana' *(Pratigya,* 1975*)* have remained evergreen. The other singers have also made huge contributions to my career. I can never forget that. But Rafi Sahab is a personal favourite.'

As versatile as Dharmendra was in his portrayal of characters, equally malleable was Rafi's voice to these characters the actor played on-screen. Gradually, all the music directors acknowledged Rafi as the voice for the earlier romantic and later macho matinee star of Hindi cinema.

The Dharmendra-Rafi combination saw its first success in 1961, with *Shola Aur Shabnam* which had gems from Khayyam such as 'Jaane Kya Dhoondti Hai' (solo) and 'Jeet Hi Lenge Baazi Hum Tum' (with Lata).

Khayyam recalled, 'In *Shola Aur Shabnam* I composed some mellow but passionate songs for Dharmendra. To do justice to the lyrics of Kaifi Azmi, I had to give it a very soothing tune. It was a challenge for Rafi as it had to be picturised on Dharmendra, the iconic action hero. I was amazed to see the chemistry they created on-screen and the songs became great hits.'

Sanjeev Kohli, Madan Mohan's son, emphasised how his father established a Dharmendra-Rafi trend in the '60s with films like *Aap Ki Parchhaaiyan* (1964), *Mera Qasoor Kya Hai* (1964) and *Pooja Ke Phool* (1964). In *Aap Ki Parchhaaiyan*, 'Main Nigaahen Tere Chehre Se' blended classical base with the intoxication of love that Dharmendra professes, especially in the lines '*…tauba tauba, tauba tauba… woh nasha hai kya bataoon kaise.*' In the same film, the composer created an unconventional tune, 'Yehi Hai Tamanna Tere Dar Ke Saamne Meri Jaan Jaaye,' where an enamoured Dharmendra entreats his love to Supriya on-screen. Rafi's voice was in harmony with Dharmendra's exuberant screen presence in both these songs. Madan Mohan repeated this magical Dharmendra-Rafi chemistry on-screen for another melodious treat 'Ab Do Dilo Ki Mushkil' (with Asha) in *Pooja Ke Phool* (1964).

Neela Aakash (1965) had the signature Madan Mohan composition 'Aakhri Geet Mohabbat Ka' where Rafi's voice poignantly expresses his bereavement. 'Aap Ko Pyar Chhupaane Ki' and 'Tere Paas Aake Mera Waqt' (both with Asha) are two memorable duets from the film.

Omi from the Omi-Sonik duo walked down memory lane to recollect how in 1966 they made their debut as independent music composers to create Dharmendra-Rafi numbers in *Dil Ne Phir Yaad Kiya* (1966), with songs like 'Kaliyon Ne Ghunghat Khole,' 'Lo Chhehra Surkh Sharaab Hua,' 'Main Suraj Hoon' (with Asha). He had observed that Rafi, with his Punjabi roots, could bring alive that Punjabi liveliness and energy that Dharmendra portrayed so well on-screen.

Sudha, Chitragupta's daughter, recounted how her father composed a pensive number for Dharmendra in the voice of Rafi 'Kahin Se Maut Ko Laao Ki Gham Ki Raat Kate' (*Mera Qasoor Kya Hai*, 1964). She also mentioned *Akashdeep* (1965) in which Chitragupta composed one of the most melodious solos in Dharmendra's career, sung by Rafi. 'Mujhe Dard-E-Dil Ka Pata Na Tha.' The song depicted the quintessential story of a poor, handsome man falling in love with a well-heeled girl. The film wasn't a box-office grosser, but the song got the attention of music connoisseurs.

When OP Nayyar composed the intense expression of love, 'Aapke Haseen Rukh Pe Aaj Naya Noor Hai' (*Bahaarein Phir Bhi Aayengi*, 1966), for Dharmendra playing a piano on-screen, it was Rafi who did justice to the melody. This chemistry, by now, was so effective that almost every composer approached Rafi to be the playback voice of Dharmendra.

Shankar-Jaikishan, like all other composers, also culled out tunes for Dharmendra in *Pyar Hi Pyar* (1969) in the voice of Rafi, who sang 'Dekha Hai Teri Aankhon Mein' and 'Main Kahin Kavi Na Ban Jaoon.'

Laxmikant-Pyarelal too gave innumerable hits with Rafi for the good-looking actor. Pyarelal remembered how in 1969, the music director duo had Rafi sing for Dharmendra in *Aaya Sawan Jhoom Ke* (1969) with popular compositions like the title track, 'Aaya Saawan Jhoom Ke' (Rafi-Lata duet) and 'Bura Mat Suno, Bura Mat Dekho;' the latter starts sans any instrumentation, with the lyrics being *'Nazar woh joh dushman pe bhi meherbaan ho...'* Another song is 'Yeh Shama To Jali Roshni Ke Liye' which also opens in the signature Laxmikant-Pyarelal style with percussions in the background, supporting Rafi's voice, that blends seamlessly with Dharmendra's suave looks on-screen. The evergreen Rafi-Lata duet in *Jeevan Mrityu* (1970), 'Jhilmil Sitaron Ka Aangan Hoga' is also a special composition.

The surviving member of the musical duo (Pyarelal) reminisced about another composition, 'When Anand Bakshi came up with the lyrics "Main Jat Yamala Pagla Deewana" for the film *Pratigya* (1975), I knew the only voice that could match the macho image of Dharmendra, playing a Jat character on-screen, was that of Rafi. Dharam*ji* did what he does best and Rafi behind the screen did the rest!'

Though the '70s saw a handful of music composers swaying with the current to record songs for Dharmendra in Kishore Kumar's voice (*Naya Zamaana* (1971), *Do Chor* (1972), *Jugnu* (1973), *International Crook*, 1974), Rafi continued to steadily contribute chartbusters to Dharmendra's career in his own inimitable ways—whether it was the evergreen song 'Aaj Mausam Bada Beimaan Hai' (*Loafer*, 1973), an all-time favourite of radio jockeys whenever there is a nip in the air, or 'Main Jat Yamla Pagla Deewana' that became the most identifiable tune with Dharmendra's free-spirited signature moves.

Rafi's last recorded song (on July 28, 1980) was for Dharmendra in *Aas Paas*.

> *Tere aane ki aas hai dost*
> *Sham phir kyon udaas hai dost*
> *Mehki mehki fiza ye kehti hai*
> *Tu kahin aas pas hai dost...*
> *Tu kahin aas pas hai dost...*
> (I hope for your arrival my friend
> Why then is the evening gloomy my friend
> The fragrant, perfumed ambience tells me
> You are somewhere closeby my friend.)

Joy Mukherjee

'Rafi Sahab had achieved the prodigious feat of building the careers of innumerable newcomers be it actors, producers, music directors or lyricists. His voice was like a magic wand…it had the Midas touch,' said Joy Mukherjee.

Rafi was the voice of Joy Mukherjee right through the latter's career. The combination along with OP Nayyar has given the industry some memorable melodies. Joy Mukherjee, who went on to establish himself as the lover boy of the '60s, made his debut with *Love in Simla* (1960), then gave the blockbuster *Love in Tokyo* (1966) and ended his career with *Love in Bombay* (1975), with Rafi as his playback voice in all of them.

Some songs from his films which are hummed even today include 'Bahut Shukriya Badi Meharbani' (*Ek Musafir Ek Haseena*, 1962), 'Gaal Gulaabi Kiske Hain' (*Love in Simla*, 1960), 'Husn Se Chand Bhi Sharmaaya Hai' (*Door Ki Awaaz*, 1964), 'Bade Miyaan Deewane Aise Na Bano' (*Shagird*, 1967).

After *Love in Simla,* which saw great success, he was paired with Asha Parekh for several hits. *Phir Wohi Dil Laya Hoon* (1963), *Ziddi* (1964) and *Love in Tokyo*. These box-office successes had fabulous renditions by Rafi such as 'Lakhon Hain Nigaah Mein,' 'Teri Soorat Se Nahin Milti Kisi Ki Soorat' and the title song 'Love In Tokyo' respectively.

The late '60s saw the rise of Dharmendra, Rajesh Khanna, Jeetendra and Shashi Kapoor and with that Joy Mukherjee faded from the limelight. It is during this time that he took to directing and producing films. He was the producer/director/actor of *Humsaaya* (1968). The Rafi and OP Nayyar combination gave some wonderful songs for the film such as 'Dil Ki Awaaz Bhi Sunn' and 'Mujhe Mera Pyar De Do' (Rafi-Asha duet), but could not save the film from being a box-office disaster.

The belief that Rafi was the voice behind the success of Joy Mukherjee is well established by the fact that all his hit films had Rafi as the playback singer. Joy Mukherjee said, 'My father Sashadhar Mukherjee, a producer and the co-founder of Filmalaya Studios, was a great admirer of Rafi Sahab. While launching me opposite Sadhana in *Love in Simla*, he ensured that 10 out of the 11 songs in the film were sung by Rafi Sahab. I was quite nervous, more so because it was my father's film, someone who was well-known for giving box-office hits. To date, I remember my father's reassuring words, "The film will be a hit as Rafi Sahab is singing the songs; he will make sure that your flaws are covered up by his voice. Just be sincere and the rest will fall into place." When the first song of the film was being recorded, I went with my father to the recording studio. He asked me to touch Rafi Sahab's feet and take his blessings. Rafi Sahab blessed me and said, "Your name is Joy and you need to bring joy to the world with your acting."

'The film became a big success and "Gaal Gulaabi Kiske Hain" became extremely popular. Even today it is considered to be one of the most popular romantic songs of the yesteryear. From there began a long journey where Rafi Sahab and I brought *joy* to millions of cinema lovers year after year and in this way he made his own blessing come true.'

Joy Mukherjee, OP Nayyar and Rafi created magic in the '60s and in the '70s. All the songs of *Ek Musafir Ek Haseena* (1962) are beautiful compositions from 'Aap Yoon Hi Agar Humse Milte Rahe,' 'Phir Tere Sheher Mein Mitne Ko Chala Aaya Hoon,' to 'Humko Tumhaare Ishq Ne Kya Kya Bana Diya' and 'Bahut Shukriya.' The songs from the Nasir Hussain film, *Phir Wohi Dil Laya Hoon* (1963) had the same magical impact on the masses. 'Banda Parwar Thaam Lo Jigar,' 'Nazneen Bada Rangeen Hai Waada Tera,' are all well-known.

Mukherjee jokes, 'I feel "Aanchal Mein Sajaa Lena Kaliyan" is so exhilarating that it can rouse fresh love in a couple who have been married for more than 50 years (*laughs*).'

In Mukherjee's decade-long cinematic career, well-marked by superhit songs, Rafi remained his default playback voice despite the fact that Kishore Kumar was his maternal uncle.

Joy Mukherjee elucidated, 'My father had blind faith in Rafi Sahab. My mother Sati Rani Devi and Kishore Kumar were siblings, yet my father chose Rafi Sahab to launch my film career and the immense popularity of songs from then on established Rafi Sahab as my voice. Moreover, *mama* (maternal uncle) was then more of an actor than a singer. Later, *mama* did sing for some of my films. But by then people identified me with Rafi Sahab just the way they would say that Rafi Sahab was the voice of Shammi*ji*.'

Of 27 films, Rafi has been Joy Mukherjee's voice in 17 films having sung a total of 74 songs in them. He also sang for the last film of his career *Haiwaan* (1977) but the song was filmed on his brother Deb Mukherjee. The last time Joy Mukherjee was seen lip-syncing to Rafi's voice was for *Umeed* (1962).

Shashi Kapoor

Shashi Kapoor, the youngest son of Prithiviraj Kapoor made an indelible mark in *Jab Jab Phool Khile* (1965), in which Rafi sung all the songs composed by Kalyan*ji*-Anand*ji*. 'Ek Tha Gul Aur Ek Thi Bulbul,' 'Pardesiyon Se Na Akhiyaan Milaana,' 'Yahaan Main Ajnabee Hoon' and the rollicking duet 'Na Na Karte Pyar Tumhi Se Kar Baithe,' hit just the right chord with the music lovers. From then on, Rafi's voice, which had established itself as the perfect foil of Shammi Kapoor's screen persona, also came to be recognised with that of his younger brother Shashi Kapoor.

Neend Hamaari Khwaab Tumhaare (1966), *Pyar Kiye Jaa* (1966), *Kanyadaan* (1968), *Pyar Ka Mausam* (1969), *Ek Shrimaan Ek Shrimati* (1969) are some of the other Shashi Kapoor hits where Rafi's mellifluous voice complemented the actor's suave on-screen presence.

Shammi Kapoor confessed, 'I was awestruck to see the way Rafi Sahab managed to adopt the mannerisms of Shashi and do justice to him as he did for me.'

Rafi became the default voice of Shashi and in all the popular Shashi-Nanda films like *Jab Jab Phool Khile*, *Mehndi Lagi Mere Haath* (1962), *Mohabbat Isko Kehte Hain* (1965), *Neend Hamaari Khwaab Tumhaare* and *Raja Saab* (1969).

Kalyan*ji*-Anand*ji* created several hit compositions for Rafi as the voice of Shashi Kapoor, be it 'Affoo Khudaya,' 'Pardesiyon Se Na Ankhiyan Milana' (*Jab Jab Phool Khile*,) or 'Mere Bechain Dil Ko Chain Tune Diya' (*Aamne Saamne*, 1967). The composer duo also got Rafi's voice for Shashi in *Haseena Maan Jaayegi* (1968), which was Prakash Mehra's debut film as a director. A melodrama set around the Chinese war, with Shashi playing a double role, it is still remembered for its melodious songs like the Rafi-Lata duet 'Bekhudi Mein Sanam.'

'O Aaye Baithe Khaaye Piye Khiske' (*Ek Shrimaan Ek Shrimati*) is an energetic rendition by Rafi, where Shashi Kapoor's jovial screen presence does equal justice to the Kalyan*ji*-Anand*ji* tune. The film also had other memorable solos by Rafi—a romantic communiqué in a moonlit night, 'Chandni Raat Mein Yoon Dil Ko Jalaa Ke To Na Ja' and the poetic love song, 'Kuchh Kahein Toh Khafaa Chup Rahein Toh Khafaa.'

Songs of *Raja Saab* had Rafi's voice impeccably moulding itself to the different on-screen shades of Shashi Kapoor, whether it was the frothy 'Kal Raat Waali Mulaqaat Ke Liye' or the sombre 'Raju Ka Tha Ek Khwaab.' Anand*ji*, on being asked why as music composers they chose Rafi as the voice of Shashi Kapoor for this particular song, replied, 'A handsome man needed a handsome voice to charm his pretty actress.'

'Likhe Jo Khat Tujhe,' is a much-hummed song from the 1969 love story *Kanyadaan*, a classic from the stable of the talented musical duo Shankar-Jaikishan. 'Thoda Ruk Jaayegi To Tera Kya Jaayega' (*Patanga*, 1971) is another melodious Shankar-Jaikishan composition which is an atypical romantic sequence beautifully captured on the mountain roads, where Rafi's voice creates the perfect mood for the young Kapoor's effervescence.

Rafi therefore played a major role in the young Shashi Kapoor garnering a significant fan-following in his heyday.

Biswajeet

Biswajeet, the Calcutta-(now Kolkata) born actor, after proving his mettle in Bengali films with *Mayamrigo* (1960) and *Dui Bhai* (1961), made it to Bombay in 1962, with aspirations to enter the world of Hindi films.

The same year, he shot to fame with his superhit film, *Bees Saal Baad* (1962). In *April Fool* (1964), Shankar-Jaikishan aptly leveraged Rafi as the voice for Biswajeet. The film turned out to be a superhit with its musical scores like 'April Fool Banaaya' and 'Aa Gale Lag Jaa' making its mark. In the same year, Ravi's composition in the voice of Rafi, 'Na Jhatko Zulf Se

Paani' and 'Kya Ajab Saaz Hai Yeh Shehnai,' in *Shehnai* (1964), repeated the success story. These two successive box-office accomplishments established Rafi as the unanimously accepted voice of Biswajeet and their combination became a hit formula for filmmakers and music composers. Rafi's voice became the default singing voice of Biswajeet just the way it had for Shammi Kapoor and actor Joy Mukherjee.

The amazing fact is that though Shammi Kapoor, Joy Mukherjee and Biswajeet worked in the same genre of films—light romantic flicks with the voice of Rafi common to all—the singer maintained a distinct style and mannerism for each of them.

Mere Sanam (1965) was a musical blockbuster where Rafi was brilliant as Biswajeet's voice. All OP Nayyar compositions, filmed on Biswajeet, were outstanding and Rafi did great justice to all the songs, some of which were 'Pukaarta Chalaa Hoon Main,' 'Humdum Mere Maan Bhi Jaao,' 'Huye Hain Tumpe Aashiq Hum,' 'Tukre Hain Mere Dil Ki Ae Yaar Tere Aansoon,' and 'Roka Kai Baar Maine Dilki Umang Ko.'

Biswajeet and Rafi became a formidable combination throughout the '60s. *Yeh Raat Phir Na Aayegi* (1966) had OP Nayyar creating a duet 'Phir Miloge Kabhi Is Baat Ka Waada Karlo' in the endearing voice of Rafi and Asha where Biswajeet is seen romancing Sharmila Tagore. In *Sagaai* (1966), Ravi gave music lovers a brilliant Rafi-Asha duet, 'Na Yeh Zameen Thi Na Aasmaan Tha,' filmed on Biswajeet and Rajashree.

The songs of *Vaasna* (1968), composed by Chitragupta and sung by Rafi for Biswajeet, also proved to be hits. The Rafi solo 'Itni Nazuk Na Bano' and the Rafi-Lata duet 'Yeh Parbaton Ke Daayre' are unforgettable tunes from this film. Biswajeet's next film *Pyar Ka Sapna* (1969) saw the Chitragupta-Rafi magic repeat itself in songs like 'Ae Meri Zindagi' and 'Tere Chehre Se Hatey Ankh Toh.'

The '70s saw the advent of Rajesh Khanna and the euphoria building around him affected the careers of the romantic heroes of the '60s. It was also the period when Amitabh Bachchan came with an angry young man image and the soft romance on-screen made way for action films. Many of Biswajeet's songs in the voice of Rafi continue to be jukebox favourites and top the *Romantic Song* charts even today.

Biswajeet said, 'Rafi is the greatest playback singer that the industry has ever seen. His contribution to my career was immense. Most of the songs he sang for me are very popular. He would make acting easy for the actor. His voice would create such an atmosphere that the audience would get captivated by it and the actor had very little to do.'

Biswajeet also acknowledged Rafi's contribution to Bengali music, 'Rafi Sahab also sang many popular Bengali songs. The song, "Pakhitar Buke Jeno Teer Mero Na," composed by Satinath Mukherjee, was sung by Rafi who later also gave his voice for the Uttam-Suchitra starrer, *Indrani* (1958), which was a Nachiketa Ghosh film; Rafi Sahab sang a Hindi song though the film was in Bengali.

'No one can ever equal Rafi Sahab in talent. He was inimitable.'

Randhir Kapoor

For Randhir Kapoor, Rafi was an unique singing genius who was beyond compare. 'Every song he has sung for me has been a blessing and some of them are played even today: "Chup Chup Kyu Baithi Ho" (*Humraahi*, 1974), "Aap Ki Kasam Ek Din Sanam" (*Lafange*, 1975), "Dil Ko Laga Ke Tujhe Kuch Na Milega" (a Rafi-Asha duet from *Ram Bharose*, 1977) and "Hum Bhi Musafir Tum Bhi Musafir" from *Khazaana* (released in 1987).'

In *Haath Ki Safai* (1974), 'Waada Karle Saajna' was picturised on Vinod Khanna but he was not pleased with the song when he first heard it. Prakash Mehra (director and producer) assured Vinod that the song was brilliant and would be one of the most popular songs of this film. The song indeed etched out a special place for itself. Randhir Kapoor who was the co-actor in this film said, 'How could Mehra Sahab go wrong, when the song was sung by a specialist like Rafi Sahab?'

Rishi Kapoor

'If Rafi Sahab was alive today, I am sure he would have been singing for my son Ranbir too!' Rishi Kapoor's admiration for Rafi's voice echoes in these words.

Rishi Kapoor's film career started at the age of 18 as the cherubic shadow of his father in *Mera Naam Joker* (1970) and later with the spectacular debut with Dimple Kapadia in *Bobby* (1973). The actor garnered a huge fan following right from the start. Successive hits at such an early stage proved that the Kapoor legacy was on able shoulders. Apart from his first few films like *Bobby*, where Shailendra Singh's songs were a rage, Rishi Kapoor, with films such as *Laila Majnu* (1979), *Hum Kisise Kum Nahin* (1977), *Sargam* (1979), *Amar Akbar Anthony* (1977), *Aap Ke Dewaane* (1979), *Karz* (1980), *Naseeb* (released 1981) and *Zamaane Ko Dikhana Hai* (released 1981) came to be inextricably linked with Rafi. It was a unique combination of two talented artistes complementing each other, even though they belonged to two different generations.

The association of Rishi-Rafi was at its peak, when it was abruptly cut short in 1980. But this went on to prove that Rafi's voice was beyond the shackles of age or generation of the actors he sang for.

'Rafi Sahab could sync his voice to the persona of any actor. The emotive quality of his voice made acting much easier for youngsters and newcomers of that period. Rafi Sahab sang for me when I was just 24. His voice will forever remain etched in our mind,' voiced Rishi Kapoor.

The '70s was a lean phase for Rafi, where many believed his career was plummeting. Post 1975, he sang for Rishi and songs like 'Parda Hai Parda' (*Amar Akbar Anthony*) and 'Dard-E-Dil' (*Karz*) became extremely popular.

'Rafi Sahab had made a huge contribution to my career. He helped me get well-entrenched into this industry and I am indebted to him. Rafi Sahab becoming my playback voice was a great honour. It challenged me as an actor when I emoted to the songs he sang for me. His voice had so many expressions, so many feelings, depicting so many different colours of our day-to-day lives; be it a highly energetic rock-n-roll song "Worli Ka Naka" from *Do Ustaad* (1959), a poor boatman's song set in Kashmir, played by Shashi uncle, in *Jab Jab Phool Khile* (1965), a youthful "Baar Baar Dekho, Hazaar Baar Dekho" (*China Town*, 1962) or a *qawwali* by a young Muslim singer (his role as Akbar in *Amar Akbar Anthony*).

'I remember Rafi Sahab was in the studio for a recording and I was secretly watching him. He very lovingly came to me, embraced me and affectionately said in Punjabi, "Son, the way you enact my songs, you look spectacular." He blessed me saying, "I am sure your prudence will take you a long way in the industry. It is a delight to sing for Laale (as Shammi Kapoor was fondly called) and now you."

'The very fact that a genius like Rafi Sahab took my name in the same breath as a gifted actor like Shammi uncle filled me with pride. His words have stayed with me forever.

'I was shooting for a film at Mehboob Studios. It was just a few days after Rafi Sahab had passed away. My thoughts went back to him again and again. I decided to take a break and visit Rafi Sahab's bungalow at Bandra. I sat there for a while and tried to connect with the voice that used to be my identity… and was no longer with me…'

11

The Stage Beckoned...

It was not only recordings that kept Rafi's schedule packed. In 1960, he also started stage performances outside India. It all began with East Africa, and he was soon travelling to other parts of the world.

Rafi was one artiste who did stage shows much before many of his contemporaries. The love that he garnered in live performances, not only in India, but across the world, inspired him to do more stage shows. As Nandi Duggal, show organiser of that period, said, 'I was fortunate to have organised a tour for Rafi Sahab in 1965, to the West Indies and Mauritius, which took the audience by storm. Kishore Kumar was also a great performer, but it took me two years (1967-1969) to convince him to do live shows. So the first show with Kishore Kumar happened in 1969 but Rafi Sahab had been performing on stage since the early '60s.'

Mohammed Rafi belonged to the masses and performing to a packed audience acted like an intoxicant for the teetotaller. If the music lovers were addicted to his voice, he was addicted to entertaining them. Shammi Kapoor rightly put it in words, 'The energy and excitement that the otherwise quiet Rafi brought to his performances is matched by none. He taught people how to get up, dance, and move with the music.'

Music director Ravi Sharma added, 'Rafi Sahab left people mesmerised with his amazing vocal range. He could hit those unbelievably high falsetto notes, which is seriously dangerous territory for any male artiste.'

Kersi Lord, who was often a part of the orchestra during the live shows of Rafi, also fondly remembered those moments of good music and *masti*.

In the '60s and '70s Laxmikant-Pyarelal conducted quite a few grand shows with at least 50 musicians on stage. Rafi was an integral part of many of these performances.

Another renowned composer duo, Anand*ji*-Kalyan*ji*, too had live shows with Rafi. Anand*ji* reminisced about those Rafi moments on stage, 'Every song that he sung would be followed by uninterrupted applause.'

Mimicry artiste and singer Sudesh Bhosle cannot forget his experience of witnessing a Rafi show, 'On stage, Rafi Sahab was a transformed man—full of energy, fun and frolic—a treat to the eyes and pleasure for the ears.'

The songs sung by Rafi continue to draw in huge crowds even years after his passing. 'Rafi has the largest number of loyal followers in the world and every show paying tribute to him is an immense success, even so many years after his death,' said singer Munna Aziz, who makes a living by singing Rafi songs on stage. Music director Usha Khanna revealed, 'Rafi would act with his voice and when he sang on stage, you could visualise on whom the song was picturised.'

It was in the '70s that Rafi's live performances were on an all-time high. As his recording schedules became less hectic than what it used to be in the earlier decades (from an average of 150 songs a year in the '50s and '60s to about 90 songs a year in the '70s), he would allocate more time to live events. There were occasions when he would be travelling for international tours for over three months.

His live shows also created a huge group of co-singers, organisers, technicians, musicians and comperes, people whose careers practically revolved around that of Rafi. In most cases, their careers started with Rafi's stage shows and ended with his demise.

Nandi Duggal

'On August 1, 1980, I went to Rafi Sahab's residence but the crowd was so huge that despite my best efforts I could not be there during the funeral,' Nandi Duggal said, misty eyed. The veteran had worked with stalwarts such as Naushad, Mohammed Rafi, Manna Dey and Kishore Kumar and organised close to 2,300 shows across the world.

He reminisced, 'My first tour with Rafi Sahab took place in 1965, to the West Indies and Mauritius. My company had collaborated with Pioneer Amusement Company, West Indies, for local logistics. Rafi Sahab performed in three cities; Trinidad, Guyana and Surinam and the tour lasted for more than three months during which 36 shows took place. The magic of Rafi took the West Indies by storm. Actually, only 30 shows were scheduled, but because of the demand from his innumerable fans, we did six additional shows. There was a show almost every evening and Rafi Sahab performed brilliantly at every instance. They were organised in theatres which had the capacity of 900-1000 seats but the shows spilled over even that capacity. I still remember the electrifying performance of Rafi Sahab at St Fernando Amphitheatre in Trinidad, when he received a standing ovation on singing "O Duniya Ke Rakhwaale." People were shouting an encore and Rafi Sahab obliged.

'From West Indies, we went to Mauritius. When Rafi Sahab entered the stage, there would be unending applause. He began with "Suno Ramzaan Ki Dastaan" (from a private album released in 1975) and there would be pin drop silence. Rafi Sahab would sing this song for 30 minutes at a stretch and as the song would reach its crescendo, the audience would be left in tears. It was the month of Ramadan. In all the 10 shows, he began the show with this song. Interestingly, I noticed that the first three rows were always occupied by the same group of people, show after show. The shows were stipulated for two and a half hours but every show, on the insistence of the audience, would go on for three and a half hours or even more. You can gauge his fan following.'

Kishan Sharma

Kishan Sharma, former announcer with All India Radio (AIR), narrates his first meeting with Rafi. During a show organised in Uttar Pradesh, young Kishan Sharma was asked to compere it. When he was asked to follow Zaheer to meet Rafi at the hotel, he was very nervous. On entering the room he saw Rafi sitting with a serene, pleasant smile on his face. Rafi did not talk about the show; instead asked him about his work so far. 'My uneasiness increased and I thought that he was probably not confident about my credibility as a compere, maybe because I was too young to be sitting across a legend like him. I stood up to take my leave when he said "*Arey, aap kahaan chal diye, hamaare programme ki kamyaabi apke upar hai.* (Where are you going? The success of our entire programme depends on you!)" I could not believe my ears.'

Kishan Sharma recollected another incident when he was compering a show featuring Rafi, Manna Dey and Suman Kalyanpur. 'Knowing Rafi's popularity Manna Dey was not sure that the audience would like to listen to him after Rafi. On the other hand, Rafi was of the opinion that after Manna Dey's performance, it would be difficult for him to hold the audience. However, the organisers decided that Rafi should begin the show. After a few songs Rafi announced how fortunate he was to share the stage with Manna Dey and presented a Manna Dey score, "Laga Chunri Mein Daag" (*Dil Hi Toh Hai*, 1963) which he said was his personal favourite. He mentioned that this was to mark his respect to the great classical singer, though he strongly believed that no one could do justice to the song better than Manna Dey himself. After the performance, Manna Dey walked up and embraced Rafi. He took the mike and announced, "*Doston, is yug mein hazaaron Manna Dey aayenge, par kabhi ek aur Mohammed Rafi nahin hoga. Rafi Sahab ne abhi mere gaaye huye geet ko behad khoobsoorti se pesh kiya. Ab main apke saamne unke gaaye huye geet ka ek kharab sa namoona pesh karunga.* (Friends, there will be thousands of Manna Deys in this era, but there will never be another Mohammed Rafi. He has just sung a marvellous version of my song. Now I will sing a not so great version of his song.)" He sang "Mann Re Tu Kahe Na Dheer Dhare" (*Chitralekha,* 1964). The mutual respect left the audience in awe and they gave a standing ovation to the two legends.'

Kishan Sharma fondly relates how, on stage, Rafi would be a bundle of verve and spirit—he would sing, whistle and do all sorts of antics on stage. 'Especially while singing "Tu Raat Khadi Thi Chhat Pe" (*Himalay Ki God Mein,* 1965) with Usha Timothy, he would gently hold her hand or play with the *chunni* (scarf) and, in many instances, we would see him whistling.'

The former announcer admitted that the inspiration of the show 'Geet Mala,' the most popular show that he had conceptualised and anchored for All India Radio stemmed from a Rafi-song. Apparently, once, on hearing 'Main Ye Soch Kar Uske Dar Se Uthaa Tha' (*Haqeeqat*, 1964), he was intrigued by the combination of Rafi's voice and the violin (which he later learnt was played by none other than Pyarelal*ji*). He decided to put together a list of similar songs—where a singer's voice coupled with a single musical instrument created a magical effect. This translated into 25 episodes of 'Geet Mala'.

Krishna Mukherjee

'My whole singing career revolved around Rafi Sahab. In each show I used to sing about four to five solos in the beginning and then Rafi Sahab would enter the stage. People would go euphoric on seeing him, be it in London, West Indies, South Africa or Mauritius.

'In many instances our troupe would include excellent dancers of our time such as Helen, Madhumati and Honey. These shows were great crowd-pullers and tickets would be sold at premium rates. Rafi Sahab made it a point to sing every song that came as a request from the audience. Once when we went to San Francisco, he fell sick with a sore throat, on landing there. We had a show that evening and the tickets were all sold out; the organisers were worried. Rafi Sahab with folded hands told the organiser that in case he was unable to sing, the show would go on with his appearance and my songs, but he would refund whatever was paid to him. Hot water and ginger did the magic; when he sang the first song on stage the crowd went euphoric. One song followed the other and the show lasted four hours. The only change that we made was that we sang more duet numbers, than usual.

'My mother belonged to Saithiya, a village in Birbhum, West Bengal. The villagers would tell her that since her daughter sang with Mohammed Rafi, she should call him to the village once for a performance. My mother humbly made this request to Rafi Sahab and to our surprise he instantly agreed. My mother offered him a token amount but he smiled and said,

"Didi, your daughter keeps my shows going and this is my small gift to you." We went to Saithiya and sang the whole night.

'I often came across the jovial side of Rafi Sahab which was unknown to many. Before going on stage he would take out his silver comb and run it through his bald head and then mischievously smile. Then he would drink a glass of cold milk. This was a regular ritual. He exhibited great energy on stage. Many a times, he would leave his harmonium and snatch the drum stick from Leslie and play the drum in the middle of a performance. During a duet, whenever it would be my turn, he would nudge me with his elbow and then smile. The hall would echo with laughter and applause.

'Among the many interesting memories are the performances in Abu Dhabi, Sharjah and Dubai. In these countries we would have two sets of performances, one for the men and the other exclusively for women. On one such occasion when we were performing in an all-ladies show, a young lady just lifted the veil of her burkha and began whistling. The entire crowd of women was in blithe spirit and danced to the tune, "Badan Pe Sitaare."

'Rafi Sahab had sung many Bengali songs as well. Amongst these, my personal favourites are the compositions of Satinath Mukherjee. "Ekhoni Biday Bolona," and "Pakhitar Buke Jeno Teer Mero Na." He has also sung more than 20 Nazrul Geetis (written by poet Kaazi Nazrul Islam).'

Usha Timothy

'My family stayed in Nagpur and I had sung in many programmes. When I was nine, Kalyan*ji*-Anand*ji* and their troupe came to Nagpur for a programme. Rafi Sahab, Mukesh*ji*, Manna*da* and Suman Kalyanpur were scheduled to sing in the musical night. For some reason, Suman*ji* couldn't make it. Kalyan*ji* was in a fix and was looking for a female voice. He conducted an all-day audition at All India Radio but could not get the right voice. My elder brother Madhusudan Timothy, a violinist with All India Radio, approached Kalyan*ji* and suggested my name. After learning how young I was, he refused saying that my voice would be too childish for duets with seasoned singers.

'I went to watch the show with my brother Ratnakar Timothy. He knew the organisers and the musicians very well. During the break, he put me in front of the curtain on stage and asked me to sing. I started singing "Rasik Balmaa" (*Chori Chori*, 1956) much to everybody's surprise, since this was not a part of the scheduled programme. After the performance, I was called to the greenroom and Rafi Sahab and Mukesh*ji* complimented me generously. The first duet I sang on stage, with Rafi Sahab, was, "Sau Saal Pehle, Mujhe Tumse Pyar Tha" (*Jab Pyar Kisi Se Hota Hai*, 1961). The stars present in the audience could not believe that a nine-year-old had sung in place of Suman Kalyanpur.

'Besides being trained by Pandit Laxman Prasad Jaipurwale and Nirmal Arun (actor Govinda's mother), in film songs, my *guru* (teacher) was Rafi Sahab. He taught me all the fundamentals of playback singing and gave me lessons on how to get the tune right, teaching me the importance of diction and the creation of a mood. I got my first break in films with a duet with Rafi Sahab, "Tu Raat Khadi Thi Chhat Pe" (*Himalay Ki God Mein*, 1965).

'Rafi Sahab was like a father; I had lost my father at the age of seven. I used to regularly go to his house for rehearsals. Both he and *Baji* (Bilquis Rafi) were very fond of me and were extremely protective too. They would always make sure that while travelling for international programmes, I was always with them; whatever was the mode of transport. At times, the whole troupe would travel separately and take side trips on days when there were no scheduled shows. I used to sometimes feel that I was losing out on so much fun as I was never allowed to go anywhere without them. But Rafi Sahab was very firm and insisted that I always accompany the family. It is only when I had my daughter that I realised why he was so protective.

'Once we were travelling to Kerala for a show; other stars like Dharmendra, Shatrughan Sinha, Navin Nischol, Hema Malini and Rekha were also on the same flight. When the plane landed, people with garlands rushed towards Rafi Sahab, ignoring the other stars. He innocently looked at me and asked, "Why are these people garlanding me instead of the great actors and stars?"

'Rafi Sahab was fun on the stage. There is a line "*...dekho dil na todo, chodo haath chodo*" in "Achhaa Ji Main Haari." Whenever we sang this song he would hold my hand to complete the act of "*...chodo haath chodo*!" For "Sar Par Topi Laal Haath Mein Resham Ka Roomal" (*Tumsa Nahin*

Dekha, 1957), he always used to carry a silk handkerchief and would do some antics with it. The audience would love it.

'During one of the shows, Baji requested for 'Teri Pyaari Pyaari Soorat Ko' (*Sasuraal*, 1960). But Rafi Sahab, in the course of fulfilling the audience requests, missed Baji's song. She took it to heart and quietly sat in a corner in the greenroom. Rafi Sahab came to the greenroom, lifted her chin, looked into her eyes, and sang "*Teri pyaari pyaari soorat ko kisi ki nazar na lage*" till she blushed and smiled.

'One of our troupe members was a young saxophone player, Kaka. He was known for his pranks. Baji had this habit of seeing Rafi Sahab's face first thing in the morning. Once during a tour Rafi Sahab had woken up early and gone for his walk. She covered her eyes with her hands and was seeking out Rafi Sahab when Kaka removed her hands from her eyes. Baji flew into a rage. Rafi Sahab arrived at the scene and with all seriousness told her, "You see my face every day, aren't you tired? Why not see someone else's face for a change? Kaka's face will bring you luck today." We did not dare to laugh, lest Baji got angry with us.' Rafi's death left the nation in tears. For a close associate like Usha Timothy, it was a loss that had an impact on her life in many ways. 'It took me a lot of time to accept that my mentor, my *guru* and my father was no more; I had lost all three in one go.'

She added, 'Rafi Sahab was not keeping well from January, 1980. During Mithun Chakraborty's show in Durgapur, he fell seriously ill. In fact he had fainted and later I was told he'd had a mild heart attack. On May 3, the same year, we did another show in a small township in Bihar where he sang very few songs. My last show with him was on May 15, 1980, at Shanmukhananda Hall, Bombay. Later in June or July, he did a show, but I could not accompany him. We spoke to each other over the phone on July 22. He was planning a tour to the Gulf and we discussed the dates and other logistics. That was the last I spoke to him.

'The gates of Rafi Villa that would normally remain closed were wide open on July 31. The house swarmed with hundreds of people. I accompanied Rafi Sahab's body to the Santa Cruz burial ground. Here, the *tabla* player, Amirbhai, convinced me to return home as women are not allowed during *daffan* (burial). That was my last journey with Rafi Sahab.'

Mohammed Rafi
December 24, 1924–July 31, 1980

The house where Mohammed Rafi, affectionately called Pheeko as a child, lived during his childhood before he and his family relocated to Lahore.

259, Alka Mansion, 2nd Floor, Ibrahim Rahmatulla Road, Near Mandvi PO, Opp. Nawab Masjid, Bhendi Bazaar—the first residence of Rafi and Hameed when they shifted to Bombay. It was tough to find a house and to afford a rent of even Rs 5.

Along with Hameed, Rafi loved spending hours with his friends, at the nearby restaurants, enjoying tea and snacks, discussing films and singing a variety of songs. He frequented the Zam Zam Hotel. Owned by Hajji Syed Haroon, it exists even today and specialises in Konkani food. Both Rafi and Hameed would never miss out on ordering shaahi tukda *at the end of their meal.*

In 1945, at a place near JJ Hospital, Hameed's sister-in-law Bilquis was married to Rafi. She happily embraced every aspect of his life and accepted Saeed, Rafi's child from his first marriage, as her own.

With his harmonium in his music room, singing for his young daughters. He was deeply attached to his three daughters and later on in life, got very emotional while rendering a bidai *song.*

Rafi loved to drive cars and even drove abroad while on musical concert tours. The first car he owned was a Fiat (above left), which was later followed by more stylish and expensive ones, like an Impala (above right).

With his son Shahid, on the youngster's birthday, along with (L-R) daughter Yasmin, wife Bilquis and daughter Nasreen.

At home, relaxing with a Bengali magazine. Rafi had sung in 14 languages (Assamese, Konkani, Bhojpuri, Oriya, Punjabi, Bengali, Marathi, Sindhi, Kannada, Gujarati, Telugu, Maghi, Maithili and Urdu), and recorded two songs in English which were released in 1968. He also sang a song in Creole when he visited Mauritius in the late '60s.

Besides patangbaazi *(kite-flying), Rafi's other sporty indulgence was badminton. He and composer Naushad regularly met up for a quick match. Here (above left), Rafi (facing the net) and Naushad (back to camera) are seen giving each other tough competition.*

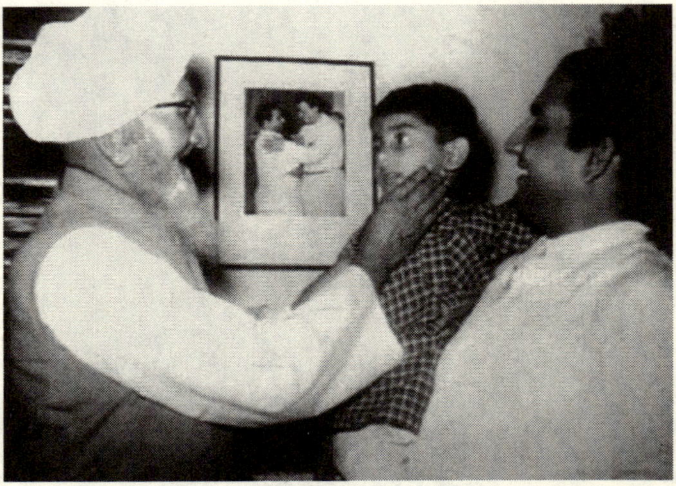

Rafi with his father Hajji Ali Mohammed at his Bombay home along with his son.

Elder brother Mohammed Deen's best friend, Hameed was Rafi's strongest support in his struggling days. He was Rafi's mentor, manager and confidante.

Enjoying a break from his hectic recording schedule. Here, he enjoys a horse ride in the hill station of Darjeeling.

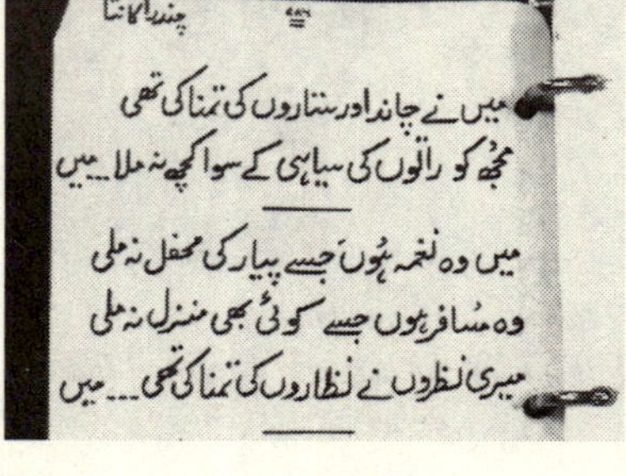

چندرا کانتا

میں نے چاند اور ستاروں کی تمنا کی تھی
مجھ کو راتوں کی سیاہی کے سوا کچھ نہ ملا ... میں

میں وہ نغمہ ہوں جسے پیار کی محفل نہ ملی
وہ مسافر ہوں جسے کوئی بھی منزل نہ ملی
میری نظروں نے نظاروں کی تمنا کی تھی ... میں

A page from Rafi's personal diary. The singer was well versed in Urdu. Hameed used to pen down the lyrics for him in that language before Rafi sang.

Learning the technicalities of television from his son Rashid.

The famous address 'Rafi Mansion' where the singer used to relax and unwind with his wife and children. If not in the recording studios, Rafi preferred to play with his children at home.

Rafi's younger brother, Mohammed Siddiqui, at Karachi, reminisced about the fun days that they spent together.

Rafi loved to eat and Bilquis loved to indulge her husband. A made-for-each-other couple, Bilquis stood like a rock by Rafi through bad times and good times.

Listening to music in his favourite corner of the house, that had all his awards and music memorabilia.

With youngest son Shahid after meeting his idol, the famous boxer Muhammad Ali.

In a one-of-its-kind rare moment, Rafi is seen here with all his grandchildren.

Naushad (above right) gave Rafi a break in Pehle Aap *(1944). Rafi and Hameed travelled all the way to Lucknow to meet Wahid Ali, Naushad's father, to get a letter of recommendation.*

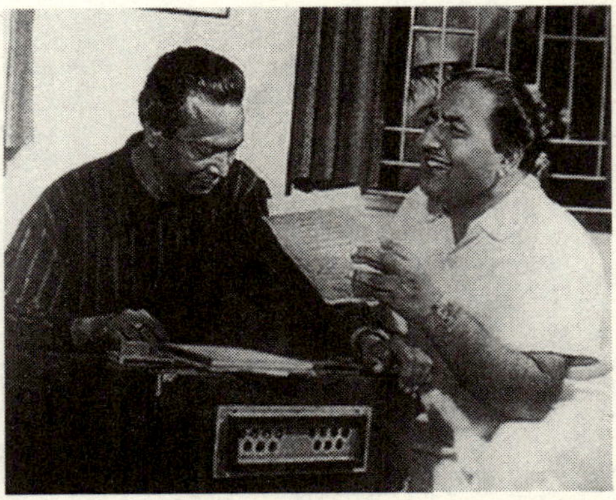

Rafi and Naushad in the latter's riyaaz *room. In those days, Rafi rehearsed a song many times till he had perfected it and then sung it in the recording studio.*

Prithviraj Kapoor wishes Rafi on his birthday as composer Jaikishan, of the famous Shankar-Jaikishan duo, looks on.

Rafi (centre) with brother-in-law Zaheer, who is shaking hands with legendary actor Raj Kapoor. Zaheer later became Rafi's manager when Hameed relocated abroad.

Besides rendering his vocals for the film Jugnu *(1947), Rafi also had a small role in the film that marked the beginning of his association with Dileep Sahab.*

Even Jammu's freezing cold couldn't keep Rafi from entertaining the jawans *of the Border Security Force in their camp.*

With music composer Sachin Deb Burman. For the iconic film Guide *(1965), SD Burman composed a variety of songs in Rafi's voice, which contributed to making the film an epic in the history of Indian cinema. The year also saw another musical hit,* Teen Deviyaan *where Rafi's voice mellifluously flows on SD Burman's compositions.*

With Khayyam(right) and VP Naik (left). The Rafi-Khayyam association was brief, with only 26 songs done together.

OP Nayyar composed some fusion scores by amalgamating Western music with Eastern melodies. And he preferred to use Rafi's versatile voice.

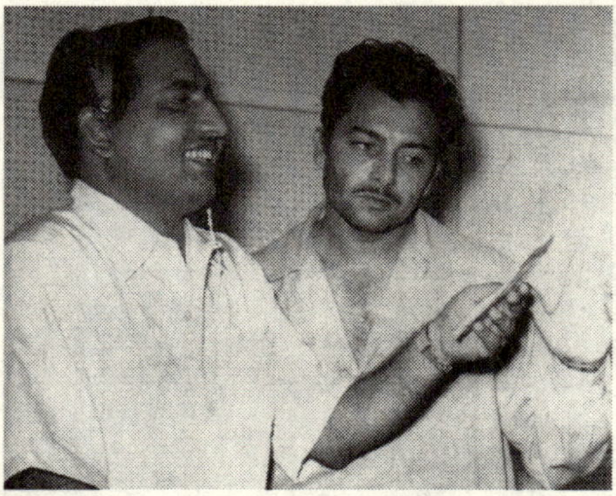

It was composer Madan Mohan's decision to have Rafi as the voice of Rishi Kapoor in Laila Majnu *(1976).*

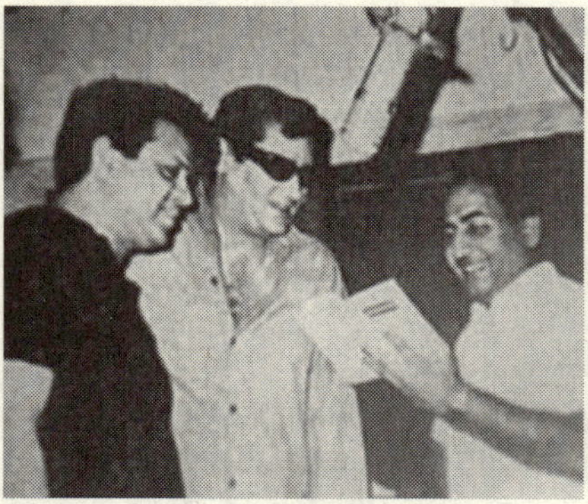

Rafi rehearses a song picturised on actor Shammi Kapoor (centre) in the presence of composer Jaikishan.

Composer Ravindra Jain (centre)sings a tune for Rafi and Yesudas (right).

Rafi's versatility could be gauged from the fun and jovial songs that he rendered for comedian Johnny Walker. In all, Rafi sung 155 songs for him.

Singers Rafi and Mukesh, who sung 13 duets together.

Comedian Mehmood with Rafi at a recording, with Shankar (left) and Jaikishan (right) conducting the orchestra.

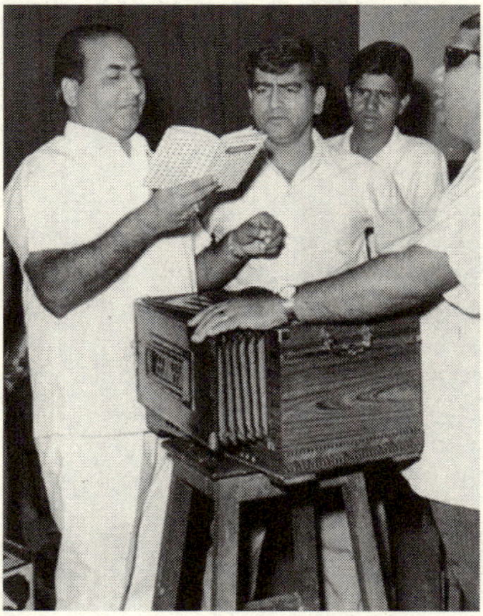

Omi-Sonik and Rafi at a rehearsal. After having worked with established music composers like Roshan and Madan Mohan, this duo independently composed in 1966 and approached Rafi hesitantly. But magnanimous as he was, Rafi readily agreed to sing for their first film.

Rafi's association with composer Ravi Shankar Sharma began with the song, 'Babu O Jaane Waale Babu Ek Paisa De De,' and lasted for over two decades, resulting in 235 songs in 79 films. The title song of Chaudvin Ka Chand *(1960) gave instant recognition to Ravi as a composer.*

Rafi with (L-R) Talat Mahmood, Indrani Mukherji, Sahir Ludhianvi and N Dutta.

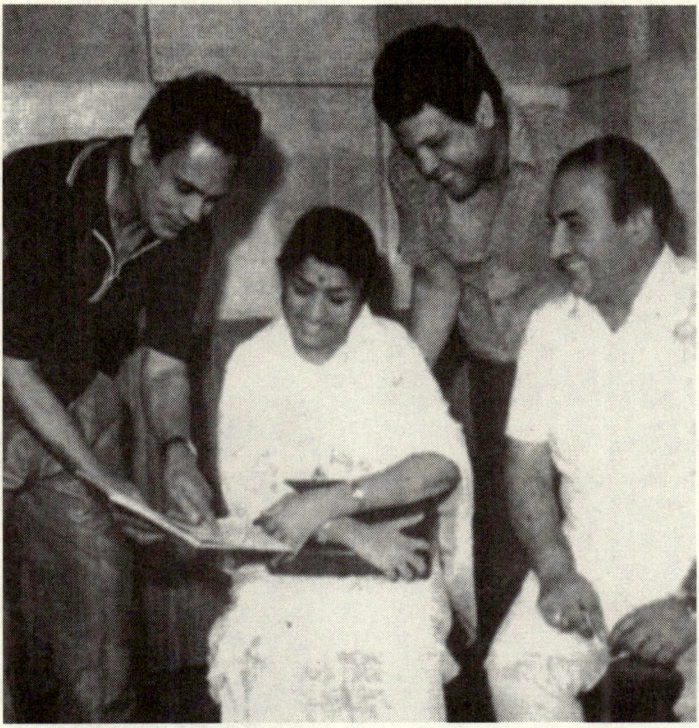

Singers Rafi and Lata are guided by lyricist Hasrat Jaipuri (left) and composer Jaikishan (second from right).

With another singing great and Rafi's contemporary, Kishore Kumar. Rafi, quiet and reserved by nature, had a good sense of humour and enjoyed the playfulness of Kishore Kumar.

With composer Salil Choudhury, who acknowledged his voice as apt for Dev Anand in Maya *(1961).*

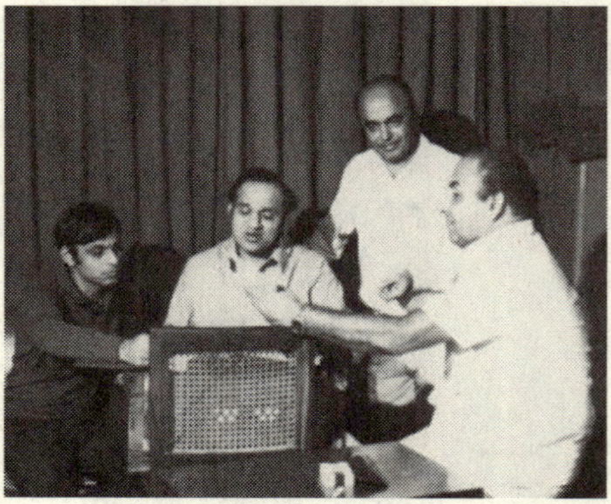

*With (L-R) Kalyan*ji*-Anand*ji, *and Ramanand Sagar, rehearsing a composition.*

Poet-lyricist Shakeel Badayuni won the sobriquet 'Geetkaar-E-Azam' from Government of India. The film Dulaari *(1949) is remembered for one of the finest songs of Rafi's career; 'Suhaani Raat Dhal Chuki,' penned by Shakeel Badayuni, and set to tune by Naushad. His songs in* Baiju Bawra *(1952) have become legendary in the annals of Hindi cinema.*

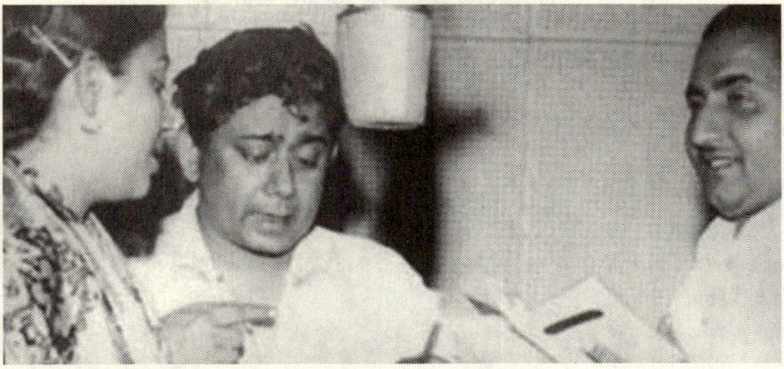

Singers Geeta Dutt and Rafi are briefed by composer Chitragupta.

Contemporaries Lata and Rafi watching the premiere show of Mughal-E-Azam.

Rafi with Shashi Kapoor and Shankar-Jaikishan at a recording studio.

In this 1975 photo (L-R), music director Pyarelal, producer Subhash Desai, Laxmikant, playback singers Mohammad Rafi, Mukesh, Lata Mangeshkar, and Kishore Kumar are joined by Manmohan Desai (in sunglasses) at a recording session for Amar Akbar Anthony.

Rafi singing with Assamese singer, Bhupen Hazarika.

Rafi at a recording with Asha Bhosle. With nearly 900 songs with Rafi—796 duets and 101 chorus songs—she has the distinction of singing the maximum songs with him.

In 1954, an album named This Is Mohammed Rafi *was released. The popularity of the album showed that people loved his new style of singing. Asha Bhosle was his co-singer in the album. During the making, each song was rehearsed nearly 18 times.*

Composer Usha Khanna with Kishore Kumar and Rafi.

Rafi with dignitaries at Jashn-E-Rafi, the silver jubilee celebrations of Rafi's musical career, 1966.

Rafi with Mubarak Begum and Jaikishan. She had sung some memorable songs with Rafi in Kamal Amrohi's Daera *(1953),* Baghdad Ka Jadoo *(1956),* Humraahi *(1963),* Fariyaad *(1964),* Qawwali Ki Raat *(1964), and* Susheela *(1966).*

Rafi at an event organised to commemorate the Silver Jubilee celebrations of the Taj Mahal.

Suman Kalyanpur and Rafi at a recording session with Naushad.

Rafi, Mukesh and Asha are briefed by composer RD Burman (extreme right) with Randhir Kapoor (fourth from left) at a recording session. Burman and Rafi shared a fruitful professional association.

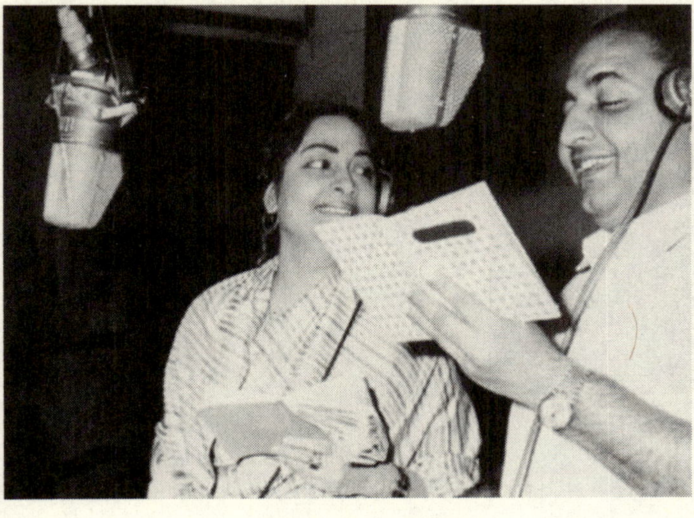

Geeta Dutt and Rafi are associated with some of the liveliest and entertaining duets in the history of Indian film music. They sang a total of 158 songs, among which was the fun-filled banter, 'Jaane Kahaan Mera Jigar Gaya Ji' from Mr. and Mrs. 55 *(1955).*

At a live show with co-singer Usha Timothy. The first duet that she sang on stage with Rafi was 'Sau Saal Pehle Mujhe Tumse Pyar Tha' from Jab Pyar Kisi Se Hota Hai *(1961). At that time, Usha was just a nine-year-old and had sung in place of Suman Kalyanpur.*

With poet-lyricists Shailendra (left) and Hasrat Jaipuri (right).

At a recording. (L-R) Shakti Samanta, Jaikishan, Sharmila Tagore, Hasrat Jaipuri, Rafi, an associate and recordist Minoo Katrak.

Rafi with the 'Main Jat Yamla Pagla Deewana' star Dharmendra. It became the most identifiable tune with the actor's free-spirited signature moves.

Usha Khanna is the only female composer in the history of Hindi film music, who has the distinction of having a successful career for almost three decades (1960-1990). She has also sung 13 duets with Rafi, 10 of which were her own compositions. Rafi and Usha Khanna have worked together in 61 films, creating a portfolio of 114 songs in Rafi's voice, of which 69 were solos.

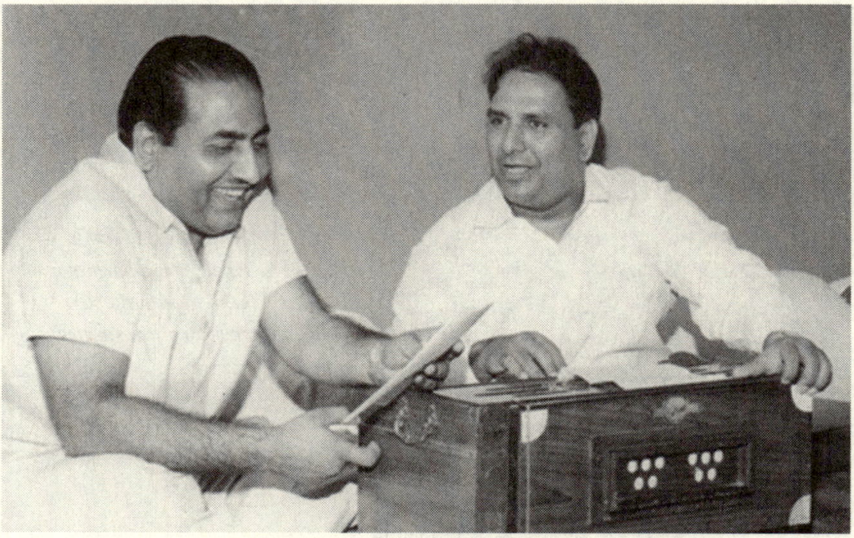

Rafi listens as music composer Shankar, of the Shanker-Jaikishen duo, sings a tune he created.

With Mahendra Kapoor, his protégé. Such was the impact of Mohammed Rafi's voice on the 12-year-old Mahendra, that one day he made it to Rafi's residence at Bhendi Bazaar and expressed the desire to be his disciple. The two shared a close bond.

The usually quiet and reserved Rafi had a major transformation on the stage during live shows. Here, he is seen in his 'Yahoo' avatar at one of his shows. Rafi would be full of verve and spirit—he would sing, whistle and perform all sorts of antics on stage.

At a recording session with percussionist Burjor Lord (playing the bongo). Rafi made sure his musicians, who travelled with him for his shows, were well taken care of.

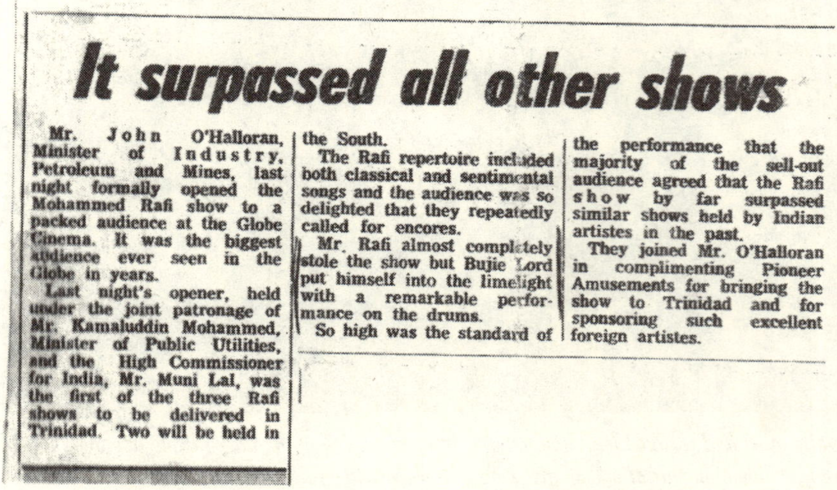

It surpassed all other shows

Mr. John O'Halloran, Minister of Industry, Petroleum and Mines, last night formally opened the Mohammed Rafi show to a packed audience at the Globe Cinema. It was the biggest audience ever seen in the Globe in years.

Last night's opener, held under the joint patronage of Mr. Kamaluddin Mohammed, Minister of Public Utilities, and the High Commissioner for India, Mr. Muni Lal, was the first of the three Rafi shows to be delivered in Trinidad. Two will be held in the South.

The Rafi repertoire included both classical and sentimental songs and the audience was so delighted that they repeatedly called for encores.

Mr. Rafi almost completely stole the show but Bujie Lord put himself into the limelight with a remarkable performance on the drums.

So high was the standard of the performance that the majority of the sell-out audience agreed that the Rafi show by far surpassed similar shows held by Indian artistes in the past.

They joined Mr. O'Halloran in complimenting Pioneer Amusements for bringing the show to Trinidad and for sponsoring such excellent foreign artistes.

Newspaper headlines on the day after the West Indies show that happened in 1966. It was a roaring success with repeated requests for encores. (Picture courtesy: Burjor and Kersi Lord)

From The Filmfare File

Glorious tour

They called him the "Suku-Suku-Man" and "the shy singer from India." This was in the West Indies and parts of South America where Mohammed Rafi gave concerts recently. It was the seventh time that the shy, perpetually busy singer went on a performing tour abroad.

He covered Trinidad-Tabago, British Guiana (which on May 26, four days after Rafi left it, became independent with a new name, Guyana) and Surinam. He also went sight-seeing in the U.S.A., visited England where his son, a qualified television engineer, works.

Record crowds—mostly comprising local Indian settlers—mobbed him at airports and at his concerts. At Atkinson airport (Georgetown) he was carried to the terminal building by an enthusiastic crowd. In Trinidad, Mr. Kamaluddin Mohammed, Minister for Public Utilities, came personally to receive the singer at the airport. Later Rafi paid a courtesy call on Dr. Eric Williams, the Prime Minister, and presented him one of his LP records.

Rafi kept up his practice of beginning his concerts with the "Hari Om" song from "Baiju Bawra." His famous song "Bapu ki amar kahani" in memory of Mahatma Gandhi, proved a big hit. There is a Gandhi statue both in Surinam and Trinidad (at San Fernando)—and Rafi visited the sites and offered floral tributes. In response to public clamour, he also sang "Bapu ki amar kahani" at the sites.

In Trinidad, with the blessings of Mr. Muni Lal, Indian High Commissioner, Rafi gave a special performance to collect money for the India Fund—in all £ 6213.

Rafi's troupe included singer Miss Minu Purushottam. His accompanists—accordionist E. Daniels, guitarist Dilip Naik, drummers Narayan Naidu, Abdul Karim and Buji Lord—won individual acclaim for their talent.

In August, Rafi is set to undertake another concert tour—a pioneering one for a non-white singer—to S. Africa.

July 22, 1966

Another newspaper cutting reporting the success of the West Indies show. (Picture courtesy: Burjor and Kersi Lord)

Manna Dey with Rafi at a stage show. Once when Manna Dey expressed his admiration for Rafi saying, 'The whole world listens to you and admires your voice, Rafi Sahab,' the latter had spontaneously replied, 'When the world listens to Mohammed Rafi, Rafi himself listens to Manna Dey.' This mutual respect and admiration translated into Rafi singing the highest number of male duets (about 60 songs) with him.

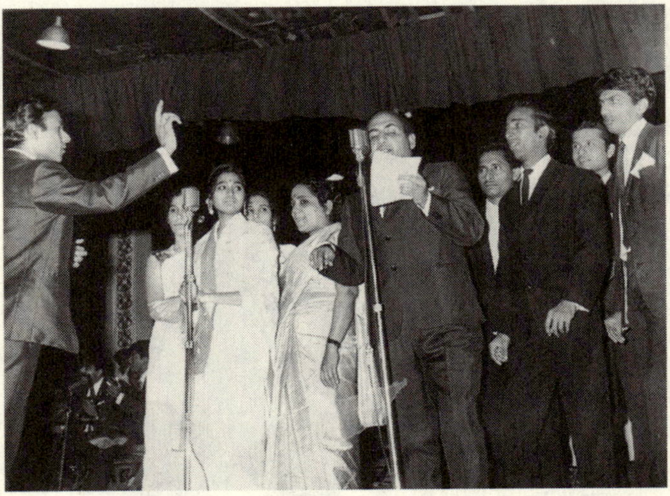

Kalyanji conducting Rafi and the chorus at a live show.

Rafi chats with actress Mala Sinha, over tea, at a function.

With composer Roshan, who established Rafi as the voice of Pradeep Kumar with six successive films, just the way OP Nayyar was instrumental in making Rafi the energetic voice of Shammi Kapoor. They worked together in 32 films and had 88 songs to their credit.

Actor David (left) and director Ramanand Sagar (centre) felicitate Rafi on the silver jubilee of Aankhen *(1968).*

Rafi won a silver medal from the then Indian Prime Minister Jawaharlal Nehru, on the first anniversary of the Indian Independence Day, for 'Suno Suno Aye Duniya Waalon Bapu Ki Yeh Amar Kahaani,' a four-part song written by Rajinder Krishan and composed by Husanlal-Bhagatram.

The Padma Shri citation in Rafi's house.

With the then President of India, Dr Sarvepalli Radhakrishnan, after being conferred with the Padma Shri, on April 12, 1967.

With Indira Gandhi after he was conferred with the Padma Shri.

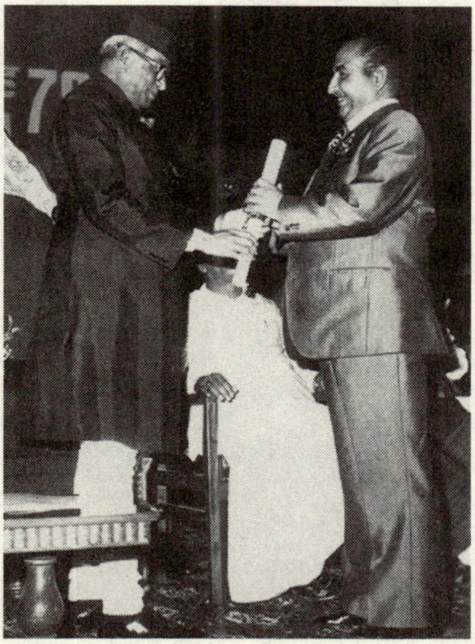

Rafi receiving the National Rajat Kamal Award from the then President of India, N Sanjiva Reddy for his song 'Kya Hua Tera Vaada' from the film Hum Kissise Kum Nahin *in 1977, the year of its release.*

Legendary boxer Muhammad Ali felicitates Mohammed Rafi during one of his tours abroad. Rafi, who loved watching boxing, requested the organisers on his tour to Chicago to get him an appointment with Muhammad Ali. Otherwise a busy man, Ali visited Rafi at his hotel room when he found out that the legendary Indian singer wanted to meet him.

Actress Mumtaz giving the Filmfare Award to Rafi; he won a total of six Filmfare Awards.

Rafi with his innumerable awards at Rafi Mansion. An immensely successful and talented singer, he remained extremely unassuming, reserved, magnanimous and grounded inspite of the fame and glamour that he achieved.

12

Co-Singers in the Studios

Rafi has had the rare achievment of singing with 78 female singers and 24 male singers.

Among male co-singers, Rafi sang the maximum number of duets with Manna Dey. The singer remembered, 'Rafi and I complemented each other very well. It was always a pleasure to sing with such a gentleman. He was a better singer than me, and I will say this—that no one came even close to him. Rafi had a powerful range that could accommodate variety. We had a great understanding and it was never about one-upmanship.'

Female Co-Singers

Asha Bhosle

> *Maine apna doosra hi gaana Rafi Sahab ke saath gaaya. Bahut hi achche gaayak aur insaan they. Mere khayaal se unke jaisa koi phir se paida naheen hoga.* (I sang my second song with Rafi Sahab. He was a great singer and human being. I think no one like him will ever be born again.)
>
> —Asha Bhosle, 'Jaimala Gold.
> Naushad on Mohammed Rafi,' 1980

With nearly 900 songs with Rafi—796 duets and 101 chorus songs (those songs where a third voice, besides Rafi's and Asha's, is identifiable)—she has the distinction of singing the maximum songs with him.

Starting from their first duet, 'Karle Kisi Se Pyar Jawaani Do Din Ki' (*Lekh,* 1949), a Krishnan Dayal composition, Rafi and Asha got sporadic opportunities to sing together between 1948 and 1957. That is till the creation of the magical OP Nayyar-Rafi-Asha team. The first composition from this trio was the duet 'Agar Baabu Dil Hai Kaabu' (*Musafirkhana*, 1955). OP Nayyar's attention to musical overtones, for films like *Tumsa Nahin Dekha* (1957) and *Naya Daur* (1957) got Asha's distinctive voice noticed by music lovers. Be it the title, tandem song of *Tumsa Nahin Dekha*, by Rafi and Asha, or the vivacious duets like, 'Dekho Kasam Se Dekho Kasam Se,' 'Sar Par Topi Laal,' each of them are a class above most duets of that time in terms of their mass appeal and idyllic youthful spirit.

Most of Rafi's duets with Asha are cavalier, teasing and spirited such as 'Deewana Mastana Hua Dil Jaane' (*Bambai Ka Babu*, 1960) and 'O Madam Nancy, You Are My Fancy' (*Basant,* 1960).

While Rafi-Asha duets under the baton of OP Nayyar are the ones that are most talked about, it is the body of work of lesser-known composers that gives a larger picture of the magic created by this singer duo. For example, the ultra-romantic 'Yeh Raat Yeh Fizaayein' (*Batwaara,* 1962); not many know that this duet, where Rafi and Asha complement each other note-for-note, was composed by little-known music director, S Madan, or that the sublime 'Dhalti Jaaye Raat' (*Razia Sultana,* 1961) was tuned by Lachhiram.

Besides OP Nayyar, the Rafi-Asha combination spelt *gold* in the capable hands of Ravi and Madan Mohan, and later RD Burman, who in *Teesri Manzil* (1966), set new benchmarks both for himself and the singing duo, by taking the music to dizzying heights, both in terms of popularity and creativity. Junior Burman could replicate his success with the duo much later in the romantic duets like 'Churaa Liya' (*Yaadon Ki Baaraat*, 1973), where he brought Rafi with Asha together overlooking his favourite Kishore Kumar. It was the light-hearted 'Poocho Na Yaar

Kya Hua' (*Zamaane Ko Dikhana Hai*, released in 1981), love-struck expression of deep love in 'Sanson Mein Kabhi Dil' (*Parchaiyan*, 1972), the sensuous club song with a tinge of Arabic feel 'Raqqasa Mera Naam' (*The Great Gambler*, 1979) or the conventional *qawwali* 'Dekhi Hazaaron Mehfilein' (*Nauker*, 1979) where the younger Burman could not overlook Rafi's vocal prowess to complement the resonating voice of Asha, though the decade saw him working more with Kishore Kumar for most of his compositions, both solos and duets.

Asha Bhosle's voice could suit the female protagonist of the Golden Era as well as the young lead actresses of the modern era. In 2011, the Guinness Book of World Records acknowledged her as the most recorded artiste in the world.

> *Rafi Sahab, aapki Himalaya ki tarah bulund awaz aur aapka namra swabhav hume phir na sunne na dekhne milega. Aapki bahut yaad aati hai.* (Rafi Sahab, your voice touched Himalayan heights. We will never get to hear you again nor will we get a chance to witness someone as polite as you. Miss you a lot.)
>
> Asha Bhosle's tweet on Rafi's 30th death anniversary

Lata Mangeshkar

> *Rafi Bhaiya was not only India's greatest playback singer but also a wonderful person. I am yet to come across another artiste so modest, dignified and unassuming. The blessings of Goddess Saraswati were with him and this was responsible, to a great extent, for his iconic success and he believed in true* sadhna *(meditative quest). Every morning, he performed his* riyaaz *like a devoted singer and rehearsed before recording each song.*
>
> —Lata Mangeshkar, July 24, 2010, *The Hindu*

Lata Mangeshkar's first Hindi solo came in the 1946 film *Aap Ki Sewa Mein*; 'Pa Laagu Kar Jori Re,' was composed by Datta Davjekar. Rafi had sung one solo and two duets in this film, but none with Lata. It was only in

1947 that Rafi and Lata sang their first duet together. The song in question was, 'Chalo Ho Gayi Taiyyar Zaraa Thehro Ji' (*Shaadi Se Pehle*, 1947); a composition by Payankar and Karnad.

In the years to come, Naushad created some rare gems for his favourite Rafi-Lata combination like 'Jhoole Mein Pawan Ke Aayi Bahaar' (*Baiju Bawra*, 1952), 'Matwaala Jiya Dole Piya Jhoome Ghata Chhaye Re' (*Mother India*, 1957), 'Do Sitaaron Ka Zameen Par Hai Milan' (*Kohinoor*, 1960), 'Mere Mehboob Tujhe Meri Mohabbat Ki Kasam' (*Mere Mehboob*, 1963), 'Ek Shahenshah Ne Banwaa Ke Haseen Taj Mahal' (*Leader*, 1964).

Some of the other songs associated with this mesmerising singer duo include, 'Yun To Aapas Mein Bigadte Hain Khafaa Hote Hain' for Naushad (*Andaaz*, 1949), 'Do Ghadi Woh Jo Paas Aa Baithe' for Madan Mohan (*Gateway of India*, 1957), 'Chali Chali Re Patang Meri Chali Re' for Chitragupta (*Bhabhi*, 1957), 'Teri Aankhon Ke Siwa Duniya Mein Rakha Kya Hai' for Madan Mohan (*Chiraag*, 1969), 'Yunhi Tum Mujhse Baat Karti Ho' for Kalyan*ji*-Anand*ji* (*Sachaa Jhutha*, 1970), 'Chalo Dildaar Chalo' for Naushad (*Pakeezah*, 1972)—just a handful from the Rafi-Lata repertoire.

The two have sung 411 duets and 37 group songs together. Lata in her own words said that she has sung the maximum number of duets with Rafi, though Rafi has sung the highest number of duets with Asha Bhosle.

Due to professional differences, in the period between 1963 to 1967, Rafi-Lata duets were not recorded. Music directors had to find ways to fill the gap; Madan Mohan for instance made Suman Kalyanpur sing with Rafi, and Talat Mehmood or Mahendra Kapoor with Lata Mangeshkar in the duets he recorded during this period, while retaining the two in the same film. Tandem song was another innovative way of substituting duets by them.

All the eminent music directors of that period experimented with the voice of Rafi and Lata to give memorable duets. OP Nayyar was one exception, as he composed extensively for Rafi and Asha.

Of the 448 songs that Lata and Rafi have sung together, over 50 per cent of the duets were from Laxmikant-Pyarelal, Shankar-Jaikishan, Kalyan*ji*-

Anand*ji*, Naushad and Chitragupta (in order of their contributions)—Laxmikant-Pyarelal have recorded the highest number (74 songs), of the Rafi-Lata duets.

In an interview, Lata had mentioned that Rafi used to treat her as his sister and he had sent someone to teach her Urdu. That's how she learnt the Urdu diction which was important while singing to the lyrics of Majrooh Sultanpuri, Sahir Ludhianvi, Shakeel Badayuni, Naqsh Lyallpuri, Rajinder Krishan and a few others, who liberally used Urdu in their songs.

On Rafi's 31st death anniversary, the Nightingale of India, as Lata Mangeshkar is often referred to, wrote in a series of micro-blogs, '*Today is our country's most talented personality Rafi Sahab's 31st death anniversary. Rafi Sahab was very honest, genuine and a nice person. He was as sweet a person as (was) his voice.*'

In another tweet, she expressed, '*Rafi Sahab was on good terms with all my family members. I am fortunate to have got the opportunity to sing several duets with him. In the (approximately) 315 films that we did together, we have sung some 440 odd duets. Such a talented artiste is not born again and again. I pay him my tribute.*'

Suman Kalyanpur

Even today, a good number of people mistake Suman Kalyanpur's voice for that of Lata Mangeshkar. Lata's fans hardly noticed the voice with such uncanny similarities to Lata for its own individuality. However, Suman has had several milestones in her career.

She recalled that 'Din Ho Ya Raat Hum Rahe Tere Saath' (*Miss Bombay*, 1956) was the first time Hansraj Behl gave her an opportunity to sing with Rafi, though the film was released a year after *Shri Krishna Bhakti* (1955) in which she rendered 'Saawan Megh Udey,' a composition by Chitragupta. She went on to sing a total of 141 duets and 14 group songs with Rafi. She admitted that she was very fond of a particular song of Rafi, 'Dil Toota Aur Armaan Loote' (*Roomal*, 1949), which repeatedly played on the radio when she was growing up. 'When I finally got to sing with him, it was a dream come true,' she remembered.

For composers trying to get a foothold in the industry, Suman Kalyanpur and Rafi were a rollicking combination. One of Kalyan*ji*-Anand*ji*'s earliest works when they entered the industry was the peppy and fun-filled composition 'Main Hoon Papa Khan' (*Post Box 999,* 1958).

For Suman Kalyanpur, the true hour of glory arrived in the mid '60s. The singer earned tremendous acclaim for her duets, especially the ones with Rafi. She was a music director's delight not only because of the resemblance of her voice to that of Lata's, but also that distinctive quality she could add to the songs that were entrusted to her. She was equally adept at delivering the springy romantic duets, typically the compositions of music directors like Shankar-Jaikishan and Laxmikant-Pyarelal and the mellow, poignant and pensive compositions of Madan Mohan. Both in terms of numbers and popularity, it was Shankar-Jaikishan (*Dil Ek Mandir* (1963), *April Fool* (1964), *Rajkumar* (1964), *Saanjh Aur Savera* (1964), *Suraj* (1966), *Chhoti Si Mulaqaat* (1967), *Brahmachari* (1968)) who best showcased the Rafi-Suman collaboration.

She recollected, 'The film industry moves on precedence and when a particular combination works well, it is accepted as a success formula. Rafi Sahab and my duets were well-accepted by the masses and most importantly, music composers recognised me as a suitable female voice to be paired with Rafi Sahab. This gave me an opportunity to sing some phenomenal songs with Rafi Sahab during that decade.'

Geeta Dutt

In a few words, Geeta (Roy) Dutt's voice could be described as evocative, emotive, soulful, and sensuous. Her first duet with Rafi was accompanied by a chorus—'Jai Hind, Yeh Hind Ki Kahaaniyan' (*Maansarovar*, 1946)—a composition by SN Tripathi. SD Burman gave her the opportunity to sing in *Do Bhai* (1947). It was 'Kaaten Banenge Kaliyan,' a contemplative group song by Geeta Dutt, Rafi, SD Batish and a few others that revealed the effectiveness of the Rafi-Geeta combination. Her voice could address, with ease, the springy, frothy duets such as the playful, 'Sun Sun Sun Sun Zaalima' (*Aar Paar*, 1954), the intrinsically hummable 'Aankhon Hi

Aankhon Mein Ishaara' (*C.I.D.* 1956) or the rock and roll song 'Dil Se Dil Takraaye' (*Love Marriage*, 1959).

Geeta Dutt and Rafi are associated with some of the liveliest and entertaining duets in the history of Indian film music. They sang a total of 158 songs; 136 duets and 22 group songs. Geeta Dutt ably matched Rafi's *adaayegi* (grace) and *harktein* (modulations) note to note, even where some songs demanded a complex rendition.

In the soulfully romantic *Pyaasa* (1957), the Rafi-Geeta combination came together for the only duet in the film, a dream sequence 'Hum Apki Ankhon Mein' where Geeta Dutt sings for Mala Sinha and Rafi for Guru Dutt. It is a song that is believed to have been added to the film at the insistence of distributors, to add a special something to an otherwise pensive tale.

The duo gave some classics filmed on Johnny Walker with his female leads: a fun-filled banter, 'Jaane Kahaan Mera Jigar Gaya Ji' (*Mr. and Mrs. 55*, 1955); a song on playful courting, 'Dekh Idhar Aye Haseena' (*12 o'clock*, 1958), and an ironic humour-laden song on the city of Bombay, 'Aye Dil Hai Mushkil' (*C.I.D.* 1956).

It is believed that Guru Dutt wanted Geeta Dutt to sing only for his own films. It was an unplanned union of Guru Dutt's favourite comrades—actor Johnny Walker, Rafi's voice and that of Geeta Dutt's—that is often seen in Guru Dutt productions. By default, Rafi was the male voice in the films by Guru Dutt. That probably explains why Geeta Dutt has the highest number of duets with Rafi.

Music aficionados cherish the rare classical 'Lag Gayi Aakhiyaan Tumse Mori' (*Jeevan Jyoti*, 1953)—an SD Burman composition based on the rare *Raaga Multani*—in the otherwise perky voice of Geeta Dutt with Rafi. 'Tum Jo Huye Mere Humsafar' (*12 o'clock*, 1958), an OP Nayyar composition based on *Raaga Pahadi*, is another unconventional classic in which the two mesmerising voices completely bowled over the listeners when it was first released and continues to be regarded as a treasure by music connoisseurs even today.

From 1946 till the early '70s, Geeta Dutt established one of the strongest associations with Rafi than she had with any other male singer; an association that came to an end with her death in 1972.

Although OP Nayyar is believed to have composed the largest number of Rafi-Geeta duets, mainly by virtue of their popularity, the composer with the maximum Rafi-Geeta duets is actually composer Chitragupta. As compared to OP Nayyar's 21 duets, Chitragupta has composed 22 duets and five chorus songs featuring Rafi and Geeta.

Shamshad Begum

Shamshad Begum opined, 'Had Rafi lived a few more years, he would have won the Bharat Ratna. He actually deserved it.'

The arresting resonance and impeccable clarity of Shamshad Begum's voice could not stay unnoticed from the doyens of music like Ghulam Haider, Shyam Sunder, Naushad Ali, OP Nayyar and others.

Pairing two of his favourite voices, Naushad went on to create some unforgettable duets like 'Kaise Baje Dil Ka Sitar' and 'Khabar Kya Thi Ki Gham Khaana Padegaa' (*Chandni Raat*, 1949), 'Door Koi Gaaye Dhun Yeh Sunaaye' (*Baiju Bawra*, 1955), 'O Gaadi Waale Gaadi Dheere Hankh Re' (*Mother India*, 1957).

OP Nayyar, who likened the dulcet voice of Shamshad Begum to the sound of bells in a temple, composed memorable Rafi-Shamshad duets such as 'Leke Pehla Pehla Pyaar' (*C.I.D.* 1956) and 'Humne Jab Dil Tha Diyaa' (*Chhoo Mantar*, 1956).

Shamshad and Rafi came together for 127 songs as the chosen voices for many other music directors in the '40s and '50s—'Aye Dil Na Mujhe Yaad Dila Baatein' (*Saawan Aaya Re*, 1949), a Khemchand Prakash composition; 'Boloji Dil Loge' (*Patanga*, 1949), a composition by C Ramchandra; 'Bheega Bheega Pyar Ka Samaa' (*Saawan*, 1959) a Hansraj Behl melody. These are just a few examples of the prolific Rafi-Shamshad vocal magic.

Recalling her association with Rafi, the late Shamshad Begum had said, 'It was somewhere in 1944 when Rafi along with his father, Hajji Sahab and Hameed came to meet me. Hajji Sahab, who was initially reluctant to send Rafi to Bombay, later accepted music as his son's destiny and personally visited me with a request. He and my father knew each other and that is how they got my reference. Hameed requested me to help Rafi get a foothold in the Hindi film industry as he was looking for a career here. The competition within the industry was cut-throat and in addition to talent, one also needed recommendations. I said that I would only recommend Rafi if I found his voice worthy. Hameed asked Rafi to take my blessings and sing a song before me. When he sang, I was spellbound. It was a serene full-throated voice that touched every chord in my heart. I told Hameed he needed no recommendation and had been created by the Almighty to rule this industry. I assured Rafi that I would introduce him to the music directors and his voice would take care of the rest.

'As he was leaving he bowed and said, "*Main aap hi ki tarah ek behtareen fankaar banna chaahta hoon.* (I want to become a great artiste like you.)" I instinctively said, "*Inshallah, aap bahut jald mere saath* duets *gaayenge.* (By God's grace, you will soon be singing duets with me.)" He did not say a word but I still remember the sparkle in his eyes. It seemed I had spelt out his dream and he was determined to make it come true. In 1945, just 11 months later, he sang his first song with me.'

The song was 'Choti Si Ek Banaayenge Naiyya' (*Hamaara Sansar*, 1945) sung by Zohrabai Ambalewali with music composed by Pandit Govindram.

Shamshad Begum continued, 'In 1946, he sang another duet with me, 'Jo Aage Badhe Use Peeche Hata De' (*Rangbhoomi*). After the recording, he humbly came to me and reminded me, "*Aap ka kehna sach nikla, sab aapki dua.* (You were right. It is all due to your blessings.)" He was an epitome of humility.

'Naushad Sahab had composed several songs for us which became very popular. Films like *Chandni Raat* (1949), *Baiju Bawra* (1952) and *Mother India* (1957) had memorable duets—"*Door koi gaaye dhun yeh sunaaye tere bin chaliya re baje na muraliya re*" (*Baiju Bawra*, 1952). I sang "Dukh Bhare Din Beete Re Bhaiya Ab Sukh Aayo Re" (*Mother India*) with Rafi, Manna Dey, Asha Bhosle and others. "Le Ke Pehla Pehla Pyar" is a catchy romantic duet from *C.I.D.* (1956), composed by OP Nayyar which he gave to me at the insistence of Asha. Another landmark song that we sang together was "Thoda Sa Dil Lagake Dekh" (*Musafirkhana*, 1955). It had a Westernised flavour.

'Once I was singing "La De Mohe Balma Aasmaani Chudiyaan" (*Rail Ka Dibba,* 1955) with Rafi. We had to sing 9-10 lines together without taking a breath in between the lines. Rafi went breathless after the fifth line. This meant the song had to be sung all over again. He faltered quite a few times. Finally when we completed the song, he walked up to me and said, "*Bahut khoob! Maan gaye aapko aapa ji.* (Wonderful! Hats off to you, elder sister.)"'

Mubarak Begum

'Mujhko Apne Gale Lagalo Ae Mere Humraahi' sang the 82-year-old in her melodious voice that was as brilliant as it was almost 50 years ago when this song was recorded for *Humraahi* (1963).

Mubarak Begum, who has seen both low and high tides in her career, spoke with great regard for Rafi. She had sung some memorable songs with Rafi in *Baghdad Ka Jadoo* (1956), *Humraahi* (1963), *Fariyaad* (1964), *Qawwali Ki Raat* (1964), and *Susheela* (1966).

'I sang seven songs in Kamal Amrohi's film *Daera* (1953). Though the film did not do too well at the box-office, the songs became popular. Rafi Sahab and I voiced a duet, 'Devta Tum Ho Mera Sahaara' in that film, which was my first song with the great singer and I treasure that moment even today. While recording, I felt that I was singing with a *devta* (divine presence). The divine voice of Rafi Sahab echoed and it felt as though we were singing in a temple.

'Much around the same time, Naushad Sahab called me to sing in *Shabab* (1954). On reaching the recording studios, I was told that I am required to sing a few lines in a child's chorus. The song was "*Mehelon Mein Rehne Waale, Humein Tere Dar Se*," a Rafi-song. Though I was perturbed to know that I was being made to sing only a few lines, I only sang it as it was a Rafi-song.

'I regret that I could only sing eight duets with Rafi Sahab. Those were the years when my career had just begun to soar. Rafi Sahab had also acknowledged during the recording of 'Mujhko Apne Gale Laga Lo,' that I really had the talent to go a long way in playback singing. This evergreen composition of Shankar-Jaikishan is one of the most popular duets even today. I only wish there were many more saints like Rafi Sahab in the industry—as fair and as humble. Had that been the case, many talents would have got their due and flourished.

'I am sad that he left this world quite early, leaving a huge vacuum in the life of many.'

Anuradha Paudwal

'When I first met him, I was in awe of him. Contrary to my notion of how such a successful singer would normally be, he was extremely grounded. Outside the recording room, he was as quiet as the blue sea and once in the recording room, he sounded like a lion with his voice dominating his surroundings. Also, he would tune to *Sa* in the medium octave with the same weight and vocal balance as he would to *Sa* in the high octave,' shared singer Anuradha Paudwal.

Rafi ruled the music industry with his voice when Anuradha Paudwal entered the industry as a novice. In the years that followed, she sang in *Phir Janam Lenge Hum* (1977), *Shirdi Ke Sai Baba* (1977), *Janam Janam Na Saathi* (1977), *Aadmi Sadak Ka* (1977), *Amar Shakti* (1978), *Mr. Natwarlal* (1979), *Lahu Ke Do Rang* (1979), *Do Premi* (1980), *Unees Bees* (1980) *Sharda* (1981), with Rafi. Some of the songs from these films like 'Raghupati Raghav Raja Ram' in *Unees Bees*, 'Payaliya Chhanki Na Chhanki Chhanki Bijuriya' in *Do Premi,* became extremely popular.

'I used to be so petrified of singing with a music mogul like him. The recording of "Zameen Dekhi Falak Dekha," a song with Rafi Sahab and Kishore*da* for *Sangraam* (1976) was my first rendezvous with the two legends. Rafi Sahab was sitting quietly on a sofa and I was wondering how an unassuming man like him would be inside the recording studio. On the other hand, Kishore*da* looked as cheerful as I had heard him in his songs. I was quite young then and my nervousness was evident and as we were entering the recording room, Rafi Sahab in his barely audible voice, said, "*Anuradhaji, aap darna nahi, apko yahaan ishwar ne bhejaa hai.* (Do not be afraid, you have been sent here by the Almighty.)" I cherish his soothing words even today. It was Burman*da* who noticed my voice and brought me to the industry. Rafi Sahab rightly identified that my entry into singing was God's gift to me.

'The day Rafi Sahab passed away is so clearly registered in my mind. That phone call from Zaheer at 6 a.m. left me stunned. I witnessed his funeral and clearly remember the last glimpse of the legend. Sadly, within a year of his death, I lost my daughter on July 30. Even on the personal front, this month of the year, proved to be the most unfortunate time of my life. Whenever the pain of my daughter's loss surfaces, I am reminded of Rafi Sahab's untimely demise.'

Sagarika Mukherjee

Her penchant for music became apparent right from childhood. At the age of five she sang her father Manas Mukherjee's composition 'Khushboo Hoon Main Phool Nahin Hoon' (*Shayad*, 1979) with Mohammed Rafi, his youngest co-singer. She shared that she used to closely observe her father practise his compositions at home and would hum whatever he composed. She recalled, 'Baba had lovingly named me tape recorder as I used to remember the tune of each and every song that he composed.'

Once the producer and the lyricist visited the Mukherjee home to listen to the song the composer had created for *Shayad*, but for some reason he could not recollect the tune. He tried different tunes on the harmonium but was unable to trace the exact tune he had composed a couple of days earlier. Sagarika smiled as she related how her father then used the last recourse. He called out, '*Miyao* (nick name meaning the mewing of a cat), *come and sing* 'Khushboo Hoon Main.' The young Sagarika could do justice to her nickname *tape recorder* and instantaneously sang the song.

The producer was quite impressed and suggested that a scene be created so that this song could be sung by her for the child artiste on-screen. Sagarika still cherishes the experience, 'I was just five and a half years old and was chosen to sing the version for the child artiste. So I made my debut with none other than Mohammed Rafi! Mummy had picked me up from school and we went straight to the recording studio. I was to sing after Rafi Sahab finished his part. The process of recording those days was quite long drawn and I fell asleep in my mother's lap, as we waited for my turn. At 11 p.m. I was finally woken up by Rafi Sahab, who said, "*Beta, sorry mujhe kuch zyada hi waqt lag gaya. Abhi aapki baari hai.* (Child, sorry I took so long. Now it is your turn.)" I was so excited that I ran to the recording room and started singing in front of the microphone. Rafi Sahab smiled and said, "*Beta, unhe microphone adjust toh karne do.* (Child, let them adjust the height of the microphone.)" Standing in front of the microphone, singing the track, putting on the headphones…it was all new to me.'

Sagarika recorded using the same microphone that had been used by Rafi, the enormity of which she realised only when she had grown up. Remembering the recording, she added, 'I began singing the line, "Main khushboo hoon, 'fool' (phool) toh nahin…" He corrected me, "*Fool nahin beta phool.* (Child, it's pronounced as phool and not fool.)" He corrected me several times and then he finally said, "Never mind what you sing; you are a beautiful blooming flower."'

Male Co-Singers

Manna Dey

> The playback singer I truly feared was Rafi. He was an instinctive singer, and I required all my training, all my grounding in classical music to match his impact. While singing duets I used to be extra careful, knowing that I have to be on my guard as the person singing with me is the one and only Mohammed Rafi.
>
> —'Manna Dey' *Bollywood Melodies*, Ganesh Anantharaman, 2008

Prabodh Chandra Dey, better known as Manna Dey and fondly referred as Manna*da* by colleagues and music lovers, is one of the profound pillars of the Golden Era of Indian film playback industry, along with KL

Saigal, Talat Mehmood, Mukesh, Mohammed Rafi and Kishore Kumar. With a portfolio of 1400 songs in Hindi films, Manna Dey is one of the exceptional contemporaries of Rafi, who despite being a senior entrant to the industry, always held Rafi's talent in high regard.

An episode often cited is that once when Manna Dey expressed his admiration for Rafi by saying, 'The whole world listens to you and admires your voice, Rafi Sahab,' the latter had spontaneously replied, 'When the world listens to Mohammed Rafi, Rafi himself listens to Manna Dey.'

This mutual respect and admiration also translated into Rafi singing the highest number of male duets (about 60 songs) with him. The first song that brought the two maestros together was 'Main Raavan Lanka Naresh, Mere Hain Dus Sheesh' (*Insaniyat*, 1955). Rafi-Manna combination for *qawwali*s also became a guaranteed hit. Music composer Roshan effectively utilised Manna Dey's voice to open the *qawwali*, a Sahir Ludhianvi creation, 'Na Toh Karwaan Ki Talaash Hai' that Rafi picks up from '*...yeh ishq ishq hai ishq ishq*' (*Barsaat Ki Raat*, 1960). The same combination of Roshan-Rafi-Manna Dey recreated this style in many other compositions such as 'Chandi Ka Badan Sone Ki Nazar' (*Taj Mahal*, 1963)—where Asha Bhosle and Meena Kapoor were the female voices, 'Waaqib Hoon Khoob Ishq Ke' and 'Dhoond Ke Laaun Kahaan Se Main'—both from *Bahu Begum* (1967) where Manna Dey and Rafi, brought out the best in each other.

It is not only *qawwali*s that made the union of Rafi and Manna Dey memorable, but also the light-hearted numbers such as 'Bahut Dinon Ki Baat The Ek Majnu Aur Ek Laila' (*Bhabhi*, 1957), by Manna Dey, Rafi and Balbeer; 'Muh Se Mat Laga Cheez Hai Buri' (*Johnny Walker*, 1957), filmed on Johnny Walker himself.

'Rafi Sahab was an introvert, so he had very few friends he would socialise with. I can't call myself a friend but I am one of his greatest admirers. His world was limited to music and he found great solace in it. He used to come to the studio, complete his recording and then go back home,' said Manna*da*. Once Rafi had said, "The universe of music is so vast, exploring it fully is just impossible in a lifetime. I am only attempting to know a part of it in this lifetime."'

When asked about his favourite Rafi-song, Manna Dey had sharply responded, 'How can one choose a favourite song of Rafi? You tell me which one will you say is the best. It would be unfair to even try to compare. All his renditions are excellent. For instance, no one but Rafi could have done justice to the Roshan composition, "Mann Re Tu Kaahe Na Dheer Dhare" (*Chitralekha*, 1964). He had developed his own unique style of singing. Then, and even today, many singers try to follow his style, but Mohammed Rafi is Mohammed Rafi.'

The legendary singer asserted, 'I am a passionate singer. I chose Indian vocal classical music as my career when I had an option to go to London to study Law, after my graduation. Even today, I practise for at least two hours every morning, but the fact is I can never do justice to any of Rafi Sahab's songs. There could never be a better singer than Rafi Sahab.'

He continued, 'Rafi Sahab was, and is, the most innovative and versatile singer the industry has ever known. Listen to "O Duniya Ke Rakhwaale" (*Baiju Bawra*, 1952) and you will notice the rendition in the high scale but without any loss of sweetness. There are innumerable examples that I can cite to exemplify the greatness of his voice.'

Kishore Kumar

While Mohammed Rafi started his career in 1944, Kishore Kumar started his singing career in 1948 with *Ziddi*, singing the solo, 'Marne Ki Duaayen Kyu Maangoon' under composer Khemchand Rakesh.

Rafi, with his versatility, became the default voice of Dilip Kumar, Bharat Bhushan, Sunil Dutt and later Rajendra Kumar, Dharmendra, Johnny Walker—that made him the leading singer of the '50s and '60s. Most importantly, during this period, he created the *Shammi genre* of music which proved to be the most prolific in Indian film music during the Golden Era.

Kishore in the meanwhile, sang his own songs for the films he acted in and also a few songs that were filmed on Dev Anand. Rafi set a record of sorts, by singing for Kishore Kumar, 'Mann Mora Bawra' in *Raagini* (1958) and 'Ajab Hai Dastaan Teri Aye Zindagi' in *Shararat* (1959).

In the '50s, Kishore is believed to have sung nearly 200 songs, of which most were composed by SD Burman. Kishore continued this association with RD Burman, all through the '70s.

In 1968, Kishore and Rafi sang a tandem song in *Pyar Ka Mausam*; 'Tum Bin Jaoon Kahaan,' composed by RD Burman. It was *Aradhana* (1969) which is considered to be the changing point of Kishore Kumar's career as a playback singer. The film saw the emergence of a *superstar*, a new term in the industry, in Rajesh Khanna, whose on-screen personality Kishore Kumar effortlessly adapted to. The Rajesh Khanna-Kishore Kumar magic caught on with the audiences to become a craze overnight. Post *Aradhana*, 15 consecutive box-office hits of Rajesh Khanna gave a fresh impetus to Kishore Kumar as his voice. The Kishore-RD Burman bonding went on to establish Kishore Kumar as the voice of Dev Anand (in the post '70s songs), Rajesh Khanna and later Amitabh Bachchan.

This post-*Aradhana* period is referred by many as the period of Rafi's decline. The press made statements like 'Rafi finished', 'End of the road for Rafi Sahab', and similar statements which displeased Kishore Kumar, who openly expressed his deep regard for the senior singer and firmly asserted that he considered Rafi to be one of the greatest singers who would always remain the legend he has been over the decades.

Sudesh Bhosle, who, like many others, was greatly inspired by Kishore Kumar and had interacted with the latter frequently, points out, 'In Rafi Sahab's context, this primarily happened because he reached a point where a singer didn't compete with anyone but himself. His own success became the benchmark for his career in the following years.'

Of the 34 duets Rafi and Kishore sang together, some notable ones include 'Do Akalmand, Huye Phikarmand' (*Akalmand*, 1966), 'Yaadon Ki Baaraat' (*Yaadon Ki Baaraat*, 1973), 'Chal Shuru Ho Jaa' (*Chupke Chupke*, 1975). Even their group songs, with female singers, had an instant impact—'Aaj Suhaani Raat Re' with Shamshad Begum (*Naya Andaaz*, 1956) is a refreshing OP Nayyar composition, with the newness that its title conveyed, where Kishore Kumar sang his own songs for his character on-screen and Rafi was the default voice of Johnny Walker.

Sudhakar Sharma, a modern day lyricist who worked with Kishore Kumar as an assistant film director, provides a glimpse of the different shades of the Rafi-Kishore relationship. He recalled that in the '70s, Kishore Kumar would usually record two to three songs a day, but the day he would have a recording with Rafi, he would reserve the entire day for just that recording. He knew Rafi was a perfectionist and they would have to practise for hours before the final recording. He added, 'Kishore*da* would incessantly crack jokes and Rafi Sahab would enjoy them in silence, adding a few words here and there which would add *tadka* (spice) to the joke. After a while Rafi Sahab would say, "*Ab gaana gaaye dada? (*Shall we sing now, brother?)" Kishore*da*, with his peculiar sense of humour would reply, "*Bilkul, main to aap hi ka intezaar kar raha tha, Rafi Sahab.* (Sure, I was just waiting to follow you Rafi Sahab.)" Kishore Kumar had made a movie *Chalti Ka Naam Zindagi* that was released in 1982. There was a *qawwali* in the film and Kishore Kumar without a second thought called up Rafi Sahab to sing it. This only expresses the deep respect that Kishore*da* had for Rafi Sahab.'

Shailendra Singh remembered that during one of the shows where Rafi and Kishore both were performing, someone approached Kishore Kumar for an autograph. He replied to his fan (pointing towards Rafi), '*Arrey mere se autograph le rahe ho bandhu, sangeet to udhar hai.* (You are seeking my autograph, my friend, there stands music personified.)' He also shared that Kishore Kumar would often sing a few Rafi-songs during his solo shows and would respectfully announce, '*Mere paas Rafi Sahab jaisi awaaz to nahin hai par phir bhi main unke kuch gaane pesh karna chahoonga.* (I do not possess the vocal talent of Rafi Sahab, but I would like to present some of his melodies.)'

Actor Biswajeet added, 'I saw the two performing together at Netaji Indoor Stadium, Kolkata (then Calcutta), and they set the stage ablaze.'

A Laxmikant-Pyarelal composition, from *Waqt Ki Deewar* (1981), with lyrics by Anjaan, captures this mutual respect and adulation in this song that Rafi and Kishore sang together.

Aye yaar teri yaari, humein jaan se hai pyaari…
Teri yaari pe jaan luta denge…

Tere saath hai jeena marna…
(Dear friend, your friendship is more valuable than my life…
I will sacrifice my life happily in the name of this friendship…
I shall live with you and die with you…)

Amit Kumar remembers…

Son of the legendary actor-singer Kishore Kumar and a singer in his own right, Amit Kumar had great respect and admired his father's contemporary, Mohammed Rafi. He spoke about the relationship between his father and Rafi. 'It is best described as that of mutual respect, perhaps the best that the industry had ever seen between contemporaries. Rafi Sahab had begun his career almost five years before my father and that was one reason why he always regarded Rafi Sahab as his senior. The adoration was evident from many instances like when Baba used to say Rafi Sahab was like his elder brother. Baba was perhaps the only person who used to crack jokes with the much-reserved Rafi Sahab. Baba's humour made Rafi Sahab laugh wholeheartedly.

'Baba and Rafi uncle would often talk on the phone. I recall how Rafi uncle refused to accept anything more than a token of one rupee for singing two songs in Baba's film, *Chalti Ka Naam Zindagi* (1982). In 1972 the media started talking of my father and Rafi Sahab's so-called rivalry. Baba and I were then in London for a show and we were invited by Rafi Sahab for a dinner at his home. I am witness to the good laugh, over a sumptuous dinner the two had on the media gossip and I remember Baba singing a few lines of a Rafi song in which he had sung as part of a chorus at the beginning of his career.

'When Mukesh*ji* passed away in 1976 and his body arrived from Detroit, Rafi Sahab and Baba were both there at his funeral. Rafi Sahab told my father, "We have lost a great singer today." Baba stood in silence, tears rolling down his cheeks. Rafi Sahab hugged him and said, "*Yehi hai zindagi.* (This is life.)" Then on July 31, 1980, Rafi Sahab left us. Baba and I rushed to Rafi Villa. Baba sat at the feet of Rafi Sahab and cried inconsolably. I had never seen him breaking down like this.'

When Amit Kumar attended the 30th death anniversary of Rafi (organised by Shahid Rafi), he fondly recollected knowing Rafi as his father's close associate and later as his own co-singer, beginning with the song from *Aandhi* (1975).

Amit had many fond memories where he had the opportunity of interacting with Rafi. 'Way back in the '70s, I was at the beginning of my career and those days I used to literally sing on the streets of Calcutta. The roadside programmes would fetch me anywhere between Rs 800-900. One of the organisers gave me an opportunity to perform in a concert where Rafi Sahab was the main singer. My happiness knew no bounds. I sang, 'Dukhi Mann Mere.' I put in my best, did everything that Baba would do on stage; danced with full energy and ended it on a climatic note. Rafi Sahab was sitting in the wings of the stage and observing all the while. When I went up to him to take his blessings, he embraced me and said, "You are a great performer. To sing live with so much energy and gusto is not easy. I am sure you have a long way to go, young man." Coming from a man of Rafi's stature, it was a great motivation. When I told my father about this episode he said, "The greatest playback singer has blessed you, what more do you want."

'I am amongst the fortunate few who had the opportunity to sing a total of 10 songs with Rafi Sahab. His voice had a *gamaka* (ornamentation used in Indian classical music performance; the unique character of each *raaga* is given by its *gamaka*s, making their role essential rather than decorative). It was refined, soothing and distinctive. It was a momentous occasion when I got to sing the *qawwali* 'Salaam Kijiye' (*Aandhi*, 1975) with Rafi Sahab and Bhupinder*ji*. Later, I went on to sing four duets with Rafi Sahab, the first being 'Bare Bare Logon Ke' (*Phande Baaz*, 1978), an RD Burman composition.

'The song "Hum Toh Aap Ke Deewane Hain" (*Aap Ke Deewane*, 1979) gave me the rare opportunity to sing with two legends—Rafi Sahab and my father.

'I can never forget the fatherly advice and affection with which Rafi Sahab would treat me during every recording. Once, after completing a recording at Mehboob Studios, I realised my car had a punctured tyre.

I was waiting for a taxi when Rafi Sahab stopped his car and offered to drop me home. I told him it would be inconvenient for him after a tiring day. But he insisted and dropped me home. I was humbled by this gesture and requested him to come inside to meet Baba. He smiled and said "I know your father better than you do. I will drop in some other day and spend some time with him." When I told Baba that Rafi Sahab had dropped me he rushed to the gate, but by then, he had left.

'Rafi Sahab was and still remains the finest of the playback singers. The lean period of his career is something that happens with every artiste. The industry is like that...there was a time when music directors, film producers, distributors and actors all chose Rafi Sahab over my father, and then in the early '70s Rafi Sahab faced the same harsh treatment. But that doesn't imply that his work deteriorated by any means. To prove the point, Rafi Sahab came back stronger than ever within a couple of years or so.'

Mukesh

Mukesh Chand Mathur, popular in the film and music fraternity as Mukesh, had the voice that enamoured millions of music lovers and went on to become the voice of the greatest showman of Indian cinema—Raj Kapoor.

RK Films primarily approached Mukesh for their songs. There were very few exceptions; the Rafi-Asha duet 'Tumhaare Hain Tumse' (*Boot Polish*, 1954) or 'Ramaiyya Vasta Vaiyya,' sung by Rafi, Lata and Mukesh (*Shree 420*, 1955) or the evergreen solo 'Yeh Mera Prem Patra Padh Kar' (*Sangam*, 1964), filmed on Rajendra Kumar and sung by Rafi. Eleven years later, when Raj Kapoor and Rajendra Kumar, in their 50s, played detectives in *Do Jasoos* (1975), Mukesh and Rafi were the playback voices for the two in 'Chadh Gayi Chadh Gayi.'

Mukesh has 1,200 songs to his credit. Amongst these, there were 14 duets and 11 group songs with Rafi. The first duet that Rafi and Mukesh sang together was a composition by Khayyam, 'Jis Pyar Mein Yeh Haal Ho' (*Phir Subah Hogi*, 1958). Omi-Sonik, the novice music directors of the '60s, brought together Rafi-Mukesh-Suman Kalyanpur in 1966 for the title song of *Dil Ne Phir Yaad Kiya*.

A landmark Laxmikant-Pyarelal song 'Humko Tumse Ho Gayaa Hai Pyar Kya Karein' (*Amar Akbar Anthony,* 1977) is a distinctively romantic composition filmed on the three lead couples of the film, had Rafi as the voice for Rishi Kapoor, Kishore Kumar singing for Amitabh Bachchan and Mukesh as the voice of Vinod Khanna, with Lata Mangeshkar as the female voice.

It was Laxmikant-Pyarelal who had the two comrades share the same mike for the duet 'Saat Ajoobe Is Duniya Mein' (*Dharam Veer*, 1977). Pyarelal*ji* remembered, 'I had no idea that it would be the last opportunity to see the two great contemporaries singing on the same platform.'

Nitin, eldest son of Mukesh and a playback singer, pointed out that there was great mutual respect and admiration between the singers in the Golden Era; the chemistry and bonding they shared, the way they appreciated each other's achievements, made them bring out the best in each other, not as competitors, but as comrades.

Nitin said, 'In Hinduism, we believe in *Ek Swarna Yug* (a Golden Era). It was perhaps due to some kind of divine plan that all those blessed with great acumen, be it in music or acting, came together during that particular time. Eminent singers like Talat Mehmood, Hemant*da*, Rafi Sahab and Papa (Mukesh) came at the same time. The greatest lyricists were also around during that time. And so did the best of actors such as Dilip Kumar, Raj Kapoor, Dev Anand and Guru Dutt, amongst others and the best of actresses such as Madhubala, Meena Kumari, Nargis, Waheeda Rehman and many others, entered the industry. Then there were the greatest of music directors such as Naushad Ali, C Ramchandra, Husanlal-Bhagatram, Ghulam Mohammad, SD Burman and Shankar-Jaikishan, again, amongst several others. This could not have been possible without some divine intervention.

'Interestingly, there was no competition amongst them. They were all genuinely appreciative of each other's work and accomplishments. In *Andaaz* (1949), unlike the usual trend, Rafi Sahab sang for Raj*ji* and my father sang for Dilip Sahab. The spirit that prevailed was only to excel.

'I remember when Rafi Sahab sang 'Din Dhal Jaaye' (*Guide*, 1965), Papa got very emotional and called him up saying, "*Rafi miyaan, kya gaaya hai apne ye geet, aisa koi gaa nahin sakta.* (How beautifully you have sung this song, no one else can sing this way.)" All through my childhood I have seen him personally appreciating Talat Sahab, Manna*da*, Kishore*da* and others.

'I used to accompany Papa to all his concerts since the age of nine, even if that meant bunking school. I would want to sing Papa's songs such as 'Dil Jalta Hai Toh Jalne De' (*Pehli Nazar*, 1945), 'Yeh Mera Deewanapan Hai' (*Yahudi*, 1958), 'Jaane Kahaan Gaye Wo Din' (*Mera Naam Joker*, 1970). But Papa would rather make me sing Rafi Sahab's songs, 'Yeh Mera Prempatra Padh Kar' (*Sangam*, 1964), 'Badan Pe Sitaare' (*Prince*, 1969), 'Aaja Aaja Main Hoon Pyar Tera' (*Teesri Manzil*, 1966). He felt that Rafi was a superlative singer and would say, "*Agar Rafi ke geet gaa sakoge, to kisi ke bhi gaa paoge.* (If you can sing Rafi's songs, you will be able to sing any song.)" In a stage show, after singing some of his songs, especially when the show had reached a certain crescendo and the audience was fully charged, he would smilingly announce, "*Dekhiye, bhaiyo aur beheno, yeh Mukesh ka beta hai aur gaane Rafi ke gaata hai.* (Ladies and Gentlemen, here is my son, but he sings Rafi's songs.)" This was the greatness of a large-hearted singer and father, Mukesh*ji*. He wanted me to be seen as a versatile singer and for that, he found no one better to emulate than Rafi.

'Immediately after Papa passed away, all the singers came forward to console and encourage me. Rafi Sahab also was amongst the first few people who came for the funeral. I remember how, crying like a child, he embraced me, assuring me that he would support me at every step of my life. Somehow, the three great singers—my father, Rafi Sahab and Kishore*da*—left this world too soon. But I really believe that their voices will live on till eternity. Have any of us heard Tansen or Meera Bai? No, since that era did not have the technology to preserve their voices for the generations to come. We are in such a blessed zone in our life that we have been able to preserve the voices of Rafi Sahab and Mukesh*ji*, and other great singers.'

Talat Mehmood

Talat Mehmood's excellent voice, diction and intonation made him an exceptional singer; the mellowness and pathos that he could induce into a composition made him an ideal *ghazal* singer and earned him the sobriquet, *King of Ghazals*. In the later years of his career, he passed on the baton of *ghazal*s to Rafi, who with his virtuosity could do justice to the genre that was otherwise considered difficult by most singers.

The four duets in the voices of the two legends, Talat and Rafi, are 'Bhar De Jholi Allah Ke Naam' (*Laila Majnu*, 1953), 'Kavita Naam Hai Gyan Ka' (*Kavi*, 1954), 'Kabhi Ansoo Bahaate Hain, Kabhi Fariyaad' (*Madhur Milan*, 1955) and 'Gham Ki Andheri Raat Mein' (*Susheela*, 1966).

Mahendra Kapoor

Such was the impact of Mohammed Rafi's voice on the 12-year-old Mahendra, that one day he made it to Rafi's residence at Bhendi Bazaar and expressed the desire to be his disciple. The visit eventually led to a very close-knit relationship between the two.

Guided by Rafi, Mahendra Kapoor started training under Pandit Husanlal and Pandit Tulsidas Sharma in classical music. It was the All India Metro Murphy competition that proved to be a winning stroke for Mahendra Kapoor. He won the competition judged by musical stalwarts Anil Biswas, Madan Mohan, Vasant Desai, Naushad and C Ramchandra. The song that made him win was a Rafi song, 'Tune Mera Yaar Na Milaaya' (*Shama Parwaana*, 1954).

Mahendra Kapoor finally got an opportunity to sing with his *guru* Rafi in *Aadmi* (1967), the song was 'Kaisi Haseen Aaj Bahaaron Ki Raat.' The song was originally recorded as a Rafi-Talat duet, but actor Manoj Kumar was keen to have Mahendra Kapoor as his voice; the song was re-recorded as a Rafi-Mahendra Kapoor duet.

Rafi and Mahendra Kapoor made a conscious decision to not sing together because of the similarity of their voices, which would have attracted unsolicited comparisons.

Mahendra Kapoor's son, Ruhan, talked about the relationship between the two singers. 'My father looked up to Rafi Sahab as a mentor all his life. He told me that he heard Rafi Sahab for the first time when he was just 12; the song was 'Yahaan Badlaa Wafaa Ka Bewafaai,' a duet with Noorjehan*ji*, in *Jugnu* (1947). The song touched him to such an extent that he went in search of Rafi Sahab's residence in Bhendi Bazaar. He was received by a man clad in the simplest of clothes. My father expressed his wish to meet Mohammed Rafi. The man replied, "*Main hi Mohammed Rafi hoon. Aap andar aaiye.* (I am Mohammed Rafi. Come in.)" My father gathered courage and replied that he loved his song in *Jugnu* and had felt compelled to come and see him. Rafi Sahab calmly asked if my father was interested in singing. Out of sheer nervousness, my father lied that it was his brother who was interested in singing. So Rafi Sahab told him to come along with his father and brother the next day.

'The next day my father told the truth to Rafi Sahab and was elated to be accepted by him as his disciple. This was the beginning of his visits to Rafi Sahab's house in the years to come. Soon Rafi Sahab took his disciple along to the recording studios as well.

'My father was 10 years younger to Rafi Sahab. When he went to sing in college competitions, Rafi Sahab would spend hours training him till he was perfect. My father used to take a lot of pride that he was trained under a perfectionist like Rafi Sahab.

'I vividly remember an instance, in the late '70s when I had accompanied my father, for his first show at the Royal Albert Hall, London. Dilip Kumar Sahab was the chief guest. The show was houseful. During the interval, a security officer came in and said that he had two visitors who said they were related to Mohammed Rafi; they were Rafi Sahab's sons, Saeed and Khalid. My father was so touched that he requested the organisers to arrange for two garlands for them. Though it was 10 p.m., they were fortunately able to arrange two garlands from a nearby temple. My father announced on stage, "Today, the Royal Albert Hall is packed and that too on my first performance. It has only happened because of my *guru*'s blessings. Though he is not present here today, two of his sons are with us and I would like to call them on stage." Saeed and Khalid Rafi hesitantly came on to the stage. My father presented the garlands to them, bowed and touched their feet. Both Saeed and Khalid Rafi were aghast, saying, "How can you touch our feet? We are much younger to you." To which my father replied that he was paying homage to Rafi Sahab, who was sitting far away in Bombay. The gesture left the audience stunned.

'Once we returned to Bombay, Rafi Sahab called up my father to say, "Your humility will take you to the highest rung of success. My blessings are always with you." Rafi Sahab used to respect my grandparents a lot. And though everyone knew him to be extremely shy, sometimes, he would call up and talk to my grandmother and express his desire to eat *choley-bhature* (a combination of spicy chick peas and fried bread made of refined flour) made by her. Whenever he felt like having some traditional Punjabi food, he would drop by at our home. Rafi Sahab would arrive on the dot, at the predetermined hour, with Hameed bhai. Then Hameed bhai would smile and say, "Have you come to just eat or will you sing something?" With my grandparents seated on the sofa, Rafi Sahab would sit on the floor with his harmonium and sing *bhajans*. 'Paaon Padu Ghanshyam,' a non-film *bhajan* composed by Khayyam Sahab was an all-time favourite and Rafi Sahab would sing it so soulfully that everybody would have tears in their eyes.

'A very interesting incident took place when Rafi Sahab and my father were returning from All India Radio, Marine Lines. Some people saw Rafi Sahab and rushed to take his autograph. He asked my father in Punjabi, "*Ki mangrey ne?* (What do they want?)" My father replied, "They want your signature." Rafi Sahab spontaneously said, "*Tu kar de.* (You do it.)" In fact, till then Rafi Sahab didn't know how to sign. As his popularity grew, he practised how to sign only for his fans, in order to give autographs and to avoid disappointing them.'

The relationship that existed between the *guru* and the disciple is best described in saint Kabir's words…

Guru Govind dono khade,
Kaake lagoon paaye,

Balihari guru aapne,
Govind diyo bataaye...
(Teacher and God both stand in front of me,
To whom should I bow first?
Well, I choose you my teacher,
Because if you hadn't been there I would have never known God's greatness...)

Shailendra Singh

'This industry functions on its own unique set of rules. It's not easy to survive here. Despite that Rafi Sahab's career spanned more than three decades. It is commendable,' remarked Shailendra Singh who sang for the film *Chacha Bhatija* (1977) with Rafi. The songs were 'Bure Kaam Ka Bura Nateeja,' 'Koi Maane Ya Na Maane' and 'Maa Ne Kaha Tha Beta.'

'Through the whole experience, it seemed to me that I had come across an institution of singing, in just three recording sessions. He was a master at what people call effortless singing.

'During one of the recordings, a musician was repeatedly making a mistake. Those were the days when several musicians practised and recorded simultaneously in the studio. When it happened a number of times Rafi Sahab got a bit irritated and said, "*Kaun baar baar galti kar raha hai?* (Who is this making an error again and again?)" He uttered that slight reprimand also in such a pleasing way that I teased him, "Rafi Sahab, it didn't seem that you were abusing someone, if you wish to, then do it the pure Punjabi way." To which he shyly replied, "*O, nai nai kakke!* (No, no, son!)"'

Udit Narayan

'*Rafi Sahab ki prashansha karna suraj ko diya dikhana jaise hai. Unki barey mein baat karney ki humaari kya haisiyat.* (Praising Rafi is like showing a lamp to the sun. What right do I have to even talk about him),' Udit Narayan said fondly.

The versatile singer markedly remembered December 18, 1979, the day he sang the first song of his career, a few lines, with Rafi (a Rajesh Roshan composition from *Unees Bees*, 1980). 'The opportunity to sing with him was like a dream come true, especially for someone who had grown up listening to his songs—a day came when he found his idol standing right beside him, as a co-singer. I spent the previous night twisting and turning in my bed, in anticipation of the morning that would be a landmark of my career. The song to be recorded was "Mil Gayaa Mil Gayaa" with Rafi Sahab and Usha Mangeshkar*ji*.'

Udit remembered an interesting instance from his second recording with Rafi and Asha, for an RD Burman composition from *Gehra Zakhm* (released in 1981). After the recording, Rafi took him to a corner and quietly uttered, 'You are so handsome. Do you know how to play a guitar?' He had sheepishly responded in the affirmative. To this Rafi joked, '*Socho apke haath me guitar aur aap stage par ho. Logon ko bahut mazaa aayega.* (Imagine how it would be if you have a guitar in your hand and you are on stage. It would be a delight for the audience.)'

'It is hard to believe that Rafi Sahab possessed such a lighter side,' Udit Narayan fondly reminisced.

13

Contentious Issues

The '60s, unfortunately, saw a discord between two notable singing voices—Mohammed Rafi and Lata Mangeshkar. Though Rafi and Lata came together again around 1967, the fallout had a defining impact on the career of some female lead singers at that time; Suman Kalyanpur was one of the beneficiaries with her dulcet voice that closely resembled that of Lata.

Terms of Royalty

In 1962, Lata Mangeshkar approached Mohammed Rafi for his support regarding royalty payments (related to sale of records). This was a period when every filmmaker's first choice, when it came to duets, was Rafi-Lata. Lata felt that Rafi's support would help establish the norm that singers be given their share of royalty, especially as no producer or music director could afford to refuse their demand. The proposition was that half the share of the five per cent royalty from the song proceeds—that film producers conceded to music directors—should go to the singers, as they too were a part of the process to create the song.

Lata Mangeshkar argued that the singer's role was equally important in creating a complete musical piece, by implementing the thoughts of a lyricist into a song, under the guidance of a music director. On the other hand, Rafi took a clear stand that his claim on the filmmaker ended on receiving the mutually agreed upon fee, at the end of the recording. He justified his stand by saying that a singer did not share the risk, irrespective of the success or failure of the film. A singer received the fee in accordance with the market price. Thus, a singer did not have the right to ask for a share when the film went on to become a box-office hit as the singers did not bear the burden of the producer's loss in case the film failed.

Rafi was of the opinion that if the film was a success the filmmaker should keep the royalty earned for it from HMV, the music record company. It is pertinent to mention here that the issue of music royalty is a complex matrix. It was not just Rafi; the entire Hindi music industry could not come to a consensus on the royalty issue. The debate continues even with the new generation of the Hindi film music industry.

It is widely accepted that in many instances, music is responsible for making a film successful. Again, there are instances when a film has flopped at the box-office but the music has done extremely well. There are quite a few films which have faded away from public memory but the songs are eternal. The music directors believed that they are the real creators of music, as the overall concept and the final outcome is the result of their efforts. They argued that the responsibility of delivering the finished product to the film producer rested on their shoulders. The role of the lyricists was limited to writing a *shayari*. Lyricists, on the other hand, clearly stated that they were the originators, as a song takes birth only with the lyrics.

Andalib, Majrooh Sultanpuri's son, said, 'A song is not hummed; it is sung using the words. People recall the song with the words, not just the tune, so lyricists have a legitimate claim on the royalty.' Both the music directors and the lyricists regard the singers as *instruments* and not as originators or creators of the music.

Anand*ji*, of the Kalyan*ji*-Anand*ji* duo, candidly said, 'The royalty issue is a serious one. We, the creators are deprived of our rightful share. This is a burning issue for every creator. In case of music, the music director and the lyricist are the creators.'

Composers Ravi and Khayyam also expressed the same view.

Simplistically, the difference between Mohammed Rafi and Lata Mangeshkar can be seen as two individuals looking at business from two different perspectives. Had Rafi and Lata stood together, perhaps the industry would have come to a consensus on this contentious issue.

Some in the industy however believe that Lata and Rafi were already having differences, since 1961, since the recording of 'Tasveer Teri Dil Mein' (*Maya*, 1961). The royalty issue only aggravated these differences. Apparently during the recording of the said song, Lata and Rafi had some argument over a stanza. Salil Chowdhury, the music director, sided with Lata. This created a rift between the two singers and they decided that they would not sing with each other.

Many in the industry feel that the ramification of Rafi's stand, in the royalty issue, continues to be felt in the music industry today. Not just that, if Rafi had agreed, his successors would have been entitled to a substantial amount in royalties, as his songs continue to be popular even today and are extensively played even on modern devices.

Perhaps Rafi's decision not to take a share of the royalty that came to the music directors and lyricists, was a completely magnanimous gesture that contributed to the survival of the many talented individuals in the industry, as in those days their careers were not highly remunerative.

As present day singer Shaan said, 'My father too was a music director and I know what their earnings were, including the royalties, and how difficult it was for them to survive and sustain their family in those days.'

The entire industry unanimously vouches for Rafi's benevolent nature—too creative to be attuned to the commercial aspects of his talent. Even if one assumes that Zaheer (his brother-in-law who was also his manager) or Rafi did not fathom the long-term implications of this decision, the legendary singer, in all probability, could not have taken this stance without discussing it with his seniors in the industry. Shahid Rafi feels that given the humane qualities of his father, he might have chosen to bequeath what he could have claimed (as royalty) to the community of music directors and lyricists for whom he had great regard.

One can assume that Rafi's decision was largely guided by his heart. As Sonu Nigam put it, 'We cannot blame only Rafi Sahab for refusing the royalty. Others could have made their own choice and fought for it if they had wanted to.' Singer Kunal Ganjawala feels, 'If Rafi Sahab had agreed to join hands with Lata*ji* and established the practice of singers getting royalty, it could have become the industry norm.'

This difference of opinion however kept the diva and the emperor of playback singing professionally apart for several years. After this incident, Rafi took a stand that he would charge the same official fee as Lata Mangeshkar did. However, Rafi often put this rule aside when he sang for a new entrant in the industry or if someone had a genuine financial problem.

The Rafi-Lata duet, 'Dil Pukaare Aa Re Aa Re' is believed to be SD Burman's attempt to bring back the early glorious days of Rafi and Lata singing together.

This issue surfaced again 50 years later, when Lata Mangeshkar spoke to a Mumbai tabloid on her patch-up with Rafi. 'Composer Jaikishan took the initiative. I asked him to get a written apology from Rafi Sahab. I got the letter and ended the cold war. But whenever I'd see him, the hurt would return.'

Shahid Rafi, voiced his objection to this remark in a press conference, that he organised at the Raheja Classique Club, Andheri, Mumbai, on September 27, 2012. 'With due regards to Lata*ji*...I am perplexed. Why is Lata*ji* bringing it up in the absence of my father after half a century? If my father had written an apology letter to her she should have treasured the piece of paper and put it in public domain as every Lata and Rafi fan has the right to see it. Moreover, every truth has to be substantiated especially when one is speaking of a national figure like Mohammed Rafi. There was no reason for my father to apologise as in the '60s, he was at the peak of his career, singing for all the lead actors of that period. If the whole feud was about royalty and he decided not to take it—which was his personal decision—and he did not stop the others from taking it, then what made him write an apology? For a moment, even if I were to believe that my father had apologised to her then that only proves his humility and justifies why the industry calls him a *farishta*. Somehow, I never heard my father ever holding any grudge against Lata*ji*, or anyone else for that matter. My father had great respect for every artiste, be it his co-singers, the musicians or chorus singers. I am clueless as to why this apology letter is being talked about in 2012 when there was enough opportunity to do so between 1967 and 1980. Even Lata*ji*'s biographies by different authors make no mention of this letter. It is hard to believe that a legend like Lata*ji* could not forget the issue in all these years.'

In the mid '60s, compositions that were envisaged as duets by Rafi and Lata turned into tandem songs. This only showed that music directors still thought of Lata and Rafi when they conceptualised the duets.

Madan Mohan was one of the composers who chose Rafi and Lata for most of his songs. His son Sanjeev Kohli elaborates, 'For songs where Rafi Sahab's voice was thought to be a must, a replacement for Lata*ji*'s voice was found in other female voices. Similarly, when composers wanted Lata*ji* in the song, they chose Mahendra Kapoor*ji*, Manna*da* and Mukesh*ji* as the male voices.'

Actor Biswajeet recollected that producer-director Subodh Mukherjee made a film *April Fool* (1964) where Saira Banu was paired opposite him and Shankar-Jaikishan were the music directors. While Lata*ji* sang the solo, 'Unki Pehli Nazar Kya Asar Kar Gayi,' she refused to sing the duet with Rafi. Subodh Mukherjee took a firm stand that he would not change the male singer, Rafi, due to which Suman Kalyanpur became the default female voice for the duets, 'Kehdo Kehdo Jahaan Se Kehdo' and 'Tujhe Pyar Karte Hai, Karte Rahenge.'

If one was to closely examine Rafi's career during that period, he had sung 857 Hindi film songs out of which 502 were solos and 308 were duets (not with Lata). Duets with Lata, released between 1963-67, were mostly recorded before 1963. From 30 duets with Lata in 1960, the number plummeted to a mere 5 duets in 1966; in 1965, there was none. The fact remains that Lata has sung more than 400 duets with Rafi, which is the maximum number of duets sung by Lata with any singer across her career as acknowledged by her. Though in case of Rafi, his maximum duets are with Asha. Even before the rift, Rafi's duets with Asha far outnumbered those with Lata. Rafi and Asha were singing an average of 43 duets every year between 1958 and 1963. Rafi's and Lata's averaged 23.

Guinness Records

In a letter to the Guinness Book of World Records, dated June 11, 1977, Rafi had challenged the claim of Lata Mangeshkar that she had recorded the maximum number of songs—*not less than 25,000,* according to Guinness.

Rafi, according to his fans, would have sung more songs than Lata—he being the senior of the two. They estimated the number of songs sung by Rafi to be anything from 25,000 to 26,000. This prompted Rafi to write a letter, in protest, to Guinness.

In an interview to BBC, recorded in November 1977, Rafi claimed to have sung 25,000 to 26,000 songs, till then. After receiving a reply from the Guinness Book of World Records, dated November 20, 1979, Rafi wrote, '*I am disappointed that my request for a reassessment vis-à-vis Ms Mangeshkar's reported world record has gone unheeded.*'

Evidently, this number, as quoted by Rafi, was also incorrect. According to industry sources, Rafi has sung 4,425 Hindi film songs, 310 non-Hindi film songs, and 328 private (non-film) songs from 1945 to 1980.

Published in 1990, *Gandhar Swar Yatra* by Vishwas Nerukar, a reknowned music researcher, details Lata Mangeshkar's Hindi film songs career (1945-1989) by saying that the singer rendered 5066 Hindi film songs till 1989; the number was far behind the Guinness claim made 15 years ago (in 1974, when this entry was introduced for the first time).

After Rafi's death, in its 1984 edition, the Guinness Book of World Records again named Lata Mangeshkar's as the one with the *Most Recordings* but also stated that *Mohammed Rafi claimed to have recorded 28,000 songs in 11 Indian languages between 1944 and April 1980.*

The Guinness Book entries for both Rafi and Lata were eventually deleted in 1991. According to the available figures, Rafi has sung 4,425 Hindi film songs, 310 non-Hindi film songs, and 328 private (non-film) songs from 1945 to 1980.

However, one has to take into account that these erroneous figures were thrown up in the absence of any official source of recorded statistics, documenting the career graph of these musical stalwarts and others in the industry.

14

End of an Era

July 31, 1980, was just another day for Rafi. Like every other morning, he woke up at six and sat in the balcony with his cup of sugarless tea and a paper which had the lyrics of a song that was to be recorded, carefully written down in Urdu, by Zaheer. Getting up to the early rays of the sun was a habit from childhood.

On that Thursday morning he entered the living room at 9 a.m. to meet two music directors, who had travelled from Calcutta to have a couple of Bengali songs recorded. During the rehearsals they were amazed to see the proficiency with which Rafi sang the songs, apart from a few corrections that were pointed out in the pronunciations. It is believed that while rehearsing, Rafi felt a pain in his chest. However, he did not reveal his discomfort, as was his nature, lest the rehearsal be disrupted.

By the time the rehearsal was over and the music directors left, Rafi's condition had taken a turn for the worse; the pain had become increasingly oppressive. He took the stairs to his bedroom on the first floor. Here, Bilquis, ill with high fever was resting. As Rafi took out a bottle of Sodamint, a common antacid, from the medicine cabinet, she asked if he was unwell. He responded that he was probably suffering from acidity and was therefore taking some medicine. After taking the antacid, Rafi walked down the flight of steps to the living room and sat down on the sofa.

Bilquis' sixth sense however told her that something was wrong. Though unwell, she walked down the steps to see where Rafi was. Downstairs she was immediately concerned on seeing his unusual posture. Though he was trying his best to conceal his pain, his countenance gave him away. In that moment she forgot her ill-health and rushed to her husband. She called for Zaheer and asked him to call Dr Alim K Chandiramani. By this time, she was massaging Rafi's back to bring him some relief. Even as Zaheer called the doctor, Bilquis noticed that Rafi's fingers had turned blue. Dr Chandiramani, general surgeon and a good friend of Rafi, who lived two bungalows down the road, rushed in.

The octogenarian recalled, 'I found Rafi Sahab in severe pain. I examined him and found that his blood pressure was quite high. He was sweating profusely. I understood that it was a heart attack. I was aware that he was a diabetic and a heart attack could be fatal and therefore after providing emergency treatment, I immediately called up cardiologist Dr Nichani at National Hospital (now Hinduja hospital) to apprise him of Rafi Sahab's condition which I knew was now critical. The ambulance arrived within 25 minutes. However, Rafi Sahab insisted on going in his Fiat driven by Qasam (his trusted driver). He was accompanied by Bilquis, his son Shahid and Zaheer. I followed Rafi Sahab's car to ensure that no time was wasted in getting him admitted to the ICCU at the National Hospital.'

On examining him, the cardiologist confirmed it was a severe heart attack. Within the next few hours, the team of cardiologists managed to somewhat stabilise him. But, the doctors came to a decision that he would need a pacemaker. Unfortunately, the hospital did not have one, so an immediate operation was not possible. It should be noted that in 1980, a pacemaker was still a rare form of treatment and was not as easily available as it is today. The cardiologist at National Hospital advised that Rafi be shifted immediately to the Bombay Hospital. Being associated with the said hospital, he was confident that a pacemaker could be arranged there. So under the supervision of several medical personnel, including cardiologists, Rafi, with emergency medical equipment, was shifted to Bombay Hospital.

On the way, between Mahim and Marine Lines, Rafi had another massive heart attack. It took about 45 minutes to reach their destination and these minutes proved to be lethal. The ambulance reached the hospital at about 6 p.m. and he was immediately rushed to the operation theatre. A panel of specialists fought against all odds to keep him alive. By this time, his relatives and a few close friends had also reached.

It was the month of Ramadan and all of them offered their evening *namaaz* for Rafi's recovery. The operation lasted for about an hour and fifteen minutes and Rafi was fitted with a pacemaker. He was brought out of the operation theatre and taken to the ICU. Bilquis, held his hand and wept, '*Ab se, aap humein chhod ke ek pal ke liye bhi kahin nahin jaayenge.* (Henceforth, you will not leave me alone even for a moment.)'

It was 9:45 p.m. when the doctors fitted him with the post-surgery intravenous care. When he finally gained consciousness, though weak, he attempted to pull out the drip lines and the oxygen pipes. Bilquis was called in. She asked him to keep calm and assured him that he would recover soon and they would go home.

When Nasreen was allowed inside the ICU, her *khaalu* (maternal aunt's husband) was reading the Quran to Rafi. She bent down to kiss her father on his forehead and said, 'You will soon get well, *Abba jaan*.' He did not respond; he simply stared at her, as if trying to say something. As she left the room, she turned and their eyes met. She remembered noticing tears in his eyes. At 10:25 p.m. Dr Modi, the cardiologist, walked up to Bilquis to inform that Rafi was no more.

Shahid, just 19-years-old then, broke down, realising that his beloved *Abba* would no longer be there to put that reassuring hand on his shoulder. Incidentally, Shahid was the only son who was with him on this fateful day as his three older sons were in London. Bilquis was still running very high temperature and with the shock of the news, she fainted. The doctors advised Shahid to take her home as she needed rest. Bombay Hospital authorities made it clear that they would take time to complete the formalities before Rafi's mortal remains could be handed over. Shahid had no option but to accompany his sick and inconsolable mother home.

The bereaved family members realised that thousands would throng to their home to have a final glimpse of Rafi and pay their homage before the funeral. They decided to entrust the hospital with the responsibility of caring for Rafi's body until the final journey, the next morning.

Zaheer and Leslie Cutihno (drummer, who often accompanied Rafi on his shows) stayed back at the hospital with the mortal remains of Rafi. They noticed that the body was not getting the due attention from the hospital authorities. Zaheer got busy with the elaborate last minute formalities that the hospital authorities insisted upon and was soon getting impatient. It was quite warm and Leslie feared that Rafi's mortal remains would get affected by the inclement weather.

It was during this time, at about 1:30 a.m. that Kersi Lord (an eminent musician, who was once Rafi's neighbour) received a call from Babloo, RD Burman's assistant, informing him of the sudden demise of Rafi. Kersi Lord mournfully recollected, 'After I received a call from Babloo, informing me of Rafi Sahab's death, I instantly called up the Rafi Villa. Baji (Bilquis) was crying at the other end and in a choked voice asked me to be with Zaheer and Rafi Sahab's body at the Bombay Hospital. I could feel her helplessness. The sons were all in London, except young Shahid, for whom it was too much to handle. Under these circumstances, without losing any time, I reached Rafi Villa and called up Bhupi (well-known singer Bhupinder). Within a short time Bhupi and music director Uttam Singh arrived at the Rafi Villa and we decided to immediately rush to the hospital.'

Kersi recalled, 'When we reached there, we found an exhausted Zaheer desperately trying to complete the formalities with the hospital authorities and he was losing his patience. We were anxious to see the mortal remains of Rafi Sahab. Finally we were led to the basement, where the morgue was located. Unfortunately, the air conditioners in the morgue were not working that evening. It was quite hot and humid and fearing that the body might start decomposing the hospital authorities had placed it on a slab of ice.'

Uttam Singh remembered, 'Death indeed is a great leveller. We got a piece of white cloth to cover up the legend. Early morning we bought flowers from a shop beside a temple and covered Rafi Sahab's lifeless body. He was then taken to the Rafi Villa in the vehicle of a friend. As we handed him over to the family members we realised our responsibility was done.'

Bhupinder took care of the final documents in Bombay Hospital while Zaheer and the others were organising the vehicle. 'That is the least I could have done,' said Bhupinder, 'At that moment, if I could, I would have given my life to him. He would have come alive again and there could be nothing better than that. He is here somewhere. We meet him every day… through his golden voice.'

It was perhaps destiny's arrangement that a man who lived in the world of music, transcending religious barriers, whose voice sang the praises of the Creator—be it Allah, Bhagwaan, Guru Nanak or Jesus—was attended to by a Hindu, a Sikh, and a Christian at the most vital moment of his last voyage.

By this time the news about Rafi's demise had started to spread amongst his relatives, friends and the entire industry. The number 533137 was dialled innumerable times never to be answered by their beloved Rafi Sahab again.

15

The Final Journey

The *Times of India* headline, on August 1, 1980, read, *Mohammed Rafi No More*. For the first time in the history of the Indian film industry, two days of mourning was declared and every activity of the film industry was suspended.

A multitude gathered outside Rafi Villa to catch the last glimpse of the great legend, who ruled their hearts. Every eye was moist.

Islamic custom requires that the burial take place as soon as possible after death and also because it was the auspicious day of Friday, and the 17th day of Ramadan, that a decision was made to not delay the funeral. So the family members in Bombay decided to not wait for the three sons and daughter of Rafi who were yet to arrive from London.

The whole industry had gathered at the Rafi Villa to pay their last respects. Wreaths piled up as actors, actresses, directors, producers, junior artistes, technicians, music directors, lyricists, contemporary singers and musicians turned up in droves to bid Rafi a final goodbye.

Rafi's mortal remains were bathed in scented water, *Al-Gushal*, and then the body was wrapped in the *kafan* (piece of white cloth). Prayers were conducted and it was placed in the *taboot* (coffin), which was decorated with flowers and *attar* (perfume) was sprinkled all over before it was placed on an open truck.

The vehicle moved inch by inch on a path that was thronged by Rafi admirers on either side. By then it was raining heavily. But the weather was no deterrent; an ocean of humanity trailed behind. The predominant colours were white and black—white clothes and black umbrellas; and a shade of grey above signifying the gloom around.

As the truck moved through the residential lanes, on its way to the Santa Cruz *kabaristan* (burial ground), people showered flowers and salutations from their terraces and balconies. At places, the crowd became unmanageable and the truck had to stop. The retinue took a break at the Jama Masjid, Santa Cruz, where a prayer was held. The Masjid had never witnessed such a huge crowd before. And on this gloomy Friday, it saw people of all religions trying to find a foothold in it.

At the graveyard, the crowd again was uncontrollable; everyone wanted to lend a shoulder to the *janaazah* (funeral shroud) of Rafi. Fearing that a stampede may occur, some of the eminent industry personalities pleaded with the crowd to step back. In response, a passionate voice from the crowd shouted, '*Hum aap logon ko parde par bahut dekh chuke, yahan toh hum Rafi Sahab ko kandha dene aaye hain. Humein rokne ki koshish na karein.* (We have seen you actors enough on-screen. We have come here to lend our shoulders to Rafi Sahab. Don't try to stop us.)' The gates of the graveyard had to be locked from inside to avoid chaos. The insistent fans climbed the high walls and jumped over the fences despite that leaving several bleeding.

The *janaazah* was led by Rafi's son Shahid. After the burial, people carried away small portions of soil from the grave as the last blessings of their icon. Amongst those who were most deeply affected by his demise, was composer Naushad. The composer mourned the loss of a friend as long as he lived. 'Rafi and I were one. So since he passed away, only 50 per cent of me has remained,' he is believed to have lamented.

The deeply aggrieved voice of Naushad touched the heart of music lovers as they sat glued to their radio listening to a special tribute broadcast on Vividh Bharti, on the occasion of Rafi's death anniversary on July 31, 1994... '*Waaqai, Mohammed Rafi aise insaan they, aise fankaar the joh zameen par kai zamaane ki ibaadat se paida hote hain.*

Woh karodon ke liye zindagi ka hissa ban chuke the, jiske gaane ke saath din shuru hota aur jiske naghmon ke saath hi raat dhalti thi. Mere saath unka bahut puraana saath raha hai, yeh sabhi jaante hain. Aisa haadsa, aisa nuksaan ho gayaa ki aisa lag raha hai jaise saat suron ke sargam se ek sur kam ho gaya, ab sirf chheh sur hi baaki reh gaye hain…'

(Mohammed Rafi was a person, an artiste, who was born after eons by the grace of Almighty. He was an integral part of the lives of millions of people, whose day would begin with his songs and the night would end with his melodies. My association with him spanned many years, as is known to everyone. It is such a tragedy, such a loss…it seems as if one of the seven musical notes has disappeared and now only six remain…)

On July 31, 1980, Naushad not only lost *the soul* of his compositions but his dearest friend; a loss that Naushad articulately poured out in his *shayari* that his sons shared…

> *Yun to sabhi aate hain duniya mein marne ke liye,*
> *Maut uski hai jiska duniya kare afsos…*
> (Though everyone who comes to this world dies one day,
> only those, for whom the world mourns, achieve glory even in their death…)

Shammi Kapoor said wistfully, 'I still remember that day when we lost Rafi Sahab. I was in Vrindavan for Guru Purnima to pay homage to my *guru*. At 4 a.m. I was proceeding towards the *ashram* (place of religious retreat, like a hermitage), when a man came running towards me and said, "*Shammiji aap ki awaaz chali gayi!* (You have lost your voice!)"

'I wondered how that was possible and replied, "I was singing *bhajan*s till late yesterday night. I am talking to you right now and you are telling me that I have lost my voice?"

'Then he said, "*Aapki awaaz chali gayi.* Rafi Sahab *chale gaye!* (Rafi Sahab has passed away!)" I started crying like a child. Rafi Sahab was an integral part of my life and without him I am incomplete. His death rendered me speechless. I lost my voice!'

~

Today, Rafi fans locate his *mazaar* (grave) by identifying the coconut tree that now overlooks it instead of the tomb that once stood there.

The Santa Cruz *kabaristan*, where the last remains of Mohammed Rafi were entombed, is also the final resting place for other luminaries of Hindi cinema, like Madhubala, Naseem Bano, Naushad, Sahir Ludhianvi, Khwaja Ahmed Abbas, Talat Mehmood, Majrooh Sultanpuri and many others.

In February 2010, the nondescript tomb of Rafi and those of other luminaries were demolished. The authorities clarified that they were forced to take this step as there was lack of space for fresh burials and that it was in consonance with *sharia* (Islamic law), which states that graves that have been in existence for 30 years or more could be removed. They further stated that according to Islam, all were equal in the eyes of Allah and hence no discrimination or preference could be made. This incident got huge media coverage and came as a colossal shock to millions of Rafi-fans.

Shammi Kapoor was particularly disturbed by a headline in a newspaper saying, *Rafi, Madhubala don't rest in peace here...* '*Agar Rafi Sahab ke liye kabaristan mein jagah nahin, toh woh mere dil mein basenge.* (If there is no place for him in the burial ground then Rafi Sahab will live in my heart),' he declared.

The family of Rafi, however, accepted this. Shahid Rafi asserts, '*Abba* lives in the hearts of millions of music lovers all across the globe. He is immortal and does not need a *kabaristan*.'

16

Rafi's Humane Side

There are numerous instances of the singer's benevolent nature. However, he never spoke about his acts of charity. Even within his limited resources, at the beginning of his career—while facing the challenge of making a livelihood in the metropolitan city of Bombay as the only earning member of the family—he was still willing to help out. At times help was in the form of lending his voice for the launch of a greenhorn in the industry. Rafi's name was a stamp of quality and there are innumerable films where his voice was responsible for making the film a great success.

The Altruistic Singer

For Mohammed Rafi, a song was a song and the remuneration he would earn was not a matter of concern.

The opportunity of having their first composition sung by Mohammed Rafi was the stepping stone to success for many music composers. Many of them went on to prove their mettle in mainstream Hindi cinema.

Rafi has the distinction of having sung for more than 200 composers, right from Shyam Sunder, Feroze Nizami and Naushad to Bappi Lahiri, Anu Malik and others.

Many of his songs have been composed by talented but 'not so well-known' composers who eventually faded away without really making a mark. On the other hand, there were many instances, where his Midas touch converted the unknown to the most popular. He often played the role of a searchlight that found talent and lit it up with his voice.

For instance, music director Nashaad, (real name Shaukat Hussain Dehlvi and not to be confused with the music director Naushad Ali) was not a well-known name in the '50s, though he had composed for a handful of films. The feelings Rafi imparted to the song, 'Aaj Gham Kal Khushi…Aadmi Woh Jo Himmat Na Hare' makes it the most memorable composition of Nashaad's musical career. Rafi did a total of 13 films for the composer.

Geeta Dutt's brother, Mukul Roy, composed music only for two films *Sailaab* (1955) and *Detective* (1958). Rafi's solo in the latter 'Chhodiye Gussa Huzoor,' is remembered even today. Dulal Sen is a composer who lent his name to just one film, *Black Prince* (1959), where Rafi sang 'Nigaahen Na Phero.'

Pyarelal Sharma (of Laxmikant-Pyarelal duo) came from a talented musical family. Of all his brothers, Ganesh was arguably the most talented, having composed music for around 10 films—starting with the Dara Singh starrer *Thakur Jarnail Singh* (1966). Today, however, he is remembered mostly for *Ek Naari Do Roop* (1973). Rafi was responsible for making the song, 'Dil Ka Soona Saaz Zamaana Dhoondega,' from this film into an evergreen hit. Even today many of Rafi fans sing a line of the song, 'Mujhko Mere Baad Zamaana Dhoondega…' while paying tribute to their idol.

Similarly, instrumentalist Brij Bhushan composed music for a handful of films and the songs sung by Rafi, 'Kahin Aisa Na Ho' (*Milaap*, 1972) and 'Yeh Shaam Hain Dhuaan Dhuaan' (*Ek Nao Do Kinaare*, 1973), are evergreen numbers.

Working as Hari-Arjun, *Aashiyana* (1974) is believed to be the only film for which Hari Malhotra and Arjun Chaabra collaborated as music directors. There were two solos sung by Rafi in the film. *Hanuman Vijay* (1974), with music composed by Ajay Vishwanath, stands out because of three Rafi songs, the most memorable being the background score, 'Kaahe Dhoondhe Ram Ko.'

There are many others who are remembered for their brilliant, but brief, encounters with Rafi's genius; composers who sparkled, much like a firefly, which shines brightly but does not have a long life. Most of the success stories are accompanied by untold anecdotes, like Rafi singing the background score for Bazmi for a notional one rupee, because the composer could not afford his market remuneration. For Rafi, the tune always came first. If not for his generosity, music lovers would have been deprived of songs like 'Subah Na Aaye Shaam Na Aaye,' 'Ek Lali Ghar Se Chali' or 'Woh Hum Na The Woh Tum Na The' (*Cha Cha Cha*, 1964) by Qureshi.

Amar Haldipur, the violinist who worked with almost every music director in the industry gave an account of an incident which left him humbled by Rafi's greatness. In 1967, when his friend Srikant, an aspiring music director, wanted to record the first song of his film in Rafi's voice, Haldipur called up Zaheer, who quoted Rs 10,000 as Rafi's remuneration. On being told that the music director would not be able to afford this, Zaheer cut down the fee to Rs 8000. Srikant's dream was shattered. Finally, they met the soft-spoken Rafi who asked Srikant what he could afford. With hesitation he said Rs 2000. Rafi called for his harmonium and sat down with Srikant to practise. Haldipur could not resist asking why Rafi even took this small amount; he could have sung for free if he finally agreed to this paltry sum. Rafi explained that he did not want Srikant to be obliged to him. The film in question was *Sant Gyaneshwar* (released in 1981).

Raju Naushad recalled his father Naushad saying that Rafi hated saying 'No' to any music director. New entrants approached him and a producer would give the music director a break in his film, only trusting Rafi's voice, which guaranteed success. These new entrants would then request Rafi to give a concession to enable the producer to afford him.

The singer is credited for having sung the maximum number of songs for *first-timers*. He literally lay the founding stone for the careers of innumerable talents.

Composer Pyarelal recollected that Rafi was the only singer who never took money for the first song he recorded for a new composer. He added that Rafi did not charge Laxmikant and him, for their maiden venture *Chhaila Babu* (signed in 1960, released in 1967) where he sang, 'Tere Pyar

Mein Mujhe Gham Milaa' and for *Parsmani* (released in1963). Even for *Dosti* (1964), he had taken just a token payment. To this day, Pyarelal acknowledges the contribution of Rafi in their career, by adding that Rafi stood by them during their most difficult times.

There is another interesting episode where composer duo Sapan-Jagmohan wanted Rafi to sing for their maiden venture *Begaana* (1963). The producer, who was a die-hard Rafi-fan, assured them that he would be able to organise the funds and Rafi was signed on. However, on the day of the recording, they failed to do so and the anxiety was written on their faces. Rafi, who had reached the recording on time, noticed it. When Jagmohan hesitantly told him what their cause of worry was, Rafi just smiled and said, '*Hum gaana record karein.* (Let's record the song.)' The resulting song is, 'Phir Woh Bhooli Si Yaad Aayee Hai.' Such was the magic of his voice and generosity.

Generosity was second nature to Rafi

Rafi's approach to life is best described in one of his favourite Urdu *nazms* (major part of Urdu poetry normally written in rhymed verse and also in modern prose style poems) by Nazeer Akbarabadi, which he had once recited to the fellow musicians when he was questioned about his simple lifestyle.

> *Yeh dhoom dharakka saath liye, kyon phirtaa hai jungle, jungle,*
> *Ik tinka saath na jaawega, mauqoof hua jab un aur jal,*
> *Ghar baar ataari, chaubaare, kya khasa, tan sukh, aur makhmal,*
> *Kya chilman, parde, farash naye, kya lal palang aur rang mahal,*
> *Sab thath padaa reh jaega jab laad chalega banjara.*
> (Why wander about from place to place, with pomp and show,
> When not a grain will accompany you in your twilight,
> The worldly pleasures of velvet, glitters, structures and chalets high,
> The luxuries of beds, drapes, inlays, or parquets,
> This glitz and glamour will be of no avail when the wanderer sets out on the final journey of life.)

Money was never the criterion for accepting an assignment. Once, CV Nagaiah, from the Telugu film industry, invited Rafi to sing in his new venture, *Bhakta Ramadasu* (1964). The film could not be released on time due to shortage of funds and Nagaiah had gone almost bankrupt. He had been cheated by fraudulent people from the industry. During that time, Rafi's voice was giving hit after hit in the Bombay industry. He approached Rafi and requested him to rescue him from this situation. Without any question, Rafi recorded the song 'Dil Ko Hamaare Darshan Dena' that was to be filmed on the character of Kabir in the film. Considering Nagaiah's circumstances, Rafi refused to accept any money. Instead, he asked the man in distress if he needed financial help to complete his movie. Not just that, he chose to travel down south at his own expense simply to help out CV Nagaiah. This incident won Rafi a place in the hearts of the South Indian film industry.

Humsaaya (1968) is remembered for Rafi's soulful song, 'Dil Ki Aawaaz Bhi Sun.' The late Joy Mukherjee was the producer/director and had also acted in the film, along with Mala Sinha and Sharmila Tagore, and it was premiered at the Maratha Mandir Cinema, Bombay. Despite the lilting compositions of OP Nayyar, it flopped at the box-office. Mukherjee was devastated. When this news reached Rafi, he met the disheartened Mukherjee and handed him an envelope, containing Rs 10,000 that he had received as his fee. Mukherjee was reluctant to accept it. Rafi patted him and hummed 'Dil Ki Aawaaz Bhi Sun. (Listen to the voice of your heart.)' The song said it all. Mukherjee couldn't refuse!

There are several other examples of Rafi's munificence; one of these was that he did not demand a fee for the songs if the film was produced by a colleague. He sang for Kishore Kumar in *Chalti Ka Naam Zindagi* ('Band Mutthi Laakh Ki') released in 1981, where he just charged a notional fee of one rupee. Kishore Kumar had offered him the ongoing charge of Rs 10,000, but he firmly refused.

Rahman Naushad narrates an interesting incident about one of the popular numbers of his father, 'Madhuban Mein Radhika' (*Kohinoor*, 1960). When Rafi heard the tune in *Raaga Hamir*, he was so moved that he decided to forego his fee. Interestingly, SU Sunny, the film's producer, wanted to remove this number, but retained it after Rafi predicted that it would be a great success; in fact, Sunny was convinced only after Rafi was willing to lay a bet that it would be a hit. It was a bet that Sunny lost happily. The song became the greatest hit of its time and many film critics credit the film's box-office success to this classic rendition. Rafi asked Sunny to buy some sweets with the Rs 500 that he had lost and distribute it amongst the musicians.

There were innumerable instances when he left huge sums of money in envelopes for senior singers who had fallen upon bad times, without letting them know that he was the one responsible for the windfall. He also encouraged new talent unperturbed by the fact that they could turn out to be a competition for him. He would distribute sweets after every recording session and would also ask the musicians if they needed any help.

A musician, who had played the *tabla* during the recordings with Rafi on many occasions, now stays in a slum. Lying on his bed, the only furniture in his one room tenement, the fragile 80-year-old, who had agreed to meet after a lot of cajoling, looks at the black and white faded photograph of Rafi on the wall. The inexplicable minutes of silence finally broke as he murmured, 'Those were the *tabla*s I played for Mohammed Rafi, Manna Dey, Kishore Kumar, and Lata Mangeshkar…' He pointed to one corner of the small room where a pair of *tabla*s lay.

On condition of anonymity, he said, 'It was on July 5, 1978, that I received Rs 200 by money order. I received the same sum of money again in August. I did not know who the mysterious benefactor was. This became a regular routine; in the first week of every month I received the money. We musicians were not paid well in those days. Rs 200 was a significant amount and I could buy medicines for my mother who was suffering from tuberculosis. I became very dependent on that money. In the month of August, 1980, I did not receive the money order which left me in total dismay. I did not know what to do. My income was hardly enough for my mother and me to have two square meals in this expensive city. I had no money to buy her medicines and her condition deteriorated. I kept waiting for the money order and started looking for my benefactor, wondering why his munificence had stopped suddenly.

'One day as I was sharing this with a friend, Zaheer *bhai* overheard and said that the *farishta* who was helping me had left this world. I was stunned. It struck me then that Rafi Sahab had passed away on July 31. I went home and told my mother and she remarked sadly that she would have wanted to thank him for keeping her alive. Three days later she passed away. Maybe she decided to meet Rafi Sahab in heaven to thank him. I then realised that Rafi Sahab must have overheard me when I was talking of my mother's illness to the music director who was chiding me for having skipped a day's session.'

The octogenarian added, '*Farishta they tabhi toh Allah ne itni jaldi bulaa liya.* (He was an angel. That is why God called him so early.)' A month after he narrated this incident, the musician passed away. It was as though he was waiting to publicly express his gratitude to Rafi, his benefactor, before taking a bow from this life.

Rafi never publicised his acts of charity. Many people in the industry received regular financial help from Rafi. The veil of secrecy was lifted only after he passed away.

People knew Rafi would never send anyone back empty-handed. There is another incident about a lady relative of Fazal Nawaz Khan Jung Bahudur, the Finance Minister of the erstwhile Nizam of Hyderabad. She was suffering from cancer of the thyroid and had come to Bombay for surgery at the JJ Hospital. She needed financial help and had knocked on every door, including that of well-known film personalities and businessmen. All in vain! She was on the verge of returning to Hyderabad without undergoing the operation when co-incidentally she met a musician in a tea shop who advised her to approach Rafi. The singer responded to her request and gave her Rs 10,000 for the surgery.

Kishan Sharma, who extensively travelled with Rafi for his shows, shared that on Rafi's first international trip for a music concert, he had sought suggestions from people regarding the places worth visiting and from where he could shop. His family gave him lists of things to be purchased. To everyone's disappointment, he returned empty-handed. His family naturally was upset, but did not say anything. After a few days, there was a communication from an overseas company regarding the shipment of something that Rafi had purchased during his trip; it was an equipment used in the treatment of cancer. He donated this to a hospital.

Haridas Prabhu, an old-time affiliate of the ISKCON temple (Juhu, Mumbai) fondly cherishes the glimpse he got of Rafi's simplicity during a 'Mohammed Rafi–Shankar-Jaikishan Night' which was organised to raise funds for the completion of the auditorium at the ISKCON temple. Haridas remembered how despite being such a sought-after artiste, Rafi immediately agreed to perform for the fund-raising event. The show, where Rafi, Manna Dey and Talat Mehmood performed, received a great response. Haridas visited Rafi Villa to thank the singer, when he enquired how the show had done in terms of collections. The amount was nearly Rs 75,000, which was an enormous amount at that time. Rafi indicated that the collection should have at least touched the Rs 1,00,000 mark and immediately wrote out a cheque of Rs 25,000.

There are several other anecdotes on the singer's benevolence and humility. Sudhakar Sharma, former assistant director with Kishore Kumar, relates an incident when a music director called Santram, who everyone fondly called Master*ji*, was going to record a song with Rafi. Master*ji* told Rafi that his wife was a great fan of his, so the singer suggested that he bring his kids and wife to the recording. On the day of the recording, Rafi left after his work. After a while, he came back to the studio. Master*ji* wondered why. Rafi had come with a box of sweets and said, '*Masterji, main bachon se milna to bhool hi gaya tha*. (I forgot to meet your children.)'

Besides his benevolence, Rafi was a very simple and unassuming man, who never let the tidings of success affect him. Sudesh Bhosle, playback singer and mimicry artist, remarked on Rafi's response when he was awarded the Padma Shri in 1967. 'If I were to get such a coveted award, I would be excited beyond comprehension and would have an infinite list of people to thank. In an interview, where Rafi Sahab was asked about the award, he said, "*Aisa sab ko mile.* (May everyone get this award.)" This can be said only by a large-hearted man.'

Sharad Waykool, a well-known painter from Kolhapur once came across Rafi, rather unexpectedly, in one of his art exhibitions at the Jehangir Art Gallery. Waykool had failed to recognise Rafi even as the latter paid for the painting he had bought. He asked for the purchaser's name and address, even as a small crowd of fans had started gathering at the counter. Rafi, with humility, stated, '*Mujhe Mohammed Rafi kehte hain*' and mentioned his address in detail. Waykool was speechless. He was later called to Rafi Villa to install the painting in Rafi's music room. This meeting was the beginning of a warm friendship, irrespective of their varied backgrounds. Waykool related how he used to wear a red shirt almost every day; not because that was his favourite but because it was his only shirt. The shirt eventually was so worn out that even the skilful darning of his wife could not mend it. One evening, Waykool was surprised to receive a suitcase full of shirts, trousers, and sarees. It was not difficult for him to guess who the sender was. The phenomenon repeated itself Eid after Eid. That was not the benevolent singer's only gift. Waykool has carefully preserved the xylophone and gramophone that Rafi had gifted to him. The manual gramophone still works!

Rahman Naushad remembered that his father, for years after Rafi's death, spoke about the Ramadan of 1980. Just a few days before his death, Rafi visited Naushad with a truck carrying *janmaaz* (mats used while reading *namaaz*). He made a request, '*Yeh Janmaaz meri taraf se Eid ki namaaz ke liye bichwa dijiyega, namaazi namaaz padhenge toh mujhe bhi uski kuch dua milegi.* (Please provide these mats to the people who will be praying at the mosque during Eid. When they sit on these and pray, I too will get some blessings.)'

Rafi passed away on July 31, on the 17th day of Ramadan. The prayers of Eid were held sitting on the *janmaaz* given by Rafi. The *namaazis* prayed for the peace of the departed soul.

Naushad Ali, Rafi's close confidante would often say, 'Rafi was someone who had a thirst for helping the poor and needy.' His was a heart that longed to give; truly a heart of gold.

The Social Side

Rafi rarely socialised. A reserved person, Rafi's life revolved around his family and the recording studios. Of the very few who found a place in the heart of the Rafi home was the Chandiramani couple.

The doctor couple, Devi and Alim Chandiramani, recalled that the Rafi family had been consulting them for years. What started as a doctor-patient relationship evolved into a rare friendship.

Devi Chandiramani recalled, 'Bilquis was my patient and then we discovered that we were neighbours, separated by just one building. Our relationship soon flourished into friendship. The whole family started consulting my husband and me. I have delivered most of Rafi Sahab's grandchildren and recently his great grandchildren as well. When his daughter, Nasreen, delivered her first child, Rafi Sahab was elated and would come every morning to our nursing home before going for his recording sessions.'

Dr Alim reminisced, 'Rafi Sahab was a man of few words. I once asked him, "Rafi Sahab, *aap itna kum kyun bolte hai?* (Rafi Sahab, why do you speak so little?)" With his usual winsome smile, he replied, "*Kya karoon Dr Sahab, baat karoon ya gana gaaoon?* (What should I do Dr Sahab? I can either sing or talk.)" implying that he conserved his energy for singing. Honestly, I could not understand the logic. Rafi Sahab must have read the confusion on my face and very soon after that invited my wife and me to attend his stage performance at the Shanmunkhananda Hall (Mumbai). We were allocated seats in the front row. I was enthralled! The atmosphere was soon charged with the resonance of his voice and the audience applauded for several minutes after each song. I then understood where he used to spend all that conserved energy.

'It was in 1976, when Rafi Sahab visited me with a carbuncle close to his spine. I told him that the carbuncle was the result of his diabetes, implying that he should stop eating sweets. He responded, "*Shaukeen hoon mithai ka, kaise chhor doon?* (I am fond of sweets. How can I stop having them?)"

'Mukesh*ji* expired on August 27, 1976, at Detroit, USA, and on August 30, his body was brought back to Bombay. Rafi Sahab was still admitted in my clinic, recovering from the carbuncle surgery. On receiving the news of Mukesh*ji*'s death, he expressed his desire to attend the funeral. I tried explaining to him the importance of post-operative caution and insisted that he wait for three more days before being discharged. But Rafi Sahab had already made up his mind. He asserted, "I have always held Mukesh*ji* in great esteem. If I am not present, the industry would misinterpret my absence and this will hurt me deeply." He returned after attending the funeral saying, "Doctor I have kept my promise."'

Dr Chandiramani recalled the morning of July 31, 1980. 'I received a distress call from Zaheer. The anxiety in his voice told me something was seriously wrong with Rafi Sahab. I rushed immediately.

'I did everything I could as a doctor (He ensured that a medical team was waiting when Rafi was brought into National Hospital and admitted to the ICCU), but Rafi Sahab's health kept deteriorating and finally at the break of midnight came the bad news from Bombay Hospital (where Rafi was later shifted).'

17

The Family Remembers

Rafi was a man who spoke very little but was the fulcrum of his close-knit family. When not in the studios, he would usually be with his wife and children at Rafi Villa.

Made For Each Other: Rafi and Bilquis

Bilquis entered Rafi's life at a tender age and when he was struggling to establish himself in the mid '40s. She was his constant pillar of support, be it good times or bad ones.

On the home front, all key decisions were taken by Bilquis which allowed Rafi to adhere to his *riyaaz*, rehearsals, recording schedules and stage performances. Shahid remembered that his mother never interfered with his father's work and was a great source of inspiration for him. Her role in the background, as the anchor of family-affairs, enabled Rafi to single-mindedly dedicate himself to his singing.

'Mom often used to tell us that a turbulent mind can never sing in a serene voice. "It is important that your father has a peaceful mind and each one of us in the family has to assure this by creating an environment of tranquility,"' recollected Shahid.

Bilquis would often joke, 'Your *Abba* would always say that it's good that you do not understand music or else you would spend all your time listening to my songs and then who would look after the kids?'

Rafi was extremely protective about Bilquis. She never attended a recording and she rarely posed for photographs with him.

'*Abba* himself was quite media shy and whenever there was an interview, he would have Zaheer *mamu* (maternal uncle) do most of the interaction and would answer just a few questions himself, and in brief,' shared Yasmin, the youngest of Rafi's three daughters, before adding, 'He always avoided socialising. Even if my parents or *Abba* alone attended a marriage reception, he would keep the car waiting at the gate so he could just bless the couple and leave.'

Bilquis would often tell the children how privileged they were to be growing up in an environment of abundance. When she got married, Rafi was at the beginning of his career and though he used to sing *ghazals* and few songs in Punjabi films, it still meant making an effort to make ends meet. But she never complained. 'I trusted your father's talent and knew he would make it big one day,' she would often say.

Life was never the the same for Bilquis after Rafi passed away. The children remembered that she would often say, 'I wish Rafi Sahab was here and would stand by me, for he always used to say, "Tell me your problems and they will all vanish" ... *Tumhaare* Abba *hote to aisa nahin hota*. (Had you father been there, things wouldn't have been this way.)' She would often recount for the children the memorable years that she had spent with him; this included talking about the family picnics and visiting their holiday home at Lonavala on weekends.

For Bilquis, Rafi was an ideal husband and the centre of her life.

Father Figure

Mohammed Rafi had seven children; son Mohammed Saeed from his first wife, Basheera, and three sons and three daughters from his second wife, Bilquis—Parveen, Khalid, Hamid, Nasreen, Yasmin and Shahid.

Saeed was born in 1942 in Lahore. When Rafi moved to Bombay in pursuit of a career, Rafi's father insisted that Saeed be shifted to Bombay. 'Bilquis had three sons and three daughters but treated Saeed as her own child,' said Siddique, Rafi's youngest brother. Saeed was later sent to London for education, where, years later, he started his laundry business. Saeed's wedding took place in Bombay in 1965 and was a lavish affair. Unfortunately, at the age of 56, he had a car accident and succumbed to his injuries in a London hospital. He was almost the same age at which his father passed away.

Rafi's second child, Parveen, was born in 1947, an eventful year when India became independent and Rafi decided to stay back in India. Her *nikaah* (wedding ceremony) with Aftab Ahmed took place in 1965, though the final *bidaai* (when the daughter leaves from her parental home after her wedding) happened in 1967. During the recording of the *bidaai* song, 'Baabul Ki Duaayen Leti Jaa' (*Neel Kamal*, 1968) Rafi is believed to have broken down; the song probably brought back memories of his daughter's *bidaai*. After the take, Rafi approached music director Ravi and apologised saying, '*Mein khudko sambhal nahin paaya.* (I could not control myself.)' Ravi recalled this incident, 'There was no need for any retake as the song sounded very natural.' The soulful song became very popular and also won Rafi an award.

Khalid, Rafi's second son, had also been sent to London for his education when he was just nine-years-old; this despite the fact that Bilquis was much against it. Rafi convinced Bilquis by promising that she could visit her sons whenever she wanted. Khalid later worked with an airline company based in Kuwait. In 1971, he married Yasmin, from Indore. At the age of 55, Khalid died of a massive heart attack.

Like his other brothers, Hamid too had been sent off to London at an early age. He later worked with the cargo department of Air India and also had his own transport business. His wedding took place in Bombay in 1975. In January 1995, during a party with his colleagues, in celebration of the New Year, they suddenly noticed him sitting quietly in a corner. They realised, to their utter shock, that he had died of a massive heart attack. He was just 40.

Of the two other daughters, Nasreen inherited Rafi's smile while Yasmin the calm and quiet nature of her *Abba*.

Abba's Girls Nasreen and Yasmin

Nasreen narrated, 'I do not remember a single instance when *Abba* raised his voice. He was a quiet man and prized us (his daughters) as the greatest gift of Khuda.'

Nasreen is a businesswoman in Mumbai now and exports designer clothing. She is married to Miraj Ahmed. Yasmin, the youngest of the three daughters of Rafi, is the only child who grew up in her parents' home and was fortunate to have got the maximum number of years in the proximity of her father. She married Parvez Ahmed in 1979 and now lives in Mumbai with her husband and two sons.

Nasreen continued, 'At home *Abba* was childlike and would play with us. He used to make me sit on his lap and plait my long hair. He consciously kept us away from the film industry. As kids we were not allowed to enter his room during his *riyaaz* or his rehearsals, which would sometimes go on for hours. Mom used to make sure that there was pin-drop silence at home lest he be disturbed.

'Once when I was really young, *Abba* was going to Madras (now Chennai) for a recording. I cried a lot so Mom said that I could accompany him to the airport. At the airport, however, I wanted to go with him to Madras and was quite adamant about it. *Abba* immediately bought my ticket and I flew with him to Madras. He had a very busy schedule, recording in the studios. I was happy playing around and getting all the attention from our host. Zaheer *mamu* took good care of me and this trip remains my most memorable one with *Abba*.

'He never allowed us to participate in any event related to the film industry. Though he was part of the glamour world, he was quite orthodox when it came to his family. After school, we daughters were not allowed to join college; he kept tutors for us and we pursued our education at home and gave private examinations. Later, I too went and stayed in London for four years. He even kept his sons away from the world of films.

'When I was about 18, I saw him performing live for the first time. It was a Shankar-Jaikishan night in Bombay, in 1969. I had accompanied *Ammi* to the show. I was stunned to see him on stage; he was a different man altogether—full of energy and fun. His performance drove the packed-house euphoric! For the first time I realised how much adulation my father commanded. He shared an amazing chemistry with Krishna Mukherjee (mother of actor Rani Mukherjee) on stage and that night, they sang some of the popular duets of Shankar-Jaikishan like "Jiya O Jiya Kuch Bol Do" (*Jab Pyar Kisi Se Hota Hai*, 1961), "Choti Si Mulaqat Pyar Ban Gayi" (*Choti Si Mulaqat*, 1967). I felt so proud that I was his daughter. It was an incredible moment to see *Abba* so gregarious on stage, as he whistled to the song "Thoda Ruk Jaayegi To" and "Badan Pe Sitaare."

'He actively participated in the selection of our grooms, though it was *Ammi* who took care of all the functions and rituals. All the marriages happened within our close family circle; Parveen *didi* and I are married to the sons of our *khaala* (mother's sister). She is settled in London and her husband is a doctor. After my wedding, I initially went to live with my husband in Aligarh where he was completing his degree in mechanical engineering. Later *Abba* insisted that we shift to Bombay and settle in Bandra as he was missing us a lot.'

Yasmin added, 'In 1977, I accompanied my parents to America, Canada and London, where *Abba* performed in several live shows in different cities. I was 17 at that time and realised how popular he was abroad—he was a great crowd-puller and everyone was elated to see him perform. Krishna Mukherjee accompanied us as the female voice for the stage performances. On weekends, *Abba* used to take us sightseeing and shopping.

'I am the youngest daughter and he would pamper me a lot. My only complaint to destiny is that within seven months of my wedding *Abba* passed away. It left me shattered! The only consolation is that *Abba* was there to bless all three of us (the sisters) when we got married. What lingers on in my memories are the words of a song that *Abba* composed especially for my wedding…

Ghar se dola chala ladli ka,
Kya nazaara hai yeh zindagi ka,
Kitne naazon se paalaa tha humne,
Har tarah se sambhala tha humne,
Haai humse judaa ho rahi hai,
Ghar ki yaadon mein wo kho rahi hai,
Aaj baabul ka rona na poochho,
Aur maa ka tadapna na poochho…

(My beloved daughter takes leave of her parents after her nuptials,
What a heart-rending scene it is of life,
We have nurtured her with so much love and care,
Now is the moment of parting,
She is lost in the memories of her childhood,
The pain of the father is inexplicable,
So is the yearning of the mother…)

Yasmin was unable to hold back her tears as she narrated the verses. Nasreen took over, 'He was diabetic and got hospitalised a couple of times but we never realised he would leave us this early. The doctor had asked him to rest. He rested for a week and got back to work. He was very fond of good food and would often indulge himself. *Ammi* used to be very strict and would restrict his diet but then he used to say, "What's the point of working so hard and earning, if I can't eat the food I like. It's futile to lead such a restricted life."

'On that fateful day, while leaving for the hospital, *Abba* kissed Yasmin and me on the forehead and said, "*Mere liya dua karna*" and he walked up to the car, which was taking him to the hospital. He waved at us through the window. Later in the evening, both of us were called to the hospital. At about 10:15 p.m. I went into the ICU. As I stood beside his bed, he kept gazing at me; his eyes were moist and I felt he wanted to say something but was unable to speak. My throat was choking and I too could not utter a word. The doctor asked me to leave. My intuition told me that this was my last meeting with *Abba*. I peeped through the curtain that had been drawn for another glance and could see his eyes searching for me. I had barely stepped out of the ICU, when the doctor came to tell us that he was no more. It was exactly 10:25 p.m.'

Yasmin added, 'As only one person was being allowed at a time, I was waiting for my turn. But unfortunately, *Abba* did not wait for me. Since *Ammi* was running a high temperature, we had to return home.'

Nasreen related how the family decided to go ahead with the burial, without waiting for her brothers to come from London, as the next day was a Friday, and it was considered auspicious.

'The greatest impact of *Abba*'s death was on Zaheer *mamu*, who was associated with him since he was 16. He used to spend most of his time in our home, going to his family only once or twice a week, though they lived in Bombay. Zaheer *mamu* was completely dedicated to *Abba*'s career as a singer; from writing the lyrics in Urdu (since *Abba* could read only Urdu) to managing his accounts. After *Abba* passed away, he rarely visited us. He used to go frequently to *Abba*'s *mazaar* and spend hours talking to himself; as if in conversation with *Abba*. Within one year of *Abba*'s death, Zaheer *mamu* also passed away; perhaps to again be with *Abba*, even in his eternal home.'

Yasmin explained how life changed after their father's death and how mishaps followed one after another, 'Our brother Hamid also had a heart attack and died young. We lost all our brothers in London. *Ammi* passed away on March 4, 1998.'

Shahid Rafi

The youngest child of Rafi and Bilquis, Shahid Rafi was born in 1961. After a few years in boarding schools, in Pune and Mount Abu, he too was sent to London, at the age of 12, to pursue his education and then his career. However, he never found himself at home in London and when he came over to attend his sister Yasmin's wedding, he did not go back to London. After a brief stint with Indian Airlines, he started his own textile business. He currently resides in Rafi Mansion in Bandra.

'In my childhood, I often wondered why people considered *Abba* so great. The realisation of his greatness dawned upon me only after his death,' said Shahid Rafi.

'He was deeply attached to the family and cherished spending time with all of us. *Abba* was a man with a lot of patience whose smile never faded. I do not remember ever being scolded or punished by him. Yet, I could not communicate openly with him; but that was more out of respect than fear. It was always *Ammi* who was the disciplinarian and who kept strict vigil on us. *Abba* often asked my mother "*Bacchey mujhse itna door kyon bhaagte hain, jab ki main inhe itna pyaar karta hoon?* (Why do children run away from me especially when I love them so much?)" Mom used to explain, "*Woh aap ki izzat karte hain.* (They respect you.)" We always used *Ammi* as our conduit to communicate our demands. Whenever he travelled abroad, he used to get gifts for all the family members.

'In his leisure hours, he would listen mostly to *ghazal*s of Mehdi Hassan and Ghulam Ali. He also spent a lot of time listening to *thumri*s (in Hindustani classical music, a light romantic song) and would play *raaga*, *ragini*s (in Indian classical music, a derivative melody related to a *raaga*) on the gramophone; listening to the *bol*s (lyrics) very minutely.

'Sundays would always be special when he would play carrom or badminton with the kids. He also spent a lot of his leisure time flying kites and watching boxing matches. In 1979, while on a US multi-city concert tour, he had the opportunity of meeting his idol, the legendary Muhammad Ali, in Kentucky, a meeting that lasted for 45 minutes where *Ammi* and I were also present. The discussion centred round both boxing and music and thus it was a classic case of *Mohammed meeting Muhammad*!

'*Abba* was a foodie and loved entertaining guests. *Ammi* was always kept busy in the kitchen as he preferred her cooking. Even on days when she was unwell, she would make it a point to cook at least one item for *Abba*, leaving the rest to Khalil *bhai*'s trusted hands; he was a part of our family and had practically grown under her guidance. *Abba*'s tea was very special. Every morning, the first thing *Ammi* would do was boil the milk with almonds, cardamom and cloves for his tea. Four to five flasks would be filled with this special concoction that he would carry to the studios. He was very particular and would have only homemade tea. Like a true Punjabi, he was very fond of milk. On days when he had no recording shifts in the evening, he would sit in the lawn and as the milkman arrived, drink at least two bottles of milk. The milkman would then complain to *Ammi* that he had now fallen short in his quota of deliveries.'

Firdaus, Shahid Rafi's wife, became a part of the family after Rafi had passed away. But she remembered how Bilquis would often mention Rafi's fondness for good food. Whenever it would rain, he would ask for *keema roti*s (a flat round bread cooked on a griddle, stuffed with mince meat) and *bhajia*s (an Indian dish of fried vegetables). Not only was he fond of good food but he also loved to treat others to good food. Bilquis was a great cook and she always credited Rafi for motivating her to cook a variety of traditional food.

When Rafi was diagnosed with diabetes, she would often insist that he take rest and not have more than one recording a day but he would ignore and say, 'The music directors come with great hope and I must sing for them.' She always felt that Rafi had neglected his health.

Shahid spoke about his father's inherent goodness. 'He never criticised anyone. He would say, "It's important to analyse ourselves first. There are hundreds of scars in us which we do not notice; while we always tend to magnify the little spots in others. It is necessary to correct our own multiple flaws before pointing a finger at others." Not only did he keep away from criticism but he would never allow anyone in the family to indulge in it. I remember how particular he was about the language each one of us used even in our day-to-day conversations. *Abba*'s spoken Hindi had a touch of Urdu and he was quite formal even at home. We siblings were never allowed to speak colloquial language at home. He was a man of few words but at times his silence spoke louder than words.

'He would go out of his way to make us happy. There is however one instance when he was discouraging. I was in the seventh standard in St Andrews and there was a singing competition in school. My class teacher told me, "Shahid, your *Abba* is a great singer. Make sure you learn a song of his for the competition. You need to win." I approached *Abba* and asked him to teach me the song 'Mere Mitwa Mere Meet Re' (*Geet*, 1970). He said, "*Beta, gaa ke sunaao.* (Son, let me hear you sing it.)" Even before I could complete the first line of the song, *Abba* patted my shoulder and said, "*Yeh tumhare bas ki baat nahin.* (You will not be able to do this.)" I was disappointed. I finally sang 'Meri Bheegi Bheegi Si,' a popular Kishore Kumar number from *Anamika* (1973). I won the second prize, defeated by a classmate who sang my father's song. In that defeat there was a lot of pride that came from the realisation that my father's song was the best.

'I remember, once in the month of July when Bombay was in the grip of monsoon, *Abba* offered to drop me to school on his way to the studio. As usual, the traffic was moving at a snail's pace and at one of the traffic signals, a beggar approached our car and held out his bowl. *Abba* did not have any coins with him and said, "*Inshallah, agli baar le lena.* (God willing, take it next time.)" The beggar peeped through the window and started singing, "*Pehle paisa phir bhagwaan, Babu dete jaana daan, dete jaana.* (First money, then God; Sir, please give alms before you go.)" This was one of my father's own songs, from *Miss Mary* (1957), which he had sung for Hemanta Kumar. He was so touched that he gave a Rs 100 note to the beggar.

'One of the things he would often say was, "*Aasmaan mein dekh kar chaloge toh gir jaaoge. Zameen par dekh kar chalo, thokar nahin khaaoge.* (If you look at the sky and walk, you will fall. Look on the ground while walking and you will not stumble.)" He considered himself ordinary even at the peak of his career, when the whole industry regarded him as a star.

'He had once gone for a recording with music director Laxmikant-Pyarelal, for a Manmohan Desai film. He returned home, exuberant and called the whole family to the living room. Then he began, "*Maalum hai aaj kya hua?* (You know what happened today?)" He then paused. We all got very inquisitive and were surprised to hear him speak so loudly. Yasmin and I asked in unison, "*Kya hua,* Abba*?* (What happened, *Abba*?)" With pride he answered, "*Humne* superstar Amitabh Bachchan *ke saath gaana gaya.* (I have sung with the superstar Amitabh Bachchan.)" He then sang the *antara* (The equivalent of a verse in Hindustani classical music), "Chal Chal Mere Bhai" (*Naseeb,* released in 1981). We were awestruck! Then he was flooded with questions. My first question was, "How tall is he and what did he wear?" Even before he could answer me, my sister asked, "Is he really handsome?" *Abba* was all praise for Amitabh Bachchan, without paying heed to the fact that he himself was a legend.'

Wherever he went people would gather around him asking for his autograph. He would politely avoid and the legion of fans used to wonder why he did so, little knowing that he did not know how to sign in English. Shahid remembered, 'He began practising his signature diligently and when *Ammi* enquired why he was wasting reams of paper, he told her that he did not want to deprive his fans and so was learning to sign his name in English. Soon he began signing autographs in English and enjoyed doing so. It came as a great compliment for all his efforts when a journalist mentioned that he had the best signature in the industry.

'One thing *Abba* reiterated was, "The joy of giving is much more than the joy of receiving." Every month he used to invite poor people from all communities to our bungalow. While my mother personally served the food, he used to sit with them and eat. At the end of the meal he would say, "*Bilquis, aaj humne bahut zyaada khaaya.* (Bilquis, I have eaten a lot today.)" *Ammi* would always laugh and give the same reply, "*Jab bhi aap inke saath khaate hai, har baar aap yehi kehte hai.* (You say this whenever you eat with them.)"

'*Abba* did not want any of his children to join the film industry. He would always say, "*Padh likh kar apna business karo.* (Get educated and then do your own business.)" He would tell us, "You all have only seen the best part of life and so move ahead and do even better. You need to achieve much more than what I have done." He made it clear to us that our career choice should in no way be allied with films. As we grew up, he sent us to London for further education. This he did, basically to keep us away from the film industry.

'When I was five-years-old, *Abba* took me to Mehboob Studio. He was recording a number with Laxmikant and Pyarelal Sahab. Lovingly, Pyarelal Sahab took me on his lap and asked *Abba*, "*Rafi Sahab, aap ka beta hai, zaroor gaana gaata hoga.* (Rafi Sahab, he is your son and I am sure he too can sing.)" *Abba* looked at me and said, "*Chal beta uncle ko ek gaana suna de.* (Come on son, sing a song for uncle.)" I recited "Jack and Jill." *Abba* smiled and said, "*Mera beta* English *mein gaata hain.* (My son sings in English.)" This was later narrated to me by Pyarelal Sahab.

'It was only after his death that I started learning Indian classical, vocal music from Ustaad Ismail Shamshi and Ustaad Taj Ahmed Khan. In 1984, for the first time, I went for a public performance in Hyderabad at Rabindra Kalakshetra. A huge crowd had gathered and the hall was jam-packed. Soon I realised they were euphoric about meeting Rafi's son and were least bothered about my singing. I understood what a great man my father was. It was surprising that *Abba* was so popular in South India where

Hindi is neither spoken nor understood very much. As I completed my performance, one of *Abba*'s fans requested me to sing one of his popular numbers. He did not know the exact Hindi words so he hummed the first few lines of the song "O Duniya Ke Rakhwaale." After I completed the song, the gentleman walked up to the stage and hugged me. He said something in Telugu. I took it to be a compliment. Later my local arranger told me he had actually said that though I could not do justice to my father's song, he felt blessed that he could embrace a part of Rafi Sahab which was in me.

'When *Abba* was touring the Gulf countries, after one of his shows, he, along with the whole group, went to attend the dinner reception at the palace of the King of Bahrain, as his guest of honour. A lady from a royal family expressed her admiration for *Abba* in a rather unusual way, "Had I known by which flight you are travelling, I would have hijacked the flight to have you as mine." My mother was sitting next to my father and she narrated this to us on their return, right at the dinner table. The lady was obviously mesmerised by his voice.

'*Abba* was a very religious and God-fearing person. He went for his first Haj in March 1970, with Nasreen and Zaheer *mamu*. It was during his second Haj in 1971, with *Ammi*, that he met a spiritual person who told him that his profession was against his religion—a sin as it was associated with the glamour world. *Abba* took it to heart. He returned to Bombay for a couple of days and then took off for London where my elder brothers were settled. A month or more went by and they were surprised why *Abba* was not making plans to return to Bombay, though the music directors were calling him frantically. It was very unusual for *Abba* to be away from the industry for more than a week, except when he was travelling for his concerts.

'My brother gathered the courage to ask *Abba* what was holding him back and *Abba* candidly said, "I want to get away from the glamour world, what I have been doing till now is *gunaah* (sin). I am retiring." My brother was taken aback! Baffled, he consulted a few of our senior family friends in London. They in turn called a spiritually enlightened person who counselled *Abba* and explained that Allah had gifted him a voice to serve mankind. It would be wrong to deprive the world of his voice. It would mean disobedience to Allah. Convinced, he got back to Bombay and continued to do what he was best at.

'One of my lifelong regrets is that I could not stay back in the hospital with *Abba*'s mortal remains. I had no choice, but to take care of my ailing mother who could not accept my father's unexpected death and had collapsed. The doctors had advised me to accompany her home and be with her. It was a difficult choice, but fear had gripped me that death might snatch away my mother too. I needed her.

'I have never seen my father without a smile. I vividly remember my last moments with him in the ICU of Bombay Hospital, the day he passed away. He was in discomfort and could not speak—just stared at my face. His eyes were flooded with tears. However, I noticed that the smile was very much there on his lips. Even today, after 34 years, I can visualise the smiling face of *Abba* in his eternal sleep.

'Within a few years of his death, our domestic help, Khalil *bhai* and *Abba*'s trusted driver, Qasam *bhai*, both left our house. Working at Rafi Villa was never the same for them after *Abba*. While leaving, Khalil *bhai* said sadly, "*Main kahin bhi jaata hoon Sahab hi nazar aate hai.* (Wherever I go in the house, I can trace Rafi Sahab's imprints.)"'

The lineage of Rafi's family continues with his 18 grandchildren, and one hopes that Rafi's enormous talent has been bequeathed to at least one of them.

> *Kaise kategi zindagi tere bagair,*
> *Paaunga har shai mein kami tere bagair.*
> (How will I lead my life without you,
> I will feel your absence everywhere.)
>
> (*Jahaan Tum Wahaan Hum*, Unreleased Film)

Mohammed Siddique

Eighty-four-year-old Mohammed Siddique, Rafi's younger brother and his only living sibling, stays in Lahore with his family. The whole family had shifted to Lahore much before Partition; Rafi chose to stay back in India.

Mohammed Siddique remembered, 'By 1947, Rafi was making a name for himself in the Bombay film industry. He loved the industry and Hameed *bhai* felt it would be unwise to uproot him from Bombay. Inspite of family pressures, Rafi decided to stay back in India permanently. Hameed *bhai* explained to our parents that the Bombay film industry in India was much ahead of the Pakistani film industry and so it would be wrong to force Rafi to leave the city where he was prospering. Moreover, talents like Naushad Sahab, Shakeel Sahab, Shamshad Begum and others all chose to stay back in the Bombay film industry. Time has proved that Rafi had made the right decision.

'He visited Lahore thrice after settling down in Bombay; could not stay away from the industry for too long at a stretch as the recording schedules would get disturbed. He was very sensitive to the fact that the producers should not face any problem because of him. He was a highly disciplined professional.

'I used to visit Bombay almost every alternate year and have also travelled all across India. A couple of times Hajji Sahab, our father, also visited India. Rafi *bhai* took *Abba* all the way to Delhi to meet Jawaharlal Nehru, the first Prime Minister of free India. He used to narrate this memorable instance to every visitor back in Lahore, till his last day. Rafi *bhai* had also taken *Abba* to the studio while recording a song. *Abba* was very impressed and, with tears in his eyes, hugged him when the recording was completed. He was the same person who was much against Rafi *bhai* singing when he was a child. Rafi put his fee in *Abba*'s *jholi* (sling bag). *Abba* blessed him, advising him to never let anyone leave hungry from his home. Rafi treasured this advice and followed it till he breathed his last. Every morning, he used to distribute a part of his earning. There were instances when the lesser privileged ones would come and say, "Rafi Sahab, we want to eat *biryani* (a dish made with highly seasoned rice and meat, fish, or vegetables)," and Rafi with his usual smile would fulfil their desire. All his life he has earned the blessings of these people.

'I remember an instance when, years ago, as we both were relaxing on a *khatia* (cot), on the terrace, I told him, "Brother, the way you sing is amazing. You just leave the world mesmerised…as if under the spell of some magic." He was quiet for a while and then said, "Brother, I learn from the music directors and the rest is left to Allah."

'When he did a stage show in Lahore, somewhere in the '60s, the Pakistani playback singer Masood Rana, who was considered "The Rafi of Pakistan," also sang a song on stage. People compared the two and Rafi was undeniably better. Masood Rana was very upset. Noorjehan called him and explained that no one other than Rafi possesses the ability to sing "Zindabad, Zindabad" (*Mughal-E-Azam*, 1960) with such gusto. It was just not possible to imitate Rafi's passionate rendering.'

18

Rafi Lives On…

Music compositions, singing style, lyrics and even technology have undergone immense change since Rafi passed away; yet, he lives on…

Some cherish the memory of having one of their early compositions in the voice of Rafi, others treasure having earned their first break with Rafi; some can't forget the moment when they met their idol for the first time, while others prize that magic moment of Rafi placing his hand on their head to bless them. From sound recordists to musicians, singers to composers, stage artistes to comperes, Rafi is revered alike irrespective of the era.

Pandit Jasraj

'The moment I hear the name of Mohammed Rafi Sahab, I feel like offering a *namaskar* (salutation) to him. *Rafi Sahab ek bahut hi manjhe huye fankaar the. Bhagwaan ne unko adbhudh shakti di thi. Woh bahut hi vinamra aadmi the. Swabhav lajawaab tha unka.* (Rafi Sahab was a fine artiste. The Almighty had blessed him with a unique vocal strength. He was an extremely polite man; a man with a wonderful temperament.)' said Pandit Jasraj, the maestro of Hindustani Classical music.

'Rafi Sahab came from a family that did not have any musical roots and his formal training in classical singing was rather short but it would certainly be wrong to say that he fell short on any yardstick. He was a singing genius and we all are proud of him. Not only his fans but his own *guru*s (teachers) took pride in his achievements. My brother was a close friend of Rafi Sahab's *guru*, Ustaad Chhote Ghulam Ali Khan Sahab. Ustaad*ji* once told my brother, "*Panditji, Mohammed bahut acha gaata hai.* (Pandit*ji*, Mohammed sings very well.)" What more could a disciple ask for than the appreciation of his teacher?

'Rafi Sahab contributed immensely to bring classical compositions into films. I want to thank Naushad Sahab for composing "Mann Tadpat Hari Darshan Ko" on the tenets of *Raaga Malkauns*. The awareness about *Malkauns* increased from there. Even those who do not understand *raaga*s, know *Malkauns*. Rafi Sahab has sung it with such excellence.

'I met Rafi Sahab in 1977 on the occasion of his nephew's wedding. All the while we were together, he went on complimenting me and I was praising him.'

Lekh Tandon

'It is sad that I did not get enough years to work with him, but I am happy that some of my best works have been with the legend, Mohammed Rafi. In fact, my first film *Professor* (a Shammi Kapoor starrer), released in 1962, and had Rafi as the male playback singer. During the composition of the songs, producer FC Mehra and music director Shankar-Jaikishan decided that the male singer had to be Rafi as the film had a very emotional story. Rafi knew exactly how to bring out the emotions of Shammi with the right modulation of his voice. "Aye Gulbadan" and "Khuli Palak Mein Jhootha Gussa" were the two memorable Rafi solos in the film. The two duets with Lata, "Main Chali Main Chali" and "Awaaz Deke Humein Tum Bulaao" became equally popular. Incidentally the film won four Filmfare nominations, of which "Aye Gulbadan" was nominated for the Best Male Playback Singer and Hasrat Jaipuri was nominated in the category for Best Lyrics.

'The roaring success of *Professor* motivated producer FC Mehra to maintain the same team for his next film *Prince* (1969). The magic of Shammi Kapoor-Shankar-Jaikishan-Rafi once again came out with flying colours. Three solos, a duet and a group song, with Rafi as the male voice, made this film one of the top grossers of the year. This time, I was absolutely sure that it was Rafi Sahab's voice that had worked wonders.'

Ram Mukherjee

Ram Mukherjee, the filmmaker, is also a key member of the famous Mukherjee family. He has made some memorable films like *Hum Hindustani* (1960) and *Leader* (1964).

'Though Kishore Kumar was my *mama*, I preferred Rafi Sahab as a male playback singer. He would stand beside me with folded arms and say, "*Main aap ke liye kya kar sakta hoon?* (What can I do for you?)" He would instruct Zaheer, "Never ask money from Mukherjee*da* and accept whatever he gives." With his songs in a film I would be confident that the film was surely going to be a hit. Rafi Sahab's association with a film meant lowering the risk of investment. His voice was well-attuned to Joy Mukherjee's (paternal cousin) on-screen presence and was largely responsible for all the recognition that he got in the industry.

'Each song he delivered for *Leader* (1964) was with absolute understanding of the situation; for instance, the way he conveys the condition of a joyfully drunk Dilip Kumar, a teetotaller in the film who had been forced to drink. The song in question is "Mujhe Duniyawaalon Sharaabi Na Samjho." For the same film, he playfully sings "Humein se mohabbat humein se ladai, arey maar daala duhaayi duhaayi" where Dilip Sahab is teasing his on-screen love Vyjayanthimala for whom he also sings the immensely romantic "Tere Husn Ki Kya Tareef Karoon."'

Sawan Kumar Tak

Sawan Kumar Tak, the filmmaker came to the city of dreams in 1956 as an aspiring actor. He later evolved into a filmmaker, making his debut with *Naunihal* (1967), a film remembered till today for its timeless music. The song 'Meri Awaaz Suno,' composed by Madan Mohan, with lyrics by

Kaifi Azmi and sung by Rafi, paid tribute to Pandit Jawaharlal Nehru (who died in 1964).

Tak narrated how, while recording the song, Rafi would weep bitterly after every fourth or fifth line. 'As a producer with restricted budget, my concern was the limited spool tape we had for the recording! This happened eight times, much to my chagrin. But, once the recording was over, the end result was electrifying and all my resentment vanished. Every pair of eyes went moist when this song was played on the silver screen,' he said.

Sawan Kumar Tak was also a lyricist. The first song he penned, 'Teri Galiyon Mein Na Rakhenge Kadam Aaj Ke Baad' (*Hawas*, 1974) had an interesting background story. The filmmaker related, 'I was a great admirer of Majrooh Sultanpuri and I had approached him to write the lyrics for my film, *Hawas*. We discussed things till lunch and then finally, he quoted a price that was beyond what I could afford as I was yet recovering from the failure of my previous film, *Gomti Ke Kinare* (1972). I requested him to reduce the fees but he was inflexible. I was extremely sad and headed home disappointed. I was so frustrated that I told myself, *Teri galiyon main na rakhenge kadam aaj ke baad* (I will never ever step in your lane, after today). I repeated this line to my wife Usha, who was the music director of the film. She said that this line was perfect for the song for *Hawas*. She instantly gave tune to the statement and it became a song. This was my first attempt as a lyricist and the song went on to become a superhit in the voice of Rafi Sahab.'

He learnt from Rafi how often this song featured in the *farmaish* (request) list of music lovers, during his music concerts. Once Rafi visited him at about 11 p.m. with sweets and gifts and said, '*Mubarak ho, Mubarak ho!* (Congratulations!)' It so happenned that Rafi had just returned from one of his international tours.

The filmmaker said, 'Wherever he went, people wanted him to sing the song. Rafi Sahab had forgotten to carry the notations of the song on this tour, but the demand for the song was so high that he asked Zaheer to get hold of a record of the song immediately. He heard it, rehearsed it, and then sang it on stage in his usual inimitable manner. Rafi Sahab was so touched by the response that he came and shared his happiness with me and my wife, Usha.'

He remembers the discipline and devotion that Rafi carried with him into every recording session, 'If the singer was Rafi Sahab, every song would be well-rehearsed, leaving no room for a music director to complain. Often, he used to skip lunch if he had back-to-back recordings. He never kept a producer or a music director waiting, though at times the producers with a small budget could not even afford to pay his fee!'

Uttam Singh

Uttam Singh spoke candidly about his interactions with Rafi Sahab, 'If he ever saw me or Bhupinder*ji* in recordings, he would call for *maalpua* (Indian pancake), *halwa* and *poori* (sweet dish with fried bread made with refined flour) and we three used to feast together. Rafi Sahab was a real foodie who not only loved eating good food but also enjoyed treating others. I still remember him serving us *halwa poori* with a smile and saying that it felt like we were sitting in Punjab.

'When I was very young I used to love the song "Suhani Raat Dhal Chuki" (*Dulari*, 1949); in fact, the song used to haunt me. I saw Rafi Sahab for the first time when I was about 16 and was completely awestruck. I prayed that I should get just one chance to meet him and get his blessings. My prayers were heard and I got the opportunity to work with him as an arranger.'

Bhupinder Singh

The singer reminisced, 'In the years I was establishing myself as a musician and a singer in the industry, Rafi Sahab was at the prime of his career; for many years we met almost every day in the studios. On meeting everyday, the first thing he would do is give a warm hug—Punjabi style, the warmth of which I remember even today. If it was an evening recording session, he would tell his driver to get *halwa poori* for Bhupi*ji*. In fact, that's how the whole industry started addressing me as Bhupi*ji*. Very few people know that he even gave me lessons in singing.

'We always used to talk in Punjabi and even shared jokes in Punjabi. I sang the first film song of my life with Rafi Sahab. The song was, "Hoke Majboor Mujhe Usne Bulaaya Hoga" (*Haqeeqat*, 1964), a film by Chetan Anand. It was a strange combination of nervousness and joy to be singing my career's first playback song with a galaxy of legends—Mohammed Rafi, Manna Dey and Talat Mehmood. Besides being the first playback song of my career, it was a memorable instance because I shared the microphone with Rafi Sahab. He infused a lot of confidence in me; spoke to me in Punjabi and in the process erased all my fears with his warm and friendly attitude. I completely forgot, for that moment, that I was a new singer.'

Anup Jalota

Known for his expertise in rendering devotional songs, Anup Jalota is acknowledged that it was Rafi who popularised *bhajan*s in films and hence among the masses. 'Some of the best Hindi spiritual songs are found in the voice of Rafi. He could sing devotional songs in different languages and his pronunciations would be immaculate. His soulful voice has stirred millions of hearts over the decades.'

The singer still cherishes memories of the opportunity he got to sing with Rafi; a *bhajan* for *Shirdi Ke Sai Baba* (1977), a Manoj Kumar film. He admits that while he was visibly nervous on seeing Mohammed Rafi from such proximity, a warm remark from the legend, '*Tu toh Punjab ka sher hai, tujhe kis baat ka dar…aur main bhi Punjabi.* (You are the lion from Punjab and what do you have to fear…and I am also from Punjab.)' made him a perennial fan of the latter's simplicity.

Anup Jalota described that Rafi and he were of almost the same height and like a child he avoided looking straight into Rafi's eyes while at the mike.

He recollected, 'In those days the producers would specifically want *bhajan*s in the voice of Rafi Sahab. Besides film *bhajan*s Rafi Sahab has sung *bhajan*s for many private albums which became very popular. For instance, a series of Krishna *bhajan*s, composed by Khayyam Sahab, was sung to perfection by Rafi Sahab. I repeatedly receive requests to sing these *bhajan*s in my concerts now.'

As for his film *bhajans*, Anup Jalota pointed out, 'In "Madhuban Mein Radhika," for instance, which is based on *Raaga Hameer*, the *taan* (a virtuoso technique used in the vocal performance of a *raaga* in Hindustani classical music) was sung by Ustaad Naiyaz Ahmed Khan. The song is a classic exception where the lyrics are in the voice of one singer and the *taan* in the voice of another. Besides a flawless rendition of a difficult *taan* by Ustaad Naiyaz Ahmed Khan, the song also exemplifies the versatility of Rafi's voice and is a song that most singers, till today, find extremely difficult to sing.'

Pankaj Udhas

'Once, during a live performance at the Brabourne Stadium, Bombay, where music directors such as SD Burman and Kalyan*ji*-Anand*ji* were also present, Shankar-Jaikishan started the show with the song "Badan Pe Sitaare." Vyjayanthimala just walked onto the stage and as she passed by, Rafi Sahab whistled! The audience, for a moment, was just stunned. Was it the same introvert Rafi they knew? The whole atmosphere in the stadium was electrifying. Somewhere within Rafi Sahab there was definitely a talented actor, who helped him to be the "Emperor of Playback Singing." The man who could create magical moments with his voice was not only an excellent playback singer but also a phenomenal *playback actor*.

'Rafi Sahab took away the very essence of playback singing from the planet with him.'

Hariharan

Hariharan is considered by many as the pioneer of fusion music. 'I have always believed in how Plato has defined music and the power it possesses—Music is a moral law. It gives soul to the universe, wings to the mind, flight to the imagination, and charm and gaiety to life and to everything.'

Hariharan commended that Rafi's versatility is inspirational, 'For a singer to successfully sing across the different genres, shows his sincerity and commitment to music. Rafi Sahab was a gift to us; one of the most treasured possessions of the Indian film industry.'

Mohammed Aziz

'I have been inspired by Rafi Sahab all my life. And though I have made constant endeavour to do justice to his songs, as I have sung them on stage, but no singer can match up to Rafi Sahab's singing,' said Mohammed Aziz.

He also felt blessed to have been the voice for a song created on Rafi's life. 'Amitabh Bachchan was to sing the song on stage in memory of Rafi Sahab in the film *Krodh* (1990). I am told that the entire team of this film, comprising composers Laxmikant-Pyarelal, lyricist Anand Bakshi, director Shashilal Nair and producer Pappu Verma, sat down to deliberate on the singer who would be able to do justice to this song. They ultimately selected me. It was a moment of great pride for me. It's like Rafi Sahab bestowing his blessings on me. Till today, I can't believe I was the chosen one to sing that song.'

The song was.

Na fankaar tujhsa tere baad aaya,
Mohammed Rafi tu bahut yaad aaya,
Suro ki surili woh parwaaz teri,
Bahut khubsoorat thi awaaz teri.
Zamaane ko jisne deewaana banaya,
Mohammed Rafi tu bahut yaad aaya.
(There has never been an artiste like you,
Mohammed Rafi, you are remembered even today,
Your flight of voice was more melodious than the musical notes,
Immensely beautiful was your voice.
One that was every music lover's choice,
Mohammed Rafi, you are remembered even today.)

Shabbir Kumar

The void created by Rafi's sudden demise compelled music directors to look for voices that were *Rafi-like*. Shabbir Kumar was one such find. He started his career with the show, 'Ek Shaam Rafi Ke Naam,' in 1980, the same year the nation mourned the loss of the legendary singer.

The singer recalled a time when as a teenager he waited for hours for a glimpse of Rafi at Famous Studios. He was a deft hand at sketching and had made a portrait of the legendary singer which he handed over to the latter. Another chance to see his idol came in 1977, during a police welfare show in Ahmedabad where Rafi was performing.

It was Usha Khanna, the music director, who trusted Shabbir's musical chords and gave him a break in *Tajurba* (1981). Producer-director Manmohan Desai, who was a great admirer of Rafi, recommended Shabbir to music director duo Laxmikant-Pyarelal, who got him to sing for some of their compositions in the films *Main Inteqaam Loonga* (1982) and *Coolie* (1983). In *Coolie*, all the seven songs were in Shabbir's voice—two solos and five duets.

On July 31, 1980, Shabbir tuned on the radio and was stunned to learn that Rafi had passed away. He left for Bombay to catch a final glimpse of his idol. He touched his idol's feet for blessings as they placed Rafi in the *kabr* (grave).

Jyoti Matwankar

Jyoti is one of the fortunate singers who have had the opportunity to sing their first duets with Rafi. The song in question was 'Mehfil Mein Tera Diwaana Aaya Hai' from *Raakh Aur Chingari* (released in 1982).

Jyoti recalled that during the 1971 Indo-Pak war, her husband was at the warfront in the Poonch district of Jammu and Kashmir. The wives of the armed-forces men would be extremely tense and in anticipation of the slightest information, would be tuned in to the radio all the time. 'All India Radio would broadcast some soulful renditions of Rafi Sahab and it is inexplicable how wives, like me, could connect with every single word that Rafi Sahab sang in songs such as "Hum Laaye Hain Toofan Se Kashti Nikaal Ke" (*Jagriti*, 1954), "Kar Chale Hum Fida Jaano Tan Saathiyon" (*Haqeeqat*, 1964), "Apni Azaadi Ko Hum Hargiz Mita Sakte Nahin" (*Leader*, 1964).

'Rafi Sahab was a pure soul and this purity could be traced even in his favourite attire—white shirt, white trousers with white footwear.'

Sudesh Bhosle

The singer was a close associate of Kishore Kumar. He recalled, 'Kishore*da* would make it a point to sing at least one Rafi-song among the first five songs with which he commenced a stage show. He would always start with the preamble, "Now, I would like to present a song of my friend Rafi." He loved to sing "Mann Re Tu Kaahe Na Dheer Dhare" in his own inimitable style. Though Kishore*da* was seen to be jocular most of the times, he would be extremely serious on some occasions. He would categorically say, "Sudesh, you are a very good mimicry artiste. But remember one thing; never disrespect the three highly respectable personalities, Saigal Sahab, Sanjeev Kumar and Rafi Sahab with your jokes on stage." I have always abided by it.'

This again highlights the mutual admiration that existed between Mohammed Rafi and Kishore Kumar.

Roop Kumar Rathod

Roop Kumar Rathod, son of late Pandit Chaturbhuj Rathod, treasures Rafi's legacy of songs and its various nuances are a lesson he learns from—his breath control, his effortlessness even in the trickiest of compositions.

He pointed out, 'Note the song, "Suhaani Raat Dhal Chuki" (*Dulari*, 1949) where in the second *antara* he offhandedly delivers a long *alaap* followed by an eloquently packed phrase, "*Tadap rahein hai hum yahaan... tumhaare intezaar mein*." No matter how many times one listens to it, it is hard to identify where he took even a slight breath. This is the reason why such songs are not composed anymore; because there isn't a Mohammed Rafi today, who can deliver such songs. Rafi Sahab did it all those years ago and that too without any kind of digital intervention.'

Himesh Reshammiya

Himesh, as a child, was fortunate to meet Rafi along with his father, Vipin Reshammiya. Though the memories are faint, he cherishes the blessings even today, 'I consider that day auspicious when Rafi Sahab had picked me up in his arms and literally invoked music in me. I was too young to remember this incident but my father told me about this and I have experienced the influence of his blessings.'

Himesh shared his views on Rafi's comeback in the late '70s and finds it a source of immense motivation. 'Most people just give up and lose hope when they go through a lean period after being at the top. It is not easy to accept the fact that the same industry which treats you like a king in your heydays overlooks you when success is not on your side. But Rafi Sahab did not lose his zest and swept the industry off its feet with his remarkable songs in *Amar Akbar Anthony* and that too for a young actor like Rishi Kapoor, which illustrated that genuine talent never fades.'

Kailash Kher

The singer, known for his soulful Sufi renditions, described the legendary Mohammed Rafi in his own unique way:

'*Rafi Sahab behadd imaandari se dusron ke hriday ke udgaaron ko apne dwara pradarshit kar paaye. Jin sangeetkaron ne Rafi Sahab se filmon mein gaane gawaaye, voh khud nahin jante ki unhone kisse kya kara liya... Unki gaayeki apko bhavsaagar paar karne ke tarike bata deti thi bas kaano ke dwaara...* (He was capable of musically portraying the heartfelt emotions with extraordinary sincerity in his songs. The music directors who made him sing are themselves unaware of what they have been able to extract from Rafi Sahab... Through his voice he could make you meditate...just open your ears and ruminate and you could tread the path of liberation...)

'*Unke* singing pattern *ko kuch shabdo mein* limit *karna uuchit nahin hoga... Agar* soulful *kahein, to bahut se* singers *ki gaayaki* soulful *thi... Kishore Kumar, Manna Dey ki bhi thi, kahin na kahin sabhi ne* soulful *kaam kiya hai... To phir Mohammed Rafi hi kyu iss duniya se niraale hain? Jab woh gaate the toh aisa lagta tha jaise gaane ke liye hi paida huye hain aur yugon yugon se gaate aa rahe ho...joh bhi gaate the shat-pratishat gaate the, chahe bhajan ho, shabad ho, ya qawwali ho... Unki gaayaki filmon se bhi badi ho gayi hai...* (His singing pattern cannot be limited in a few words. If we talk about soulful singing, there are many singers who sang soulfully, like Kishore Kumar and Manna Dey. But how is Mohammed

Rafi unique? A listener feels that he was born into this world to only sing; whatever he sang, he sang it to perfection, be it a *bhajan*, a *shabad* or a *qawwali*. There are innumerable instances where his songs are bigger than the films concerned.)

'*Jahaan shabd aur vichaar maun ho jaaye, wahaan se prarambh hota hai Mohammed Rafi ki gaayaki ka safar...* (Where resonance and silence become unanimous, where words become secondary, where thought fades into insignificance; from there begins the musical journey of Mohammed Rafi.)'

Javed Ali

Javed Ali grew up in a musical atmosphere with his father, Ustaad Hamid Hussain, a known *qawwali* singer. Javed Ali admired Rafi's vocal range and considers him as his role model in playback singing.

'An aspect that even a well-trained singer can learn from Rafi Sahab is voice control—how he modulated his breath, his voice, the throw—to match the appropriate mood of the song. In whichever range he sang—low, medium or high—there was never a distortion; rather his voice seemed to bloom in the higher octaves.

'There are some singers who sing from their throat and some who sing from their *naabhi* (navel—implying the depth of the voice). Rafi was one such singer who used to sing from the *naabhi*. If one listens to his songs, especially the *bhajans* and other religious compositions, one can easily trace the *naad*—the cosmic sound—echoing in his voice.

'From my experience as a jury member in reality shows like *Sa Re Ga Ma Pa Li'l Champs*, I can tell you that in today's world, if the younger generation is opting to sing Rafi Sahab's songs; it only shows how big an artiste he was. Our grandfathers have sung his songs, our fathers have, we have and our children and grandchildren will continue to sing his songs.'

Sonu Nigam

'Rafi Sahab is my musical father. He forever holds my finger,' acknowledged Sonu Nigam. He set himself in the Rafi mould at a tender age. He emphasised, 'I fell in love with music when I was three. Ever since, we have been in love—music and I—nothing has ever come between us.'

Vocalist Agam Nigam, Sonu's father, did a number of stage performances in his youth. As a performer, his quest for variety drew him to Rafi's vast repertoire. It was only natural that these Rafi songs were played at the Nigam home most of the time. During one of Agam Nigam's stage performances, four-year-old Sonu walked up to his father and insisted that he wanted to sing along with him. The song was 'Kya Hua Tera Waada,' a Rafi-song from *Hum Kisise Kum Nahin* (1977). Though Sonu had never been on stage before, he grabbed the mike and began singing '…*bhoolega dil jis din tumhe, wo din zindagi ka akhri din hoga*.' The audience was in raptures. Soon it became a regular practice for Sonu to sing at least one *antara* with his father during most of his performances. When this graduated to singing complete songs, Agam Nigam realised that his son was really gifted and decided to give him serious vocal training.

It is intriguing that Sonu concentrated on singing Rafi's songs rather than that of any other singer from that era, especially when his formative years, the '70s and '80s, were the decades which saw the upsurge of Kishore Kumar. The young singer opined, 'Choosing the mentor can make all the difference between success and failure in what one wants to achieve. I wanted to be a versatile playback singer and so chose Rafi Sahab as my musical mentor, and I have never regretted it since.'

Commenting on the oft seen trend that today's generation prefers to sing Kishore Kumar's songs rather than Rafi's songs on stage or in reality shows, Sonu said, 'They have been brought up on the popular songs of the '70s and '80s and hence, Kishore*da*'s songs are more popular. Rafi Sahab's songs are more difficult to sing due to their pitch and classical base, for instance, "Madhuban Mein Radhika Naache Re" or "Akhiyaan Sang Akhiyaan Laagi." Do you think today's generation can do full justice to Rafi Sahab's songs? I perceived that Rafi Sahab's voice belonged to a purest level compared to most of the leading singers of that era.'

Epilogue

Writing this book on the life of a legend such as Mohammed Rafi was an interesting journey. Anecdotes from the various sources added up to create a beautiful picture of a great human being who had not only captured the hearts of millions with his songs but who had touched the hearts of his colleagues and friends and those he came in contact with, sometimes quite accidentally. They all vouched for the singer's benevolence and humility.

It all began with a journey to Kotla Sultan Singh, a small village, 24 kilometres from Amritsar in Punjab. As Shahid *bhai* and I landed at Amritsar, we were amazed to see a host of Rafi-fans waiting to receive us with bouquets and garlands. Gurdeep Singh drove us all the way to Kotla Sultan Singh, a journey during which he left us in no doubt that he was one of Mohammed Rafi's greatest fans.

At the village, Sardar Kundan Singh Samra, was ecstatic to meet Shahid Rafi, the son of his childhood friend, Pheeko, and we were treated to *lassi* (a sweet or savoury Indian drink made from a yogurt or buttermilk base with water); I was actually served the tallest glass when I told them I was making an attempt to put together Rafi's life story. To our delight, he had an impeccable memory. He could chronologically narrate most of the incidents of Rafi's childhood. We also met Sardar Bakshish Singh Samra, another childhood friend of Rafi who upon learning the reason for our visit, insisted that we must highlight that his friend was no ordinary human being; he was a messenger of God. There were more surprises: at the school Rafi attended, the headmaster took us to a classroom where Rafi used to attend classes and where the children now sang, 'Yeh Desh Hai Veer Jawaanon Ka' for us. At the end of the song, a seven-year-old said to us with great pride, 'Do you know who sang this song, it's him! (*Pointing to a framed photograph of Rafi on the wall.*) And he used to study in this school.'

An attempt to sketch out the life of the legend also meant reaching out to Rafi's only living sibling, younger brother, Mohammed Siddique, who lives in Lahore. Samina, a documentary filmmaker from Pakistan, helped us trace Siddique *Chacha* (paternal uncle) and his interview was captured on video as we were connected on phone. It gave us a glimpse of the boy who came to Bombay with dreams in his eyes.

Later, as we walked up the staircase to the second floor of Alka Mansion—in Bhendi Bazar—to the one-bedroom home that Rafi shared with Hameed *Bhai* some seven decades ago, it was not difficult to visualise the time when the two young men had taken the first tentative steps into Bombay with the hope of realising a long cherished dream. Not much has changed; the place still retains its original character. Nasim Bano, the current lady of the house, informed us that the building that once housed one of the greatest legends of Indian music is in the process of being demolished.

A major challenge was to get a clear picture of what happened on July 31, 1980, at the Bombay Hospital, particularly after his family had to leave his mortal remains there for the night.

Very little facts could be retrieved from the old records as 1980 was not the era of computers, and written records had fallen prey to the ravages of time. That is till a gentleman from the accounts division mentioned an elderly staff member who might be of some help. I could finally trace him and learned that he worked as a ward boy at the very hospital in 1980.

He remembered the night when Rafi passed away, urging me on to Uttam Singh (the only name he remembered from the three who were at the hospital that night) who was present with Rafi Sahab's mortal remains.

Another interesting serendipity connected us to Dr Chandiramani, who had been called on that fateful night when Rafi passed away.

It so happened that Anupriya mentioned that she had noticed a Dr Chandiramani's clinic in Bandra. We called the clinic and got connected to the senior most Chandiramani. On being asked if he knew Rafi, the aged doctor seemed to read the question in our mind and told us that he was the doctor who was called to check on Rafi when he had literally collapsed on July 31, 1980.

Meeting Rafi Sahab's colleagues was a major challenge as many of them are particularly media shy. For instance, it took over two months and more than 20 calls to convince Suman Kalyanpur for an interview. Suman Kalyanpur finally agreed. Charul Agny, her daughter, revealed that this was the first time her mother had opened up about a contemporary, that too a legend of that era.

It was not easy to track down Shamshad Begum and even more difficult to convince this elusive legend for an interview. Had it not been for Usha Ratra, her only daughter, this interview, which was her last heart-to-heart conversation about her career and Rafi Sahab, would not have been possible.

There were other breakthroughs, like a conversation with the legendary singer Manna Dey; the legend had specified that it should be a short conversation but in actual fact, it went on for over an hour when the singer began to talk about his contemporary Mohammed Rafi, the man with whom he had shared the mike and stage on several occasions.

On February 3, 2011, at the premier show of the coloured version of the evergreen film *Hum Dono* (1961), Dev Sahab enthusiastically explained that he had insisted to music director Jaidev that Rafi should be his playback voice.

As the song 'Main Zindagi Ka Saath Nibhata Chala Gaya' played on-screen, he hummed along and remarked, 'This is the magic I was talking about; this song in the serene voice of Rafi has been the philosophy of my life and my inspiration. This is what has kept me going on and on from 1941.'

On visiting Shammi Kapoor it was difficult to accept the fact that the iconic Yahoo-man was confined to a wheelchair. But his unbeatable spirit took over as soon as he started sharing his experiences about Rafi Sahab.

Joy Mukherjee narrated his close association with Rafi, overflowing with gratitude for the voice that established him as the romantic hero of the '60s. Little did we know that this was to be our last interaction; Joy Mukherjee passed away exactly a month later.

There were other memorable interactions. The one with Khayyam Sahab was an opportunity to revisit history, when the Partition divided the population of Punjab between India and Pakistan; like Rafi, Khayyam was born in undivided Punjab (Rahon, a village in Nawanshahr District). Both the musical geniuses had showed a strong inclination towards music right from childhood. The interview began with a birthday cake; it was Khayyam Sahab's 85th birthday. An appointed 30 minutes tête-à-tête with the composer went on for hours where Khayyam spoke about the Golden Era, when Mohammed Rafi ruled the recording studios.

The interviews with Rishi Kapoor and Randhir Kapoor, sons of Raj Kapoor, took place at the RK Studios—the place that once witnessed its creator, the legendary Raj Kapoor, seamlessly juggle the roles of actor, director and producer. As Shahid Rafi and I waited amongst the banners, vintage posters and props of another time for the Kapoor brothers to join us, the ambience grew on us, so much so that we almost felt as if we would find Raj Kapoor himself sitting inside the studio office, when a voice called out saying, '*Kapoor Sahab aap ke intezaar kar rahe hain*. (Kapoor Sahab is waiting for you.)' The moment passed just as fleetingly as it had arrived.

Rafi belonged to the masses and his popularity continued unabated even three decades after he passed on; this fact was brought home to me again in the most unusual of circumstances.

On August 12, 2011, on a visit to Kolkata's New Market, I parked my car and walked down the crowded area. The breeze was infused with the aroma of *biryani* from Aminia Restaurant. Following the fragrance, I noticed a *paan* (betel leaf) shop with a huge cloth banner which read Taj Mahal Paan Shop; proprietor, Mohammed Munir Uddin. What stopped me in my tracks were the huge framed photographs of Mohammed Rafi in the shop. I approached the small boy at the counter and enquired about Munir Uddin. Since it was Ramadan, I was told that his father would come only after 9 p.m.

At close quarters, I also noticed the enlarged laminated newspaper cuttings on the walls. They were articles from different magazines and newspapers which had interviews of Munir Uddin. Each article eulogised him as a great fan of Mohammed Rafi. An old article spoke of his collection of Rafi-songs and how his *paan* shop played only the songs of the musical legend all day. Noticing my interest in the articles the boy proudly pointed out a huge photograph of the singer with his father. The pride was evident in his eyes.

The next day I reached the *paan* shop 10 minutes ahead of the appointed hour. Exactly at eight, a lean man, in his 70s, came and introduced himself as Munir Uddin. He related that 40 years ago, he was a spot boy at Filmistan, Bombay. (He had come to Bombay from Calcutta in search of a job.) In 1972, he met Rafi, who had come to the sets to meet Dilip Kumar, who was shooting for *Dastaan* (1972). From then on Rafi used to pat his shoulder every time he visited the studio.

A few years later, he shifted to his hometown, Calcutta, and opened a *paan* shop. Rafi visited the city seven years later. Munir Uddin learnt that Rafi had asked the organisers to find him. The photograph was taken to capture that golden moment, the greatest moment of Munir's life. After that, Rafi would inevitably ask for his special *paan*, whenever he visited his shop. Munir related how once Rafi had walked into his shop and said, '*Jaldi se ek paan dena, gala kharab hai aur mujhe show mein gaana hai.* (Quickly give me a betel leaf, my throat is bad and I need to sing at the show.)' He gave him a *paan* with cloves and cardamom. Rafi had it and instantly said his throat felt better. Munir packed a few more *paans* for him. Maybe the sincere love of Munir worked more than the *paan*.

Munir's eldest son Mohammed Javed took me through their huge collection of Rafi's songs. Munir offered me a *paan* and said, '*Allah ne Rafi Sahab ko kum umr di aur yehi maksad se bheja ki, geet gaao, sab ke dil jeeto aur chaley aao.* (The Almighty sent Rafi Sahab with a short life. He was sent to sing and win the hearts of people and then return to his heavenly abode.)'

That was the moment my mind was made. I would dedicate this book to the fans of Rafi, who exist in the lanes and bylanes of every city in India and beyond.

Awards and Honours
Mohammed Rafi

Civilian Awards

1948 Silver medal from then Indian Prime Minister Jawaharlal Nehru, on the first anniversary of the Indian Independence Day, for 'Suno Suno Aye Duniya Waalon Bapu Ki Yeh Amar Kahaani,' a four-part song written by Rajinder Krishan and composed by Husanlal-Bhagatram. The song mourned the death of the 'Father of the Nation.'

1967 Padma Shri Award, India's fourth highest civilian award, from the Government of India.

National Film Awards

1977 'Kya Hua Tera Waada' (*Hum Kisise Kum Nahin*), music by RD Burman and lyrics by Majrooh Sultanpuri.

Filmfare Awards

The Filmfare Awards did not initially have a distinct category for playback singers, since its inception in 1953. The contribution of Rafi however can be traced in the awards that were won by the music directors of the films he was associated with; this is for the period, 1953-57.

1953 Best Music, composed by Naushad for *Baiju Bawra*.

1958 Best Music, composed by OP Nayyar for *Naya Daur*.

It was in 1958 that a distinct category for Best Singer was introduced; a common award for both male and female playback singers.

1960 'Chaudhvin Ka Chand' (*Chaudhvin Ka Chand*), music by Ravi and lyrics by Shakeel Badayuni.

1961 'Teri Pyaari Pyaari Soorat Ko' (*Sasural*), music by Shankar-Jaikishan and lyrics by Hasrat Jaipuri.

1964 'Chahoonga Main Tujhe Saanjh Savere' (*Dosti*), music by Laxmikant-Pyarelal and lyrics by Majrooh Sultanpuri.

1966 'Bahaaron Phool Barsaao' (*Sooraj*), music by Shankar-Jaikishan and lyrics by Hasrat Jaipuri.

It was in 1967 that the Best Singer Award was split into two categories—Best Male and Best Female Playback Singer.

1968 'Dil Ke Jharoke Mein' (*Brahmachari*), music by Shankar-Jaikishan and lyrics by Hasrat Jaipuri.

1977 'Kya Hua Tera Waada' (*Hum Kisise Kum Nahin*), music by RD Burman and lyrics by Majrooh Sultanpuri.

Other songs nominated for Filmfare Awards

1961 'Husnwale Tera Jawab Nahin' (*Gharana*), music by Ravi and lyrics by Shakeel Badayuni.

1962 'Aye Gulbadan Aye Gulbadan' (*Professor*), music by Shankar-Jaikishan and lyrics by Hasrat Jaipuri.

1963 'Mere Mehboob Tujhe' (*Mere Mehboob*), music by Naushad Ali and lyrics by Shakeel Badayuni.

1965 'Chhoo Lene Do Nazuk Hothon Ko' (*Kaajal*), music by Ravi and lyrics by Sahir Ludhianvi.

1968 'Mein Gaaon Tum Sojaao' (*Brahmachari*), music by Shankar-Jaikishan and lyrics by Shailendra.

1969 'Badi Mastani Hai' (*Jeene Ki Raah*), music by Laxmikant-Pyarelal and lyrics by Anand Bakshi.

1970 'Khilona Jaan Kar' (*Khilona*), music by Laxmikant-Pyarelal and lyrics by Anand Bakshi.

1973 'Hum Ko To Jaan Se Pyaari' (*Naina*), music by Shankar Jaikishan and lyrics by Hasrat Jaipuri.

1974 'Achha Hi Huva Dil Toot Gaya' (*Maa Bahen Aur Biwi*), music by Sharda and lyrics by Qamar Jalalabadi and Vedpal Varma.

1977 'Parda Hai Parda' (*Amar Akbar Anthony*), music by Laxmikant-Pyarelal and lyrics by Anand Bakshi.

1978 'Aadmi Musaafir Hai' (*Apnapan*), music by Laxmikant-Pyarelal and lyrics by Anand Bakshi.

1979 'Chalo Re Doli Uthao Kahaar' (*Jaani Dushman*), music by Laxmikant-Pyarelal and lyrics by Varma Malik.

1980 'Mere Dost Kissa Yeh' (*Dostana*), music by Laxmikant-Pyarelal and lyrics by Anand Bakshi.

1980 'Dard-e-dil Dard-e-jigar' (*Karz*), music by Laxmikant-Pyarelal and lyrics by Anand Bakshi.

1980 'Maine Poocha Chand Se' (*Abdullah*), music by RD Burman and lyrics by Anand Bakshi.

Bengal Film Journalists' Association Awards

1957 *Tumsa Nahin Dekha*, music by OP Nayyar and lyrics by Majrooh Sultanpuri.

1965 *Dosti*, music by Laxmikant-Pyarelal and lyrics by Majrooh Sultanpuri.

1966 *Arzoo*, music by Shankar-Jaikishan and lyrics by Hasrat Jaipuri.

Film World Magazine Awards

1974 'Teri Galiyon Mein Na Rakhenge Qadam' (*Hawas*), music by Usha Khanna and lyrics by Sawan Kumar Tak.

Sur Sringar Awards

1964 'Mann Re Tu Kaahe Na Dheer Dhare' (*Chitralekha*), music by Roshan and lyrics by Sahir Ludhianvi.

Posthumous and Honourary Recognitions

Seven Hindi films have been dedicated to Mohammed Rafi in their title credits: *Naseeb* (1981), *Desh Premee* (1982), *Coolie* (1983), *Mard* (1985), *Allah Rakha* (1986), *Aas Paas* (1981) and *Heeralal-Pannalal* (1999).

On January 7, 2001, Rafi was honoured as the 'Best Singer of the Millennium' by Hero Honda and *Stardust* magazine.

In 2007, the *Times of India* released a special 12-page supplement, to mark the 60 years of Indian Independence. *Makers & Shakers*, as the supplement was called featured SUPER 60; eminent politicians, philosophers, social reformers, industrialists, legal luminaries, scientists, spiritual *gurus* and dignitaries from the film fraternity, who have contributed immensely to India's history. One of the *Makers & Shakers* selected from the music fraternity was Mohammed Rafi. He was credited for changing the face of playback singing.

In June 2010, Rafi was voted the most popular playback singer in the *Outlook Music Poll*, conducted by *Outlook* magazine, along with Lata Mangeshkar. The same poll voted Rafi's 'Mann Re Tu Kahe Na Dheer Dhare' (*Chitralekha*, 1964), as the number one song.

On May 15, 2003, the Department of Posts, Government of India, issued a set of postage stamps, to honour four great musical legends of yesteryears: Mohammed Rafi, Kishore Kumar, Mukesh and Hemanta Kumar.

For a detailed discography, please visit the following websites:

http://en.wikipedia.org/wiki/List_of_songs_recorded_by_Mohammed_Rafi

http://rateyourmusic.com/artist/mohammed_rafi

http://www.discogs.com/artist/386904-Mohammed-Rafi

Appendix

1. Rafi's renditions for lesser known music composers.

Year	Film	Composer	Song
1964	*Cha Cha Cha*	Iqbal Qureshi	'Subah Na Aayee'
1965	*Sangram*	Lala-Assar-Sattar	'Main Toh Tere Haseen Khayaalon Mein'
1965	*Adventures Of Robinhood*	GS Kohli	'Maana Mere Haseen Sanam'
1965	*Chor Darwaza*	Frank Fernandes	'Tum Jahaan Jaaoge Mujhko Bhi Wahaan Paaoge'
1974	*Thokar*	Shyam*ji* Ghanshyam*ji*	'Apni Aankhon Mein Basaa Kar Koi Ikraar Karoon'
1975	*Mrig Trishna*	Shambu Sen	'Nav Kalpana Nav Roop Se'
1962	*Naqli Nawaab*	Baabul	'Tum Poochte Ho'
1960	*Lambe Haath*	GS Kohli	'Pyar Ki Raah Dikha Duniya Ko'
1964	*Punar Milan*	C Arjun	'Paas Baitho Tabiyat Behel Jaayegi'
1978	*Pal Do Pal Ka Saath*	Shyam Sagar	'O Chupke Se Peeche Se Aake'

2. The information below provide a glimpse of Rafi's career, when he and Lata Mangeshkar were not singing together.

Year	Total Hindi film songs	Total solos	Duets with Lata Mangeshkar	Duets with Asha Bhosle	Duets with Suman Kalyanpur
1958	173	63	10	52	3

1959	179	68	27	41	6
1960	237	91	30	58	14
1961	154	62	24	31	14
1962	150	61	20	38	14
1963	181	93	24	35	9
1964	204	120	7	37	23
1965	159	107		27	9
1966	174	98	5	39	7
1967	139	84	12	18	6
5 year average (1958-63)			22.5	42.5	10
10 year average (1958-67)			17.6	37.6	10.5

Duets with Lata Mangeshkar that were released between 1963 and 1967 were mostly recorded before 1963. The information above gives a clear picture of Rafi's career in conjunction with the three main female singers of that period.

3. Rafi's overall career

Categories of Songs	Number of songs
Solos (Hindi Film)	2036
Duets (With Male Singer)	205
Duets (With Female Singer)	1909
Mixed songs	275
Total Hindi Film Songs	4425
Non-film Songs (all languages)*	328
Regional Language Film Songs	310
Total Rafi-songs (1944-1980)	5063

*Non-film songs include songs in Hindi and other languages.

4. Rafi's duets with major female co-singers

Co-Singer	Number of duets
Asha Bhosle	796
Lata Mangeshkar	411
Suman Kalyanpur	141
Geeta Dutt	136
Shamshad Begum	127
Others	288

NOTE: The 'Others' category includes female singers with whom Rafi might have sung just one song.

5. Rafi's duets with major male co-singers

Co-Singer	Number of duets
Manna Dey	58
Kishore Kumar	34
Balbir	15
Mukesh	13
Talat Mehmood	4
Hemanta Kumar	1
Others	92

NOTE: The 'Others' category includes male singers with whom Rafi might have sung just one song.

6. Rafi's voice behind the scenes

Name of Actor	Number of Songs
Shammi Kapoor	190
Johnny Walker	155
Shashi Kapoor	129
Rajendra Kumar	112
Dharmendra	109
Dev Anand	100
Jeetendra	100
Mehmood	85

Bharat Bhushan	80
Dilip Kumar	77
Joy Mukherjee	74
Sunil Dutt	69
Pradeep Kumar	63
Sanjeev Kumar	58
Biswajeet	47
Manoj Kumar	38
Rajesh Khanna	30
Rishi Kapoor	29
Sanjay Khan	27
Guru Dutt	26
Feroze Khan	25

Any discrepancies in Rafi's ultimate tally of songs can be attributed to factors like:

i. Films that never reached the box-office but the music was released.
ii. Non-film songs (all languages) in the form of albums that were released by music label companies but data for which is not available.
iii. Regional film songs (many of which remain unreleased) without any means of authentication.
iv. Shelved films whose songs were recorded, but are available only with a handful of collectors connected to the music industry in some way.
v. Some songs, though present in the original film soundtrack, were not released in the record format.
vi. Some unpreserved songs, lost to posterity.